O Let Us Howle Some Heavy Note

O Let Us Howle
Some Heavy Note

Music for Witches, the Melancholic, and
the Mad on the Seventeenth-Century
English Stage

Amanda Eubanks Winkler

INDIANA UNIVERSITY PRESS

Bloomington and Indianapolis

This book is a publication of

Indiana University Press
601 North Morton Street
Bloomington, IN 47404-3797 USA

http://iupress.indiana.edu

Telephone orders   800-842-6796
Fax orders   812-855-7931
Orders by e-mail   iuporder@indiana.edu

The paper used in this publication meets the minimum
requirements of American National Standard for Information
Sciences—Permanence of Paper for Printed Library Materials,
ANSI Z39.48-1984.

MANUFACTURED IN THE UNITED STATES OF AMERICA

Library of Congress Cataloging-in-Publication Data

Winkler, Amanda Eubanks.
O let us howle some heavy note : music for witches, the melancholic, and the
mad on the seventeenth-century English stage / Amanda Eubanks Winkler.
    p. cm.
Includes bibliographical references (p.   ) and index.
ISBN 0–253–34805–6 (cloth : alk. paper)
1. Dramatic music—England—17th century—History and criticism.
2. Operas—England—Characters. 3. Theater—England—History—17th century.
4. Purcell, Henry, 1659–1695. Dido and Aeneas. I. Title.
ML1731.2.W56 2006
782.10942'09032—dc22
                                                            2006008072

1 2 3 4 5 11 10 09 08 07 06

For my family

Contents

Acknowledgments

This book benefited tremendously from astute and probing commentary by Louise Stein, Naomi André, Richard Crawford, Valerie Traub, and Steven Whiting. At a pivotal moment in developing the manuscript, I was honored to receive a long-term fellowship, funded by the National Endowment for the Humanities, to conduct research for this book at the Folger Shakespeare Library. During my year at the Folger I benefited from having access to the library's rich resources (the reader will note the various illustrations I have gleaned from the Folger's ample collections). Thanks are due to Werner Gundersheimer, the former head of the Folger, the helpful library staff, and particularly Sarah Weiner, assistant to Werner, and an excellent early-music oboist who became a good friend during my tenure at the library. While at the Folger, I was pleased to work side by side with a wonderful and distinguished group of scholars. In particular, I thank Anna Battigelli, Vincent Carey, Marika Keblusek, Stephen May, Gail Kern Paster, and Linda Woodbridge for their interest in my work and their helpful suggestions. In addition, I must also warmly thank the staffs of the following research institutions for their assistance and, in some cases, permission to publish materials from their collections: the British Library; the Bodleian and Christ Church Libraries, Oxford; the Fitzwilliam Museum, Cambridge; and the Huntington Library. I must also thank Novello and Company for permission to reproduce excerpts from the Purcell Society edition of *Dido and Aeneas*.

My institutional home as I completed this project has been the Department of Fine Arts at Syracuse University. I wish to thank my department chair Wayne Franits, Dean Cathryn Newton, and Frank Macomber, trustee of the Fleming Fund, for their financial support; Stephen Meyer, who read and commented upon this manuscript in its early stages; and Laurinda Dixon for her helpful suggestions. All of my colleagues in the Department of Fine Arts have been supportive of this endeavor and I appreciate their friendship. Outside the Syracuse community, I must give special thanks to my dear friend Rose Pruiksma for her careful reading of my manuscript and to Linda Austern, Michael Burden, Kathryn Lowerre,

Anthony Rooley, and Andrew Walkling—I have learned a tremendous amount from all of you.

The suggestions of Steven Plank and the anonymous reader who commented on the project for Indiana University Press strengthened this book immeasurably. Finally, a word of gratitude to the wonderful people at IU Press: editor Suzanne Ryan and assistant editor Donna Wilson, who shepherded this project to timely completion, and my first editor, Gayle Sherwood, who supported this project from a very early stage.

On a personal note, I am extremely fortunate to have a wonderful, understanding husband, Jason Winkler, and daughter, Emma, who, during the first year of her life, had to cope with her mother completing a book manuscript. I am also blessed with a mother, father, and sister who offered to provide childcare during this crucial time and in-laws, the Winklers, who have been a constant source of steadfast love and support. For these reasons, I dedicate this book to my family.

Note on Transcriptions

When transcribing quotations from seventeenth- and eighteenth-century English texts, I have retained original spellings, capitalization, and punctuation. I have, however, changed the *y* used as a thorn to *th*, and *i, j, u,* and *v* have been modernized as necessary for ease of reading. Readers should be aware that the orthography of quotations from modern editions of seventeenth- and eighteenth-century texts has sometimes been updated.

In the musical examples I have also retained original spellings, note values, time signatures, and figured basses unless otherwise stated in the text. Punctuation has sometimes been lightly adjusted for clarity. Clefs have been modernized where indicated. All added barlines are notated with dotted lines, and other editorial additions are indicated with brackets. For ease of reading, I have removed slurs indicating melismas and have replaced them with protraction lines.

Library Sigla

GREAT BRITAIN (GB)
Cfm.   Cambridge, Fitzwilliam Museum
Lbl.   London, British Library
Ob.   Oxford, Bodleian Library
Och.   Oxford, Christ Church Library

UNITED STATES (US)
NYp.   New York, Public Library at Lincoln Center, Music Division

O Let Us Howle Some Heavy Note

1

Music and the Macrocosm: Disorder and History

> For Musicke is none other than a perfect harmonie, whose divinitie is seene in the perfectnesse of his proportions, as, his unison sheweth the unitie, from whence all other, (concords, discords, consonancies, or others whatsoever) springeth, next his unitie, his third: (which is the perfectest concord that is in all Musicke) representeth the perfect, & most holie Trinitie; his fift, (the most perfect consonance in all Musicke, for that it is the verie essence of all concords) representeth the perfection of that most perfect number of five, which made the perfect atonement, betweene God, and man.[1]

Although Thomas Robinson, in his didactic *The Schoole of Musicke* (1603), finds analogies between concords (the unison, third, and fifth) and the deity, he also recognizes that music is not all about order and consonant harmonies. From the "unitie" springs *all* music, including the less aurally pleasant intervals. What of this discord? How can we understand its meaning within seventeenth-century English culture? In 1605 playwright Samuel Rowley, reflecting the thinking of many of his contemporaries, compared discordant music to society:

> Yet mong'st these many stringes, be one untun'd
> Or jarreth low, or hyer than his course,
> Not keeping steddie meane among'st the rest,
> Corrupts them all, so doth bad men the best.[2]

For Rowley, musical dissonance was analogous to "bad men"—and in both cases these disorderly elements were dangerous, as they corrupted.

Little systematic analysis, in either musicology or literary studies, focuses specifically on the fascinating ways those in the seventeenth century understood music and disorder: thus, this volume considers the theatrical music for those who disrupted the fabric of the kingdom, those who were neither harmonious nor obedient, those who did not keep a "steddie meane." The seventeenth century proves to be fertile ground for a study of disorder, as chaos reigned supreme throughout Europe. Even a brief summary of large-scale political events in England provides a clear sense of the upheavals that characterized the era: the end of Elizabeth's reign and the anxieties about the Virgin Queen's successor, whispers about the immoral activities at James I's court (r. 1603–25), Charles I's disastrous rule (which began in 1625 and ended with his execution at the hands of his subjects in 1649), the closing of the public theaters by Parliament in 1641, Civil War (1642–49), the puritanical Commonwealth and the Protectorate of Oliver Cromwell and his son Richard (1649–60), the restoration of the monarchy with Charles II (r. 1660–85), the reopening of the public theaters in 1660, the problematic kingship of Charles's Catholic brother, James II (r. 1685–88), the Glorious Revolution (1688–89), and the concomitant accession of William and Mary to the throne (r. 1689–1702). Furthermore, as cultural theorist José Maravall claims,

> individuals acquired relative consciousness of the phases of crisis that they were undergoing. They also showed a difference in their attitude . . . toward the events they were witnessing: an attitude not limited to passivity, but postulating an intervention.[3]

Given this proactive approach, it is not surprising that cultural producers during this era were preoccupied with the question of disorder and how it might be mediated and contained.

To enact my own order upon the potentially limitless material from this tumultuous century, I've chosen to examine the vocal music and dances for three disorderly character types that appeared repeatedly on the public and private stages: the witch, the melancholic, and the mad. These three character types are richly multivalent. They remained popular throughout the seventeenth century, and their representations were intertwined with crucial debates that significantly reshaped religious, political, and social ideologies.

Of course, for those in the seventeenth century, the representation of disorder in music presented an inherent challenge, as music could be aurally intelligible only if sound was ordered. Was the very idea of disorderly music oxymoronic? Was it noise? Composers working within a modal or nascent tonal framework couldn't have imagined using dodecaphony to represent disorder. So how was disorder portrayed and why did certain musical and theatrical conventions emerge? These are the questions at the heart of my study. The way music represented these characters also changed over the course of the century. As this book will argue, there are many reasons for these changes, having to do with both shifting musical tastes and alterations in the way people understood these characters.

Although my selection of witches, the melancholic, and the mad may seem somewhat arbitrary, in actuality the discourses about these three types of disorderly subject frequently entwined. For example, debates over witchcraft sparked debates about the nature and definition of mental illnesses. In the late sixteenth century some skeptics began to question the existence of witches—why, they asked, would the Devil consort with poor, decrepit old women? These authors claimed that such women couldn't have access to the supernatural; instead, they must suffer from melancholy. For some it was easier to believe in female irrationality than in a female with supernatural powers. Johann Weyer first made this case in *De praestigiis daemonum* in 1563, and by 1584 this controversial argument—an argument that had serious religious implications—had been taken up by Englishman Reginald Scot in his *The Discoverie of Witchcraft*:

> If anie man advisedlie marke their words, actions, cogitations, and gestures, he shall perceive that melancholie abounding in their head, and occupieng their braine, hath deprived or rather depraved their judgements, and all their senses: I meane not of

coosening witches, but of poore melancholike women, which are themselves deceived. For you shall understand, that the force which melancholie hath, and the effects that it worketh in the bodie of a man, or rather of a woman, are almost incredible. For as some of these melancholike persons imagine, they are witches, and by witchcraft can worke wonders, and doo what they list: so doo other, troubled with this disease, imagine manie strange, incredible, and impossible things.[4]

According to Scot, many so-called witches did not actually have access to magic; rather, melancholy played tricks with their imagination, deceiving them into thinking they had demonic power. As important and influential as Weyer and Scot were, not everyone agreed with their relatively enlightened perspectives on witchcraft and melancholy. James I wrote his *Daemonologie* (1597, reprinted 1604) to refute the perceived atheism of Scot's book, and the king ordered all copies of Scot's *Discoverie* burned upon his accession to the throne.[5] Although James I protested that Scot's views were heretical, the seed of doubt had been planted.

Besides the fact that Weyer and Scot's claims were potentially heretical, for followers of Aristotle's influential *Problemata*, which associated melancholy with mental acumen, Weyer and Scot's theory that women suffered from the disease was deeply troubling: women simply could not be geniuses! In response to the problem of female melancholy, Edward Jorden, a medical doctor and star witness in witchcraft trials of the day, wrote *A Briefe Discourse of a Disease Called the Suffocation of the Mother* (1603). He blames the wandering womb for many of the "melancho-like" symptoms supposed witches displayed.[6] One cause of this womb sickness, Jorden explains bashfully, was the retention of the menses or sperma (which in the early seventeenth century women, as well as men, were thought to have) due to sexual frustration. Jorden then cites the authority of Galen, who suggests marriage as a possible cure for this species of the disease.[7] Similarly, Robert Burton discusses womb sickness in his highly influential *Anatomy of Melancholy* (1621). He associates the melancholy of maids, nuns, and widows (all women abstaining from sexual intercourse) with "fits of the mother."[8] Judging from play and song texts, delusional women of all sorts frequently display the typical symptoms of womb frenzy.

Aristotle's *Problemata* notwithstanding, melancholy wasn't always a glorious malady for men, and the onstage portrayal of afflictions that called masculine reason into question was fraught with anxieties. Lovesickness, the most common cause of mad or melancholic behavior on the seventeenth-century stage, was particularly transgressive. In 1672 the physician Gideon Harvey articulated the longstanding belief that the behavior of lovesick men was problematic; after describing several historical cases of male lovesickness, he proclaimed, "these passages that resent so much of natures impression, do in no wise merit to be admired at."[9] As overt displays of unbridled emotion were considered womanly, a man who fell victim to melancholy or madness was, according to Jacobean courtier Sir Thomas Overbury, "a man onely in shew, but comes short of the better part; a whole reasonable soule, which is mans cheife preeminence."[10] Similarly, onstage auditors derided men who sang their lovesick complaints, and associated their musical discourse with effeminacy, particularly later in the century.

New ideas about gender increased the anxiety over male lovesickness. In 1651 William Harvey published *Exercitationes de generatione animalium*, which began to challenge the old Aristotelean and Galenic notions that women were less perfect or inverted men. He discovered the female egg and acknowledged that, contrary to previous modes of thought, the woman had a significant role in reproduction of the species, or, as Harvey would have it, "ex ovo omnia."[11] This discovery, and others in the latter half of the seventeenth century, undermined what medical historian Thomas Laqueur calls the "one-sex" model—the notion that men and women were not truly separate sexes, biologically or ideologically.[12] As this one-sex model was eroded by new anatomical discoveries, women increasingly had their own sphere of influence, albeit a lesser one than their male counterparts, as they were still hampered by their "natural" emotionalism and irrationality.[13] In this new gender economy, the emotionalism of a man who suffered from lovesickness marked him as womanlike—a man who transgressively crossed into the realm of the other sex.

Although understanding some of the major discourses surrounding these disorderly subjects is helpful, to fully comprehend the *musical* portrayal of witches, the melancholic, and the mad, we must naturally turn to seventeenth-century ideas about the power of music to promote harmony and well-being or, alternatively, to sow discord. Music was believed to have mystical properties, properties that—if used properly by a skilled practitioner—could perform all sorts of miracles, even curing illness, as musical harmony affected the humors.[14] According to humoral theory, four fluids, or humors, circulated within the body, and each one corresponded to a temperament: blood (sanguine), phlegm (phlegmatic), yellow bile (choleric), and black bile (melancholic). An excessive amount of any one humor, or an overheating of a humor, turning it black (adust), caused mental and physical illness.[15] Music, it was believed, counteracted the deleterious effects of such humoral imbalances. To return to Robinson:

> But that Musicke is Phisical, it is plainlie seene by those maladies it cureth. As it cureth melancholie, it much prevaileth against madnesse; If a man be in paines of the gout, of any wound, or of the head, it much mittigateth the furie therof: and it is said, that Musicke hath a salve for everie sore.[16]

This passage, which amusingly details music's ability to cure melancholy, madness, and even gout and head wounds, demonstrates early modern culture's deep belief in music's therapeutic qualities. The abilities of an individual brilliant musician could cure the afflicted, soothe savage beasts, and even pacify unruly subjects. A panegyric published in 1610 for James I elucidates the wonderful power of music, if wielded by a benevolent master musician:

> Behold, how like another *Orpheus*, *Amphion*, and *Arion*, he draweth to the true knowledge of God, very salvage Beasts, Forrests, Trees, and Stones, by the sweet Harmony of his harp: the most fierce and wilde, the most stupid and insenced, the most brutish and voluptuous, are changed and civilized by the delectable sound of his Musick. The which may transport and ravish our eares, at his mellodious touchinges and concordes and not tickle them with any delicate noyse, tending unto voluptuous and sensuall pleasure: but rather such, as by well tempered proportions are able to reduce all extravagant rudenesse, and circuites of our soules, though they had wandered from the right way, to the true path of dutie, and settle all thoughts in such a harmony, as is most pleasing unto them.[17]

But music, as this passage indicates, could also be dangerous; just as harmonious music could cure, its opposite could provoke political and religious dissent and bodily disharmony in all its forms. Discord produced discord. "Delicate noyse" incited "voluptuous and sensuall pleasure." Music could also do harm, a conceit we see enacted on the seventeenth-century stage in representations of disorderly characters.

Given the potent effect music was thought to have upon the auditor, certain elements of seventeenth-century society were anxious to control its use. Puritan anti-theatricalists enumerated the dangers of disorderly musical representations, believing they led audiences into sin and degradation, even illness and derangement. As Linda Austern has demonstrated, music occupied a contested space within early modern English culture.[18] While Puritans believed devout music could direct the listener to pious thoughts, they were anxious that certain kinds of music might seduce the ear, as a beautiful woman seduced the eye. During Elizabeth's time, Phillip Stubbes wrote heated diatribes against the music he perceived as dangerous because of its ability to emasculate men. Music, like a beautiful woman, communicated directly to a man's passions, which, overstimulated, supplanted his reason—the hallmark of masculinity—thereby reducing the ravished man to a womanish (i.e., overwrought) emotional state. Despite the dire predictions about disorderly music's potential to produce moral decay, it proved popular with audiences: transgression was tremendously entertaining.

The two stages considered by this study—the court stage and the public stage—featured different kinds of disorderly musical entertainments. In the masque, the primary genre performed at court during the reigns of James I and Charles I, disorder was carefully regulated. Music's healing harmonies were used as tools of political pacification. Sweet music and elegant dance reproduced the supposed harmony present in the happy state of England, in turn inspiring the king's subjects to be harmoniously obedient in their relations with their monarch. The creators of the court masque believed that their endeavors provided insight into the true nature of the universe, a conceit they borrowed from Neoplatonic philosophers.[19] Through the orderly movements of courtiers, harmonious music, and expertly crafted costumes and scenery these artists captured, with visual and musical harmony, the harmony of God's universe.[20] Creators of the court masques sought to replicate and foster within obedient subjects the idealized harmonies that were thought to exist between internal and external, human and divine. This idea, that the microcosm imitated and affected the macrocosm, was part of what philosopher Michel Foucault has called the doctrine of "resemblance." As Foucault states, "representation—whether in the service of pleasure or of knowledge—was posited as a form of repetition: the theatre of life or the mirror of nature."[21]

But the masque was not all harmony and order: at the court of James I, Ben Jonson introduced an antimasque in which disorderly characters paraded forth, only to be banished from view by the order and harmony of the masque proper. Historian Kevin Sharpe eloquently explains the relationship between the antimasque and masque, order and disorder, in *Criticism and Compliment: The Politics of Literature in the England of Charles I.*

> Neo-Platonic philosophy postulates an ascent of cognition from the plane of senses and material objects to a loftier stratum of knowledge of forms and ideas, of which objects were but an imperfect material expression. The Caroline masque enacted that philosophy in the transition from antimasque to masque. The world of sense and appetite was represented in the masque by images of nature as an ungoverned wilderness, threatening, violent, ignorant and anarchic; the sphere of the soul was depicted as nature ordered and governed by the patterns of the forms. So in the Caroline masque the transcendence is most often a transformation of nature—from chaos to order and from disjuncture to harmony—through the understanding of the philosopher-kings.[22]

English court masque production can therefore be viewed as an attempt to contain social discord (which was relegated to the antimasques) through the triumph of musical concord and monarchical power. As Sharpe would have it, "The theme of the masque was the imposition of order and peace on chaos and fury through the agency of the king and queen."[23] However, as this book demonstrates, the enchantment of the disorderly antimasque proved too potent. Disorder, once presented, could never be fully contained.

Despite its lofty goals, the court masque did not quell discord. The regicide of Charles I in 1649 seriously challenged old notions of the relationship between the microcosm and macrocosm that lie at the heart of the court masque. From medieval times, the king was thought to have "two bodies": his physical body and the body politic, which, although materially separate, were mystically connected.[24] As Louis XIV pithily claimed, "L'État, c'est moi." The relationship between the king's body and the kingdom incorporated analogies of sickness and health to explain the connection between the two. If the head of the kingdom were diseased (i.e., the king were corrupt), then the kingdom would suffer in kind through plagues and famine. Disorder among his subjects was also explained in pathological, analogical terms. If there was political and religious dissent and discord, there was disease within the body politic.[25] The regicide of Charles I—the forcible removal of the head of state— permanently demystified kingship and rendered notions of the relationship between microcosm and macrocosm, between king and kingdom, outmoded. Thomas Hobbes's contract theory advanced in *Leviathan* (1651) reflects this demystification. In a radical departure from the previous doctrine of divine right (the king as God's representative on Earth), Hobbes claims that the king ruled by the consent of the people, not by divine dictate. And people could overthrow their ruler; subjects *chose* to obey the sovereign only as long as his "power lasteth, by which he is able to protect them."[26]

Although the debate about kingship did not die with Charles I, in a post-regicidal world the relationship between monarch and subject could never be the same, and neither, by extension, could the old analogic model of understanding the world: a model that heavily informed early seventeenth-century notions of disorder. Divine right was relegated to the world of myth. A king considered unfit for the job could be overthrown. Even after the Stuart Restoration of 1660 disharmony and faction seemed a permanent condition of the kingdom, so the most a monarch could hope for wasn't the containment of discord (not that it was ever really a possibility) but escape from it. At the end of John Dryden and Louis Grabu's *Albion and Albanius* (1685), for example, Charles II ascends into the heavens, providing a welcome release from the earthly plagues of faction and civil strife.[27]

The court masque enjoyed only intermittent support after the Civil War, but throughout the seventeenth century the public stages of London were important venues for negotiating the anxieties about the disorderly elements of society. Although the court masque influenced the treatment of disorderly characters on both the early and even the late seventeenth-century public stages, other conventions emerged that were specific to the musical genres that flourished in the public theater: songs within plays and after 1660 dramatick operas (or semi-operas), entertainments that interpolated lengthy masques into spoken drama. The English never embraced through-sung opera as their continental counterparts did, and music was usually reserved for scenes where its presence did not break the rules of verisimilitude. Music in an otherwise spoken play was a heightened form of discourse, a potent communicative medium frequently used when invoking the supernatural or by those in an altered psychological state, such as madness or melancholy.

Historical forces also shaped musical practices on the late seventeenth-century public stages. A puritanical Parliament closed the public theaters in 1641; while musical and theatrical activities continued after the Restoration of Charles II in 1660, the theaters' closure and the mid-century social unrest had a profound effect. Many of the musicians and playwrights who had been engaged in the production of public and court entertainments before the Civil War experienced significant hardships during the Interregnum. Court musician William Lawes, a man who created music for several court masques and for the public stage, was killed in battle in 1645. Others, such as the musician Matthew Locke and the playwright/impresarios Thomas Killigrew and William Davenant, had been in exile on the Continent. Furthermore, the boys who had played women's roles on the early seventeenth-century stage found their voices breaking during the long fallow season when they could not ply their trade. A paradigm shift was inevitable.

After the reopening of the public theaters by Charles II in 1660, women appeared for the first time as professional actresses in England: an innovation that gave scenes involving women, including the disorderly women considered by this book, a potent verisimilitude. Actresses were allowed to perform for many reasons, both material and ideological.[28] Practically, as noted above, there was a dearth of trained boy actors, but other, ostensibly moral, considerations informed the decision to allow women to perform. According to the patent granted to Killigrew in 1662:

> And for as much as many plays formerly acted do contain several profane, obscene and scurrilous passages, and the women's parts therein have been acted by men in the habit of women, at which some have taken offence, for the preventing of these abuses in the future, we do hereby strictly command and enjoin that from henceforth . . . we do . . . permit and give leave that all the women's parts to be acted in either of the said two companies for the time to come may be performed by women, so long as their recrea-

tions, which by reason of the abuses aforesaid were scandalous and offensive, may by such reformation be esteemed not only harmless delight, but useful and instructive representations of human life.[29]

As indicated by the language of the patent, boys performing women's roles, while marginally acceptable in a world that viewed both boys and women as imperfect, was problematic. Much antitheatrical sentiment among Puritans had been created earlier in the century because of the potential of beautiful boys to lure unsuspecting men into the wilds of same-sex desire and even acts of sodomy (a fear that reemerges in the early eighteenth-century controversy over Italian castrati).[30] As the reactionary Presbyterian William Prynne had ranted during the 1630s:

> Yea witnes . . . *that players and play-haunters in their secret conclaves play the Sodomites;* together with *some modern examples of such, who have been desperately enamored with Players Boyes thus clad in woman's apparel, so far as to solicite them by words, by Letters, even actually to abuse them.*[31]

It was probably hoped that putting women onstage would quell this old Puritan objection to the public theater. But the problem of desire was not solved by the introduction of actresses. As Elizabeth Howe notes, the bawdiness of the Restoration stage resulted in part from the desire to exploit the charms of these women.[32] The introduction of actresses also allowed the lament and the mad song to flourish: two musical genres that showcased the erotic potential of the women who performed them.

In this age of conflict, this century that completely reformulated the relationship between monarch and subject, between man and woman, between the macrocosm and microcosm, how did music, dance, and theater negotiate this obvious social tumult? I would argue that as a public discourse it was central to the working out of these problems. But I must emphasize that this was a process of *negotiation*, not containment. If one hopes to find disorder banished with finality, completely expunged through musical and theatrical catharsis, one will be sorely disappointed by the analysis that follows.

The history of musical disorder is riddled with ambiguities. Theatrical and musical sources from the period are fluid, existing in multiple and sometimes imperfect copies. And one cannot rely solely on the remaining sources as an absolute record of how disorder was portrayed in the theater. Performance played a crucial role in the construction of musical and theatrical disorder. While a song as presented in a contemporary manuscript may seem to adhere to standard compositional rules, performers might have chosen to interpret the piece in an inharmonious, disorderly way (indeed, some stage directions suggest this was the case).

This ambiguity of representation doesn't exist only because of the imperfect or incomplete nature of the remaining sources or the style of performance. As we shall see, playwrights and composers used certain dramatic and musical devices that emphasized the ambivalent place these characters occupied in early modern society. In their discussion of transgression within early modern culture, Peter Stallybrass and Allon White, echoing Mikhail Bakhtin, observe, "Again and again we find a striking ambivalence to the representations of the lower strata (of the body, of literature, of society, of place) in which they are both reviled and desired."[33] The same can be said of musical disorder, and its slipperiness, its richness of meaning, made it compelling entertainment.

My study of disorder resisted containment within the margins of any single discipline or methodology. The reader will note a range of influences upon my thinking. My unruly book fits somewhere between the realms of literary criticism and musicology. In critical theory I have found the tools of social analysis, while musicology has provided a range of meticulous studies into the history of English song and theatrical music.

The main body of the book is organized into three main sections, each one devoted to one of the three primary character-types considered by this study. Chapter 2 examines the ideological contradictions in musical representations of witchcraft. The witch, representative of political and religious rebellion, social decay, poverty, ignorance, and the gender trouble presented by unruly women, was domesticated for the pleasure of audiences, singing and dancing in public, private, and court theaters for monarchs and plebeians alike. Musical witches play prominent roles in entertainments such as Ben Jonson's *The Masque of Queens* (1609), Thomas Middleton's *The Witch* (1615–16), seventeenth-century revivals of *Macbeth*, and plays based on actual witchcraft cases: Thomas Dekker, John Ford, and William Rowley's *The Witch of Edmonton* (1621), Thomas Heywood and Richard Brome's *The Late*

Lancashire Witches (1634), and Thomas Shadwell's *The Lancashire Witches* (1681).

An analysis of the music in these works shows how musical and dramatic conventions marked witches as disorderly, rural, ignorant, sexually profligate, and poor. Performed by cross-dressed adult men who imperfectly represented the female body and voice, witches sang bawdy ballads, danced rustic rounds, morrises, and jigs, contorted their bodies with antic postures, ineptly mimicked religious ritual, and produced "rough" dissonant music. These performance traditions placed musical witchcraft within the larger English tradition for portraying carnivalesque figures symbolic of inversion and disorder.

This chapter ends with a consideration of witches' music for the Restoration stage, including Henry Purcell's *Dido and Aeneas* (ca. 1687).[34] Particularly after the mid-century, science, rationalism, and empiricism prevailed among the elites. Prosecutions of witches became less frequent, and Catholics emerged as the primary threat to English society; in fact, witches and Catholics were frequently conflated, on- and offstage.[35] While many of the same musical strategies for witchcraft continued on the late Restoration stage, musical gestures became increasingly stylized as Purcell and others wrote artful and sometimes elaborate approximations of rustic songs and dances instead of actually quoting the "real" thing. After the mid-century, witches' onstage musical practices were separated from lived experience, and their antics were transmuted into theatrical fiction. But theatrical fiction still can be persuasive and powerful; in Purcell's coven, comedy and subversion make natural bedfellows.

Engaging in witchcraft undoubtedly violated early modern notions of normative feminine behavior. In contradistinction, the mentally distressed female characters considered in chapter 3 did not challenge contemporary ideas about the female nature: women were supposed to be irrational creatures. Yet these portrayals, both in the medical literature and in musical-theatrical productions, were still problematic for two main reasons. First, while the irrational behavior of afflicted women corresponded to notions that they were the weaker sex, a debate raged about whether women could be melancholic, mostly because it was an affliction associated with two things that were gendered male: genius and scholarship. Because of the reluctance to associate female mental disorders with melancholy, a rhetorical strategy developed that associated melancho-like disorders with womb frenzy, a move that sexualized female mental illness. Of course, this created a second site of tension. The sexual nature of female mental disorders invited the erotic objectification of sufferers and prompted scorn from moralists, who decried the inherently lustful nature of women.

Sexual desires were caused by a restive womb, and conversely a womb could be set to wandering by unfulfilled erotic longing. Given this relationship between lust and female mental illness, it is understandable why so many of the disturbed, disorderly women on the seventeenth-century stage suffer the loss of a lover or desire consummation with a partner who, through death or design, is unattainable. This chapter first considers the music for deserted women, such as the lament for Echo in Ben Jonson's early play *Cynthia's Revels* (1600) and Desdemona's famous "Willow Song" in William Shakespeare's *Othello* (1604). Both these women are silenced, Echo by Mercury, who, in a departure from mythological precedent, tires of her moaning and robs her once more of body and independent voice, and Desdemona by the jealous hands of her husband. Other afflicted women go mad before they die, giving them license to unleash a tirade of semi-lucid, sexually inflected commentary. These musical madwomen often sing snatches of bawdy ballads (Ophelia being the most famous example), a doubly subversive practice when performed by a female character—she sings music below her class that invites the audience to question her chastity. Perhaps because female musical performance was so problematic, these songs are sometimes ventriloquized by lower-class servants or by boy pages, so deserted women could retain a small shred of dignity.

After the Restoration, dignity, for the most part, was not a primary consideration. Female singers performed for the first time on the public stage, and their charms were such that composers and playwrights accentuated the titillating qualities of female mental disorder. Even Dido of Henry Purcell's opera exhibits the typical musical and dramatic symptoms of lovesickness. Female singers, in ever swelling numbers, performed sexually provocative mad songs, a development that is reflected in the careers of Moll Davis and Anne Bracegirdle, who benefited from their ability to "sell" the pathos and eroticism of musical disorder. Moll Davis, if we are to believe prompter John Downes, was elevated from obscurity, in part because Charles II took a liking to her performance as the mad Celania in William Davenant's *The Rivals* (1667 revival). Bracegirdle was an even more intriguing figure. While she maintained the appearance of chastity in her offstage life, rumors circulated about her supposed liaisons, and composers and playwrights frequently made her a victim of lovesick madness onstage, allowing the audience to indulge their fantasies as they viewed the spectacle of Mrs. Bracegirdle "in love." She increased her fame with her performance of John Eccles's "I Burn, I Burn" in Thomas D'Urfey's *Don Quixote, Part II*, and her popularity was such that Gottfried Finger and Henry Purcell wrote musical odes to her brilliant and pathetic portrayal of musical madness. As Finger's and Purcell's reactions demonstrate, singing madwomen had real musical power. But again the interpretation of female mental disorders cannot be simple. To celebrate "I Burn, I Burn" or Dido's lament without acknowledging that these musical outpourings, within their dramatic contexts, hastened the characters' inexorable journeys to silence or death erases the complexity of these artworks.

Unlike the women who suffered from mental instability, a man who succumbed to melancholy or madness was deficient because he had forfeited what playwright Thomas D'Urfey called "the charter of his kind" (his reason). Chapter 4 considers these male unfortunates. But, as with witchcraft, there was no single hegemonic perspective on the subject of male melancholy and madness. Melancholy was a particularly problematic affliction. It was simultaneously critiqued as an affliction of weak-brained, effeminate men and celebrated as a sign of genius, a position articulated at length in Robert Burton's *Anatomy of Melancholy*, which described the myriad manifestations of the disease. Madness, while seldom imbued with the glamorous properties of melancholy, still occupied an ambivalent space, as it was frequently conflated with its less acute sister, melancholy, or was viewed as an affliction that could potentially give the sufferer access to higher realms or modes of thought.

This chapter examines the musical language of male melancholy and madness, focusing on three related strands: politics, class, and gender. First, I examine how the music of melancholy and madness was associated with political disorder, particularly early in the period, when Neoplatonic models of the body politic were central to the understanding of the relationship between ruler and kingdom. In plays such as John Marston's *The Malcontent* (1604), John Webster's *The Duchess of Malfi* (1614), and Richard Brome's

The Antipodes (1638) the noisy and disruptive music of melancholy and madness signified macrocosmic disorder. In addition to the political critique frequently associated with melancholy and madness, class issues also came to the fore, particularly when the afflicted characters were of the nobler sort. I suggest connections between Castiglione's indictment of aristocratic public performance of music with mad and melancholic men who sing music in inappropriate situations or perform bawdy songs that debase them.

One of the most problematic kinds of malady, lovesickness, is the central consideration of the final section of this chapter. I examine various ways playwrights and composers negotiated the problematic status of the male erotomaniac, who suffered from a species of melancholy consistently reviled, both in the medical literature and onstage, for causing indecorous and effeminate behavior. If the erotomaniac has not succumbed to madness, his musical outpourings of grief are foisted upon a young boy servant, an acceptable "feminine" mouthpiece for the lovesick gentleman's lament. If the lovesick swain completely lost his reason, he sings himself, his musical outburst making clear his effeminacy and irrationality.

The music composed for these disorderly subjects resists simplistic moralistic interpretations, in part because seventeenth-century England itself was so disorderly: so many competing discourses about religion, politics, and gender informed these characters. Although onstage witches, melancholics, and the mad behaved transgressively, the music for these characters, while constituting their disorder, also, paradoxically, provided some of the most compelling dramatic and musical moments on the seventeenth-century English stage, seducing even their creators. But what had appealed to seventeenth-century tastes did not always appeal to those in the eighteenth century. The final chapter of this study briefly considers what happened to the musical portrayal of disorder after the turn of the century. I begin with an examination of the continued popularity of William Davenant's musical *Macbeth* and the role of the witch in other early eighteenth-century entertainments. As belief in witchcraft rapidly declined, the musical and theatrical witch continued her transformation into a beloved and comical figure—pure entertainment with very little menace.

I then consider the change in thinking about madness and melancholy that occurred in the late seventeenth and early eighteenth centuries and corresponding changes in the portrayal of these disorders on the musical stage. New theories of mental illness emerged, ones that clearly delineated madness from sense. Also exerting a considerable influence on portrayals of madness and melancholy were late seventeenth- and early eighteenth-century moral reformers, who decried the excessive (and sometimes bawdy) outbursts of these characters. Even Ophelia, whose madness had inspired so much sympathy in the past, now troubled antitheatricalists such as Jeremy Collier because of her supposed licentiousness. Indeed, in the eighteenth century her role was sanitized, excising the bawdy. The popularity of Italian opera at the beginning of the eighteenth century also had a profound effect on the reception and portrayal of all these disorderly characters. Although native English entertainments did not disappear overnight and many older portrayals of disorder were present in theatrical revivals or concert performances, a new disorderly subject emerged. Using critical discourses from the period, I demonstrate that, for early eighteenth-century operagoers, the castrato became one of the most prominent symbols of disorder, of nature subverted. Unnatural and grotesque like the witch, humorally unbalanced like the melancholic or madman, these singers gained power through their vocal innovations, simultaneously inciting audience fascination and revulsion.

2

"Stay, You Imperfect Speakers, Tell Me More"

In William Shakespeare's *Macbeth* (1603) the witches greet Macbeth and his companion, Banquo, on the heath with strangely paradoxical prophecies. Intrigued, Macbeth beseeches them, "Stay, you imperfect speakers, tell me more" [I.iii.70]—an exhortation redolent with meaning.[1] "Imperfect" did not simply mean the opposite of perfect. Macbeth's description also told seventeenth-century audiences that the witches were "wanting," potentially evil, and "not fully instructed or accomplished" in their mode of speech.[2] Their cryptic predictions are riddled with contradictions and lack the clarity and logic prized by rhetoricians.[3] Their charms imperfectly replicate religious formulas; in particular, they bear a resemblance to Catholic rituals, already demonized in anti-Catholic propaganda and witchcraft treatises.[4] Their moral imperfection is also evident. They engage in bawdy talk and celebrate chaos. For Shakespeare's witches, "Fair is foul, and foul is fair" [I.i.11]. While others weep at misfortune, witches sing, dance, and rejoice.

As the brief catalogue of the witches' behavior in *Macbeth* suggests, Shakespeare's witches and other theatrical hags played an integral role in seventeenth-century religious and moralistic discourses. The English witchcraft beliefs that informed the creation of singing and dancing hags drew upon Anglo-Saxon lore, classical mythology, Neoplatonism, and contemporary anxieties about heresy, Catholicism, and the nature of women.[5] This chapter unpacks these divergent influences, showing how they coalesced into a disorderly musical character who was simultaneously entertaining and troubling.

The Witch's Body and Voice

Anxieties about gender, religion, and even politics shaped the body and voice of the theatrical witch. On the early seventeenth-century stage, boys usually portrayed women's roles because professional actresses were forbidden to appear. As Stephen Orgel and others have noted, boys "passed" for women in a theatrical context, perhaps because in seventeenth-century England both women and boys were economically subordinate objects of desire for adult males. Indeed, according to the venomous claims of anti-theatricalists, the boy actors' performance of femininity was all too successful; with their narrow hips and flat chests, these latter-day Ganymedes seduced spectators with their approximation of idealized female beauty.[6] But hags were neither beautiful nor desirable, and boys, the "women" of the early seventeenth-century English stage, did not play witches, or other older, sexually experienced women, such as procuresses, nurses, and bawds. Adult men, frequently the comedians of the company, took these parts.[7] This tradition carried over onto the late seventeenth-century stage, with men continuing to play these roles. As Banquo says, "You should be women / And yet your beards forbid me to interpret / That you are so" [I.iii.45–47].

The assignment of these roles to adult actors marginalized the theatrical hag from the normative onstage female body (ironically, in the early seventeenth century, a boy's body). Banquo acknowledges that the witches he sees are not quite women. Indeed, female witches, both on- and offstage, were regularly accused of being overly masculine or androgynous.[8] There are many reasons why the witch was thought to be masculine. Many of the women accused of witchcraft were elderly and therefore past childbearing age. According to humoral theory, a young woman was thought to be cold and wet, while a man was hot and dry. As people of both sexes aged, they became colder and drier. Thus, an older woman, as she became drier, would gain certain masculine traits such as facial hair and a deep voice.[9]

The masculine physical attributes of the witch could be interpreted as a visual signifier of her usurpation of masculine privileges through her pact with the Devil. Through witchcraft she controlled the will of men. She eschewed patriarchal dictates about chastity and silence, cursing freely and engaging in twisted sexual acts with her familiars and even with the Devil himself. While her monstrous appearance seemed to preclude the possibility of sexual satisfaction, by resorting to unnatural demonic means the witch procured her own sexual partners, enabling her to chart her own sexual destiny outside the traditional procreative family unit.

For most of the seventeenth century certain behaviors were thought to have an effect on one's body, even one's biological sex. According to the one-sex model, which held sway among the educated, women could actually turn into men.[10] Women, as less perfect men, retained their genitals inside because of a lack of vital heat. If a woman became hotter through some means (great exertion, excitement, etc.), her internal genitalia were expelled, changing her into a man. Thus, the witches' onstage personification by adult men could have reflected such beliefs, which were widespread in seventeenth-century England.[11]

The blatant androgyny of the onstage witch provided physical evidence of her internal spiritual deformity: her grotesque outside reflected her tainted soul. Indeed, the witch's body, onstage and off, corresponds to the well-known Bakhtinian description of the grotesque body. It is unbounded (possessing masculine and feminine qualities, moving in unexpected, unregulated ways), is connected to the earth, excrement, and vermin (the ingredients she uses in her disgusting rituals), and emphasizes the lower bodily stratum (her overt sexuality).[12] The onstage body of the witch subverted symmetry and harmony of form. The movements of her grotesque body were jerky and malformed, completely bereft of feminine grace. Indeed, real-life women accused of witchcraft often had some visible physical handicap or flaw. It was apparently comforting to think that women in league with the Devil could be easily identified through their physical abnormalities.

If the supposed witch's somatic deformity wasn't immediately apparent, zealous officials interested in proving witchcraft resorted to a full body search, seeking a Devil's mark, an extra teat from

Figure 2.1. Witches with Familiars, from *The Wonderful Discoverie of the Witchcrafts of Margaret and Philip* [a] *Flower* (1619), 59371. This item is reproduced by permission of *The Huntington Library, San Marino, California.*

which her demonic familiar sucked, a perversion of the "natural" maternal role.[13] These invasive investigative practices continued throughout the century. An account of a witchcraft trial from 1670 describes how a midwife and other women deposed in court searched the bodies of the accused witches and "found several large Teates in the secret Parts of their Bodies."[14]

In a purely theatrical sense, the adult male transvestite performance tradition gave witches' scenes a certain comic potential; however, even when witchcraft was obviously played for laughs, anxiety percolated beneath the surface—an anxiety about the witch's improper usurpation of power, the topsy-turviness of the grotesque hag who bewitches and controls her betters through magical means. Anthropologists who study ritualized behavior (and the theater is but another sort of ritualized behavior), suggest that role reversal—in this case the representation of a woman by an adult male actor—reinscribes order and stability in a hierarchical society, clarifying the proper structure by reversing it.[15] On the other hand, this performance tradition could also undermine established hierarchies. The male theatrical reenactment of inappropriate female behavior for entertainment allows the audience to consider and possibly enjoy the spectacle of unruly women. Although having adult males perform witches' roles might inspire laughter or cause the audience to recoil at their less-than-ideal female form, the witches' onstage presence allows the spectator to consider the possibility that women *could* wield fantastic power.[16] And within patriarchal seventeenth-century culture, this possibility was troubling.

The physical reality of the adult men who performed witches' roles also colored the performance of the witch's voice. An adult male singer had two performance choices: he could either sing the role using his natural range or he could use a falsetto voice. As the usual performers of these roles were the comedians of the company, they might have been inclined to use a humorous, cracking falsetto. This manner of performance seems plausible, as witches (both on- and offstage) were described as having unattractive, squeaky voices, characteristic of elderly women. Authors of anti-witchcraft treatises used the ugliness of the witches' voices to question the efficacy of their charms, decrying the muttering, cursing, and incomprehensible nonsense that made up their incantations. In 1646, John Gaule sarcastically describes the typical woman accused of witchcraft:

> every old woman with a wrinkled face, a furr'd brow, a hairy lip, a gobber tooth, a squint eye, a squeking voyce, or a scolding tongue, having a ragged coate on her back, a skullcap on her head, a spindle in her hand, and a dog or cat by her side; is not only suspected, but pronounced for a witch.[17]

Beyond the fact that Gaule's physical description of the supposed witch perfectly fits the women pictured in the woodcut of figure 2.1, his derisive description of the witch's "squeking voyce" reinforces the notion that witches aren't just ugly in appearance—the *sound* they produce is ugly as well. These ideas may have inspired comedians to adopt a creaky falsetto, mocking the "scolding tongue" of the women accused of witchcraft. By envoicing the witch in such a fashion, the actors undermined the power of the offstage witch, transforming her incantations into comedic fodder.[18]

On the other hand, it is equally possible that actors playing witches would have used their natural range; late seventeenth-century evidence indicates that basses or baritones frequently sang witches' roles.[19] In addition to the obvious humor of a deep voice emanating from an ostensibly female body, the use of a lower voice could also be a further sign of the witch's monstrous usurpation of masculine power—the aural analogue to Banquo's beard. This performance practice may have also reflected the social reality that postmenopausal women—women with naturally lower voices— were often accused of witchcraft.

Regardless of the specific manner of vocal performance, the theatrical witch as embodied by an adult male actor would have had an imperfectly feminine voice—perhaps even an aesthetically displeasing voice. The imperfection or even ugliness of the witch's voice is crucial for understanding her onstage incantations, incantations that were frequently sung. The act of singing was literally imbedded within the word incantation (*cantare*), reflecting the belief that sound and song were essential tools of the magician's and the witch's trade.[20] According to occult philosophers, by using appropriate music, a magician could alter the natural world or summon supernatural help.[21] This idea—sympathy, or the belief that like summons like—was one of the essential tenets of early modern occult philosophy. As the influential Renaissance magician Heinrich Cornelius Agrippa describes musical sympathy:

> Such like verses [as the hymns of Orpheus] being aptly, and duly made according to the rule of the Stars, and being full of signification, & meaning, and opportunely pronounced with vehement affection, as according to the number, proportion of their Articles, so according to the form resulting from the Articles, and by the violence of imagination, do confer a very great power in the inchanter, and sometimes transfer it upon the thing inchanted, to bind, and direct it to the same purpose for which the affections, and speeches of the inchanter are intended. Now the instrument of the inchanters is a most pure harmoniacall spirit, warm, breathing, living, bringing with it motion, affection and signification, composed of its parts, endued with sence and conceived by reason.[22]

Although new models for understanding the world emerged, the idea of musical sympathy continued to hold sway in some quarters throughout the seventeenth century. In 1677, radical sectarian and occultist John Webster, while profoundly skeptical about the existence of witches, acknowledges the power of music to perform magical wonders:

> There is no one thing . . . that hath more induced me to believe that there is some natural virtue in words and charms composed in a right way or Rhythme, than because those that are stung, or bitten with the *Tarantula* or *Phalangium*, are cured with Musick, and that not with any sort of Musick, but with certain proper and peculiar tunes, which are diversified according to the colour of the *Tarantula* that gave the venemous prick or bite, and so by dancing they sweat forth the poison. And *Kercherus* further tells us not only that those that are stung with the *Tarantula* are cured with Musick, but that the *Tarantula's* themselves will dance, when those tunes are modulated that are proportionable and agreeable to their humors. Now if tunes modulated in proportionable and sympathicizing ways agreeable to the humours, do cure those that are stung, then much more may words and charms rightly composed and joined together, and that in a due selected time under a powerful constellation, produce such effects as to cure diseases, and move animals to divers and various motions; for betwixt the prolation of words putting the Atomes of the air into a fit motion, site, figure, and contexture suitable to perform the end intended, and the vibrating and various figuring the air in its motion by musical tunes, there is no difference at all in respect of the material or efficient cause, and so either of them may produce like effects.[23]

The witches' songs discussed in this chapter certainly do not conform to the elevated, "reasonable" Orphic hymns described by Agrippa, yet, as we shall see, the notion that one can "bind and direct" by using charms that correspond in "number" and "proportion" to the thing enchanted shaped onstage representations of witchcraft. The aesthetic imperfection of the witch's voice and the frequent nonsensical and irrational nature of her incantations were the perfect magical mediums for performing her demonic rituals, summoning powers from hellish realms.[24]

Beyond the general performance practices associated with musical witchcraft, specific musical conventions represented the witch's transgressive qualities. Although the significance of witches changed over the course of the century, composers and playwrights consistently marked witches as disorderly by rendering them incapable of producing harmony, portraying them as rustic bumpkins bereft of graceful movement or music, or conflating sexual, political, and spiritual transgression through the setting of treasonous lyrics to bawdy or sacred-sounding music.

The Symbolism of Noise

Noisemakers or dissonant music frequently accompanied witches on both the court and the public stage. How might we understand this phenomenon? As discussed in chapter 1, Neoplatonism had a significant influence on seventeenth-century musicians and dramatists, particularly those involved in the creation of court masques, a form that frequently used Neoplatonic symbolism to contrast the harmony of the king and queen (the masque proper) with the disorder of those who might threaten that harmony (the antimasque). In the court masque, musical harmony represented divine harmony and the harmonious relationship between divinely appointed monarch and subject. Dissonant or harsh, noisy sounds symbolized violence, conflict, and subversion.[25] Ben Jonson's highly influential *Masque of Queens* (1609), performed for James I and his court, uses this trope to great effect. The hags, Jonson tells us, represent ignorance, suspicion, and credulity: all things opposed to Fame. He describes their entrance in terms that manifest, in physical and aural terms, their personal deficiencies:

> *These witches, with a kind of hollow and infernal music, came forth from thence. First one, then two, and three, and more, till their number increased to eleven, all differently attired: some with rats on their head, some on their shoulders; others with ointment pots at their girdles; all with spindles, timbrels, rattles or other venefical instruments, making a confused noise, with strange gestures.* [lines 25–30][26]

Jonson cites noisemakers as being appropriate for the witches' "hollow and infernal" music. To complement this unharmonious soundscape, Jonson visually emphasizes the hags' physical disorder, as they appear haphazardly, make "strange gestures," and wear ragged attire emblematic of their low social status.

Later in the masque, when the witches request music for dancing, Jonson reinforces the notion that their music lacks harmony, citing demonological literature for support in one of his many footnotes:

> Nor do they want music, and in strange manner given them by the devil, if we credit their confessions in Remy, *Daemonolatria*

I.xix, such as the Syrbenaean choirs were, which Athenaeus remembers out of Clearchus, *Deipnosophists* XV.[697F], where
everyone sung what he would without hearkening to his fellow,
like the noise of divers oars falling in the water. But be patient
of Remy's relation: "They are mixed up and disordered there in
marvelous ways, nor can it be sufficiently expressed in any words
how they make confused, harsh and discordant noises." [note to
line 323]

It would seem that Jonson's comparison of the witches' music to
"the noise of divers oars falling in the water" is a fanciful way of
describing inexpert singing—singing that is discordant, out of tune,
each line so independent that it cannot be incorporated into a co-
herent whole. Indeed, the description from Remy supports the association between witches' music and aural chaos ("mixed up,"
"disordered," "confused," "harsh," "discordant noises"). The onstage singing of the hags in the *Masque of Queens* should, then,
reflect the beliefs of the authorities cited by Jonson.

But Jonson takes a different approach to represent the witches'
inherent disharmony. The witches do not sing at all, either in their
incantations or to accompany their dances. While he cites a variety
of sources that describe the witches' discordant singing, Jonson
does not grant them this ability. As Peter Walls observes, the hags'
incantations effectively function as spoken songs, but they fail to
capture the spiritual power of true religious ritual. Instead, they
are poetically irregular and ineffectual charms.[27] Sung music and
its special magical powers are reserved for the noble participants
of the masque proper.[28]

Later plays also perpetuate the notion that witches lack harmony, sometimes portraying musicians as unable to produce music
in the presence of witches or having the coven themselves perform
unpleasant, confused music. In Thomas Dekker, John Ford, and
William Rowley's *The Witch of Edmonton* (1621) the fiddler, Sawgut,
cannot coax any sound from his instrument in the presence of the
witch's evil familiar, Dog. In Thomas Heywood and Richard
Brome's *The Late Lancashire Witches* (1634) the witches musically
disrupt an occasion that should be a harmonious communal activity, a wedding. The bewitched wedding musicians cannot play in
the presence of the evil coven. Thomas Shadwell's *The Lancashire
Witches* (1681) features a coven of witches that descend into aural
chaos. After a sung invitation to mischief, the witches perform a
spoken incantation to conjure a storm, an incantation that is heav-

ily indebted to Jonson's charms for his hags in *The Masque of Queens*.[29] When their spoken invocation is unsuccessful ("Not yet a Storme?") the coven resolve to "wound / The Air with every dreadful sound, / And with live vipers beat the ground."[30] The coven then "beat[s] the ground with Vipers, they bark, howl, hiss, cry like Screetch Owles, hollow like Owls, and make many confused noises."[31] These "confused" and bestial noises, like the confused noise of the hags in Jonson's *Masque of Queens*, are aural manifestations of the witches' disorder. The coven then sings a charm song, "Now the Winds Roar," which, with its noisy adjectives ("roar," "crack" "howl") and, one assumes, appropriate music, draws forth the fury of nature.[32] Of course, storms frequently signified unruly passions and disorder (most famously in Shakespeare's *Tempest*).[33] The disharmony of the Lancashire coven thus serves a dual purpose: to illustrate the witches' internal disorder and to summon and harness the chaotic power of the natural world, using bestial noises and evocative music to "wound the air": an onstage demonstration of the power of sympathy.

Rusticity and Authority

The dissonance of witches' music, like the witches themselves, resonated on multiple levels. As we have seen, the noisemakers and dissonant sounds associated with witchcraft portrayed in aural terms the wretched physical and spiritual deformity of the witch, summoned the disorderly elements of the natural world to do their bidding, and in the court masque signified their estrangement from the elite aristocrats, who were accompanied by harmonious sounds as they danced a ritualized bodily display of order.[34] But other meanings can be ascribed to this unharmonious music. Although an idealized Arcadian England was celebrated in plays, masques, and music of the period, the countryside also held more troubling associations.[35] The witches' songs and dances frequently drew upon the musical practices of seasonal folk festivals in which normative social hierarchies were overturned and for the day peasants took power that wasn't ordinarily theirs, just as the witch took power that didn't rightfully belong to her. In his description of the witches' dancing from *The Masque of Queens*, Jonson records that timbrels and rattles accompanied the hags. A timbrel is another name for a tambourine, a noisemaking instrument that audiences would have instantly associated with country dancing and folk festivals. The rattle was also a standard aural signifier of disorder featured in village rituals: the skimmington, in which cross-dressed men portrayed unruly women and hen-pecked husbands were punished and humiliated; and charivaris, a rite in which inappropriate marriages were mocked.[36] Shadwell's *The Lancashire Witches* makes explicit the connection between these sorts of village festivals and witchcraft. The hag Mal Spencer, spurned by the clown Clod, rides him like a horse—a practice similar to the Lady Skimmington ritual in which a man is ridden through town.[37] As Terry Eagleton and others have noted, authorities actually licensed and sponsored such festive disorder to purge dissent from the system.[38] The association of witches with rusticity, then, might be read as a reenactment of the festive ritual that purged or contained problematic elements through licit entertainment.

The portrayal of witches as rustic bumpkins also had class implications. It is important to remember that most of the people who consumed these theatrical witchcraft entertainments were city dwellers. The noisemakers and dissonance that accompanied the witches' onstage antics may have also sought to marginalize the witches from the urban elite of London. Portraying witches as rustic allowed theatergoers to take comfort in the notion that such demonic nastiness was something that mostly happened outside fair London or the elite environs of court. For aristocratic audience members in the public theater and the masquing hall the witches were not only separated from them by virtue of their rusticity— they were also separated from them by class. Watching the witches in *The Masque of Queens*, noble spectators probably felt somewhat smug—confident that they were superior in class, sophistication, and bodily movement.

Historical evidence further contextualizes the seventeenth-century desire to mark witches as rural and lower class. In seventeenth-century England many of the people accused of witchcraft *were* rural peasants from such places as North Berwick, Lancashire, and Edmonton.[39] Indeed, playwrights often used actual witchcraft cases as source material (most explicitly in *The Witch of Edmonton* and *The Late Lancashire Witches*). Thus, the witches' association with musical rusticity may have been an attempt at journalistic accuracy.

We can see this relationship among class, musical rusticity, and theatricality resonate in remarkable and complex ways in the tract *Newes from Scotland* (1591). One of the probable sources for Shakespeare's *Macbeth*, *Newes from Scotland* demonstrates how real-life

witches' singing and dancing inscribed their social status, deline-
ating their separation from the elite.[40] In this description of the
malicious activities of a coven based in North Berwick, Scotland,
music functions as a signifier for the witches' lower-class status,
religious nonconformity, and ethnicity. The author recounts a fascinating episode in which James, King of Scotland and future King
of England, encountered a few of his more disorderly subjects:

> Item, the saide *Agnis Tompson* was after brought againe before the
> Kings Majestie and his Counsell, and being examined of the
> meetings and detestable dealings of those witches, she confessed
> that upon the night of *Allhollon* Even last, she was accompanied
> as well with the persons aforesaide, as also with a great many
> other witches, to the number of two hundreth: and that all they
> together went by Sea each one in a Riddle or Cive, and went in
> the same very substantially with Flaggons of wine making merrie
> and drinking by the waye in the same Riddles or Cives, to the
> Kerke of North Barrick in Lowthian, and that after they had
> landed, tooke handes on the land and daunced this reill or short
> daunce
>   . . . At which time she confessed, that this *Geilles Duncane*
> did goe before them playing this reill or daunce upon a small
> Trump, called a Jewes Trumpt, untill they entered into the Kerk
> of north Barrick. These confessions made the King in a wonder-
> ful admiration, and sent for the said *Geillis Duncane*, who upon
> the like Trump did playe the said daunce before the Kings Ma-
> jestie, who in respect of the strangenes of these matters, tooke
> great delight to bee present at their examinations.[41]

The women accused of witchcraft in *Newes from Scotland* were rural
peasants—poor servants living on the margins of polite society.[42]
According to the account, as part of their ritual they danced a
reel—an ancient Scottish folk dance frequently performed in a circle.[43] To accompany their celebration, Geilles Duncane plays a
small "Jewes Trumpt" (also known as a Jew's harp) that by its very
name denotes religious nonconformity.[44]

Newes from Scotland also describes the rustic type of vocal music
appropriate for witches. According to the treatise, Geilles Duncane
and her companions danced toward the church, accompanied by
their own singing. The author claims the witches sang "all with
one voice" the words, *"Commer goe ye before, commer goe ye, / Gif
ye will not goe before, commer let me"*.[45] The coven's rustic quality is

accentuated as their song is in dialect.[46] Their musical charm is simple, unlearned, and repetitive. It is not sung in learned counterpoint, but rather is sung "all with one voice"—in unison.

From this short description we can begin to conceive how music and dance marked individuals as belonging to a certain social group or class. Geilles Duncane and Agnis Tompson are not professional musicians. They have not mastered the elegant courtly dances performed by the aristocracy (and they probably had no interest in doing so). They do not sing learned music. Their musical practices are of the folk. From the king's perspective, their activities are grotesque and strange, yet he took "great delight" experiencing their unusual performance.

Many of the issues raised in *Newes from Scotland*—the relationship of king to subject, musically rustic witches as entertainment for the elites (to fill them with "great delight")—are translated into theatrical spectacle on the seventeenth-century stage. We know the real-life "witch" Geilles Duncane danced a reel for the king, but what rustic dances did theatrical witches perform for their audiences, and how might we understand their cultural meanings? One of the most common types of witches' dance was the round. While round dances performed in a clockwise fashion mimicked the motion of the spheres and replicated divine harmony in bodily movement, witches' rounds were often perversely performed counterclockwise and back-to-back.[47] The tendency to associate witches with backwardness, identified by Stuart Clark, is here made physically manifest.[48] The witches' backward dancing also resonates with earlier criticisms of round dances accompanied by singing, such as the carole. From medieval times, the carole had been indicted in clerical discourses as a dangerous folk tradition, a remnant of paganism, and a tool of the Devil, provoking lasciviousness, particularly when performed "backwards."[49]

Ben Jonson featured this type of devilishly backward round dancing in his *Masque of Queens*. Jonson's masque is directly concerned with the relationship between the aristocracy and unruly Others. Within the masque the witches are musically and physically represented as grotesque, antic foils to the order represented by the Queens. The witches' marginalization from the beauteous Queens, and, by extension, the harmonious body politic of James's court, is sealed when they begin their antic dance. Drawing on classical and contemporary sources, Jonson describes their terpsichorean deformity:

Figure 2.2. Woodcut from *The Kingdom of Darkness* (1688). By Permission of the Folger Shakespeare Library.

At which, with a strange and sudden music they fell into a magical dance full of preposterous change and gesticulation, but most applying to their property, who at their meetings do all things contrary to the custom of men, dancing back to back and hip to hip, their hands joined, and making their circles backward, to the left hand, with strange fantastic motions of their heads and bodies. [lines 327–32]

This description of witches' round dancing encapsulated common ideas about witches' terpsichorean practices, ideas that can be seen in virtually all seventeenth-century depictions of witches' round dancing, theatrical and otherwise. For example, witches in the anti-witchcraft tract *The Kingdom of Darkness* (1688) still dance a round, back-to-back, accompanied by a bagpiper in a tree. (See figure 2.2.[50])

"The Second Witches' Dance" found in GB-Lbl. Add. MS 10444 may have been used to accompany the backward round dance, "full of preposterous change" in *The Masque of Queens*.[51] The piece is certainly metrically unstable; the time signature changes four times, with three of the changes occurring in the second strain.[52] The music seems irrational, unable to sustain musical coherence. The first section is rhythmically regular. Once this regularity is established, expectations are subverted as the rhythmic pattern is disturbed by two long blasts. After this disruption, the music shifts into a triple meter, and temporarily becomes more regular, but this new rhythmic profile is very short-lived; the meter changes and rushing eight notes appear in measure 14, a musical analogue to the witches' jerky, strange, and unpredictable movements described by Jonson. The final section presents a rhythmically regular rustic dance, complete with a drone-like accompaniment (perhaps alluding to a bagpipe), first on a repeated F in the bass and then moving downward, landing on a repeated C. (See example 2.1.[53])

While the witches' dance is undoubtedly grotesque, unpredictable, and unruly, it travels through chaos toward some degree of regularity, from uncontrolled disorder to mockable rusticity, drawing a musical line between the lower-class witches and the beauteous Queens, played by Queen Anna and her ladies. The witches' subordination, their place in the social hierarchy, is further clarified at the end of the masque as they enter bound, yoked to the Queens' chariots. In Jonson's *Masque of Queens*, then, music, dance, and stage action serve to mark the hags as rustic, lower class, and grotesque, in opposition to the elegant, refined aristocratic body.

While the preposterous round in *The Masque of Queens* clearly contrasts the hags' bodily inferiority with the elegant pageantry of the aristocratic queens, the witches' round and the relationship between witch and aristocrat is treated with more ambivalence in entertainments for the public theater. Thomas Middleton's *The Witch* (1615–16) presents an overtly comical, but ultimately more troubling, variety of onstage witchcraft. Possibly banned by the censors, Middleton's play features Hecate, a bawdy and grotesque witch who serves an aristocratic clientele, creating disgusting concoctions to manipulate their sex lives (in particular, she sells a potion to promote impotence, a vivid demonstration of her emasculating powers).[54] Thus, *The Witch* presents a disturbingly symbiotic relationship between witch and noble.

Although courtiers consult Hecate (and even sleep with her), in many other respects Hecate and her coven are marginalized from the court. Hecate is explicitly of lower-class status; she is addressed by her betters as Goody Hag, Goody being short for Goodwife, a term applied to a married woman of the poorest class.[55] Her lack of education is evident; while occasionally using Latin charms from the learned tradition, she frequently misapplies

Example 2.1. "The Second Witches' Dance," GB-Lbl. Add. MS 10444. By permission of the British Library.

them or gets them wrong (her love charm misquotes Virgil's *Eclogues*)—she too is an imperfect speaker.[56] Furthermore, Hecate and her clan reside in an undisclosed location, away from the court, establishing a comforting spatial distance between courtier and witch.

While Hecate exists on the margins of the drama, her witches' round is not banished as in *The Masque of Queens*. Although *The Witch* uses the same musical materials as *The Masque of Queens*, the dramatic context causes us to read the scene of witches' dancing quite differently. Rather than place witch in opposition to aristocrat, the final scene of musical witchcraft in act 5, scene 2, of the play emphasizes the disturbing relationship between the world of the courtier and the world of the witch. A murderous Duchess approaches Hecate for a potion to kill her former lover. Hecate agrees, and the witches sing "Black Spirits and White" to prepare the aristocrat's deadly charm. No music survives, but Hecate's son Firestone describes their incantation as "the tune of damnation" [V.ii.81].[57] After the charm song, Hecate commands the "air to strike our tune," [V.ii.83] to provide accompaniment for their dancing. John Cutts has posited that a witches' dance from *The Masque of Queens* was used here, and if it was, then the witches' last moments onstage would have been spent dancing a grotesque antimasque dance, which, in its original context, musically and visually emphasized the hags' estrangement from the idealized harmony of the aristocratic body.[58] However, unlike Jonson's hags, Middleton's coven is not dispelled by courtly order, by the loud music of Fame. Hecate and her cohorts simply disappear. They are not punished for their deeds; in fact, they prosper. The treatment of the relationship between aristocrat and witch, in this case, is wholly ambiguous.

Likewise, in the 1623 folio of William Shakespeare's *Macbeth* the inclusion of a round dance forces a consideration of the power dynamic between witch and noble. In the first printed edition, witches' music was interpolated from Middleton's *The Witch*.[59] Some commentators believe the addition of the bawdy and comical music from *The Witch* rendered Shakespeare's weird sisters considerably less ominous; this may be so, but I would argue that they actually have more power, not less, by virtue of their musical performances.[60] In particular, their round dance in act 4, scene 1, while undoubtedly suggesting the witches' alignment with the common folk, simultaneously demonstrates their power over Macbeth (much as Geilles Duncane had the power to delight James I). After conjuring a show of eight kings, Hecate notices Macbeth's consternation and decides to provide a musical performance. She tells her sisters, "I'll charm the air to give a sound, / While you perform your antic round: / That this great King may kindly say / Our duties did his welcome pay" [IV.i.129–32].

This possible allusion to the dance performed by the North Berwick coven for James seems politically dangerous; if one were to make allegorical substitutions, the illegitimate king, Macbeth, would represent James, and the powerful weird sisters would represent Geilles Duncane and her troupe. But there is a crucial difference between the historical incident and the dramatic one: in the historical narrative the king summons Geilles Duncane to perform. As Diane Purkiss has noted, Geilles Duncane's music is for James's consumption and occurs at his pleasure. Through his kingly prerogative, James transforms Duncane's powerful charms into empty spectacle (although I would argue one must acknowledge Duncane's power to entertain).[61] In contrast, the witches in *Macbeth* decide to dance for the king. *They* control the spectacle and music; they do not dance in obedience to a kingly command. While the inclusion of their antic round makes the difference between the rustic witches and aristocrats physically manifest, their ability to provoke wonder in their king suggests that through their music and dance they ruled his passions as well as his destiny in the 1623 folio of *Macbeth*.

Another dance linked with disorderly festive conduct, the morris, also plays a complex and multivalent role in articulating the relationship between witches and the elite. Morris dancing is at the center of the comic subplot of Thomas Dekker, John Ford, and William Rowley's journalistic play, *The Witch of Edmonton* (1621), which draws on the real-life witchcraft case of Elizabeth Sawyer.[62] While often played for laughs, the morris occupies an ideologically contested space, and its performance suggests a disturbing fluidity among the world of the corrupt aristocrat (Sir Arthur Clarington), the rustic clown (Cuddy Banks), and the witch (Elizabeth "Mother" Sawyer).

The morris, itself a fluid genre, crossed social boundaries, as it was performed not only in rustic settings by peasants, but also at court by aristocrats. It did not have a set form; rather the name applied to any grotesque dance performed in bell-laden costumes and occasionally with blackened faces (the name "morris" might have been a reference to the Moors). Accompanied by the pipe and tabor (a small drum), a common version of the dance involved a galloping hobby horse, Robin Hood, and a man cross-dressed as Maid Marian encircled by prospective suitors (for an illustration of some of these characters, see figure 2.3). The hobbyhorse was overtly disruptive, breaking the circle and charging at random, while the mock wooing between Robin Hood and his mistress was disruptive in a more subtle way. The Maid of the Morris, in direct opposition to the stereotype of the virtuous courtly lady, was neither a woman nor chaste. Her bawdiness and her role as sexual aggressor was the source of much humor, and, among Puritan reformers, much anxiety.[63]

While the morris had in the past enjoyed church sponsorship, by the late sixteenth century it had increasingly drawn fire from Puritans. After 1630, the church stopped sponsoring morris dancing altogether, although both James I and Charles I claimed it was a harmless pastime, as long as their subjects went to church first.[64] By supporting the right of the folk to indulge in such entertainments, the Stuarts formed an unlikely and ultimately unstable alliance with the rural peasantry, who, by the mid seventeenth century, were the primary performers of the dance.[65]

One of the Puritans' main objections to morris dancing and other country games and sports was that many of these festive practices were holdovers from Catholicism and even earlier pagan festivals.[66] In a passage strikingly similar to the description of the witches' dancing procession toward church in *Newes from Scotland*, Puritan polemicist Phillip Stubbes lavishes his unadulterated disgust upon the morris dance:

> Thus all things set in order, then have they their Hobby-horses, dragons & other Antiques, togither with their baudie Pipers and thundering Drummers to strike up the devils daunce withall, then marche these heathen company towards the Church and Churchyard, their pipers pipeing, their drummers thundring, their stumps dauncing, their bels jyngling, their handkerchefs swinging about their heds like madmen, their hobbie horses and other monsters skirmishing amongst the route: & in this sorte they go to the Church (I say) & into the Church (though the Minister be at praier or preaching) dancing & swinging [t]heir handkercheifs over their hede, in the Church, like devils incarnate with such a confuse noise, that no man can hear his own voice.[67]

Figure 2.3. Morris Dance. Engraving of Sixteenth-Century Window in the House of George Tollet, Esq., sixteenth century. Art File M875#1. By Permission of the Folger Shakespeare Library.

The morris's aural confusion, its lack of predictability, its ability to disrupt even a minister's prayers, lies at the heart of Stubbes's anxiety. In short, the morris resists control, even ecclesiastical control. Given such objections to the dance, it is but a small step to explicitly connect the unruly morris with witchcraft. A few decades later, Samuel Harsnett does precisely that in his description of a bewitched girl in *A Declaration of Egregious Popish Impostures* (1603):

> *Frateretto, Fliberdigibbet, Hoberdidance, Tocobatto* were foure devils of the round, or Morrice, whom *Sara* in her fits, tuned together, in measure and sweet cadence. And least you should conceive, that the devils had no musicke in hell, especially that they would goe a maying without theyr musicke, the Fidler comes in with his Taber, & Pipe, and a whole Morice after him, with mostly visards for theyr better grace. These foure had forty assistants under them, as themselves doe confesse.[68]

The problematic nature of the morris is clearly articulated in the climax of *The Witch of Edmonton*. Instead of the aristocrat being presented in virtuous opposition to witchcraft, as in Jonson's *Masque of Queens*, Sir Arthur Clarington actually hosts the morally suspect morris.[69] The aristocrat's sponsorship of the potentially demonic dance may have appealed to those in the audience inclined to critique the excesses of the upper classes. But *The Witch of Edmonton* also indicts the lower-class clown, Cuddy Banks. Cuddy has clearly been tainted by demonism as he brings Dog, the Witch of Edmonton's familiar, to the morris. As the dancers take their places, the fiddler strangely cannot produce any sound from his instrument: the presence of evil also robs virtuous people of harmony. Banks takes the fiddle and gives it to Dog, who promptly plays a tune to accompany the morris. The devilish Dog literally leads the morris dancers in their measures. This moment is profoundly disturbing, as the morris, sponsored by a nobleman and performed by the folk, is unambiguously the dance of the Devil. Both upper and lower classes are tainted by demonism. Here the moral implications of class are not clear.

Although festive folk dances such as the morris frequently featured carnivalesque transvestite characters such as the cross-dressed Maid Marian, another dance performed by witches, the jig, seems to have been specifically associated with fluid gender boundaries and perhaps even spiritual transgression. From Elizabethan times "jig" was a broad generic term used to describe a dance and song, sometimes performed by men in drag or other grotesque costumes, full of bawdy, low humor.[70] Over time, the jig developed a characteristic rhythmic profile that complemented the leaping movements of the dance. An analysis of the jigs in John Playford's *English Dancing Master* (1650) demonstrates that while the time signature could be duple, triple, or compound, a lilting rhythmic pattern (either half note–quarter or dotted quarter–eighth) was almost always present.[71]

The jig's inherent bawdiness and undignified leaping movements made it vulnerable to accusations that its performance led to various kinds of deviance and disorder. The anonymous author of *Hic-Mulier* (1620) associated the jig with uppity women, women who refused their proper place. According to the pamphleteer, the jig was a favorite dance for the sartorially subversive "Masculine-Feminine," a woman who, in an attempt to be fashionable, donned elements of male dress:

> You have . . . exchang[ed] the modest attire of the comely Hood, Cawle, Coyfe, handsome Dresse or Kerchiefe, to the cloudy Ruffianly broad-brim'd Hatte, and wanton feather, the modest upper parts of a concealing straight gowne, to the loose, lascivious civill embracement of a French doublet, being all unbutton'd to entice, all of one shape to hide deformitie, and extreme short wasted to give a most easie way to every luxurious action: the glory of a faire large hayre, to the shame of most ruffianly short lockes; the side, thicke gather'd, and close guarding Savegards [an outer skirt or petticoat worn by women to protect their dress when riding], to the short, weake, thinne, loose, and every hand-entertaining short basses [plaited, knee-length open skirts]; for Needles, Swords; for Prayer bookes, bawdy Jigs; for modest gestures, gyant-like behaviours, and for womens modestie, all Mimicke and apish incivilitie.[72]

In this short passage, the anonymous author manages to associate the jig with sartorial subversion, gender-role transgression, and religious deviance (instead of praying, the Masculine-Feminine jigs). One can understand, then, why the jig was a favorite dance of the theatrical witch.

In Heywood and Brome's *The Late Lancashire Witches* (1634), a journalistic witchcraft play specifically concerned with the subversion of hierarchies—wives rule their husbands, children rule their parents, servants rule their masters, and witches rule good Christians—the unruly female coven use a jig to subvert masculine exercise. Presaging a line from Nahum Tate and Henry Purcell's *Dido and Aeneas*, they perform a dance charm "to spoyle the Hunters sport."[73] The lilting dance rhythms of the jig also pervade the extant settings of the witches' dance song in William Davenant's revised version of Shakespeare's *Macbeth* (ca. 1663). Davenant's textual and musical alterations and additions to *Macbeth* increase the stage presence of the witches, who are particularly subversive as they celebrate regicide with jigging dance songs.

Richard Leveridge, a composer, actor, and singer who began his lengthy career on the London stage in the late seventeenth century, was probably responsible for the most famous musical setting of the witches' scenes (1702). The other Restoration musical incarnations of Davenant's *Macbeth* include two dances, possibly by early Restoration composer Matthew Locke (probably for the 1663–64 revival) and a complete setting from around 1694 or 1695 by John Eccles, the house composer for Lincoln's Inn Fields.[74]

All three composers use jig dance rhythms to set one of Davenant's original witches' songs, "Let's Have a Dance upon the Heath."[75] Indeed, the settings, although separated by decades from each other, are remarkably similar, being diatonic, triple meter, and major key, and use similar jig dance rhythms (one of the sources for Locke's dance, *Musicks Delight on the Cithren*, labels it "A Jigg called Macbeth"). Late seventeenth-century audiences continued to understand the jig as a sexual and potentially comical dance. The actresses Moll Davis and Nell Gwyn pleased the libertine Charles II with their performances of the dance,[76] while Restoration-era music theorist Thomas Mace highlighted its frivolous qualities: "*Toys* or *Jiggs*, are *Light-Squibbish Things*, only fit for *Fantastical* and *Easie-Light-Headed People*."[77] (See examples 2.2,[78] 2.3, and 2.4.)

How would Restoration-era audiences have understood this jig, ostensibly a light-hearted dance, which contains the disturbing lyric, "We gain more lives by Duncan's death"? The lilting major-key music directly contradicts the menace of the text. Yet, if the witches of Davenant's *Macbeth* were viewed as comical, oversexed, lower class, or just generally transgressive, this portrayal was facilitated by the use of the jig. With this strategy of musical class marginalization, the threat of the weird sisters might have been somewhat mitigated. On the other hand, it is possible that the

Example 2.2. Matthew Locke, "Let's Have a Dance," *Apollo's Banquet* (London, 1669).

Example 2.3. John Eccles, "Let's Have a Dance," mm. 3–10. GB-Lbl. Add. MS 12219. By permission of the British Library.

Example 2.4. Richard Leveridge, "Let's Have a Dance," mm. 1–6. GB-Cfm. Mu MS 87. By permission of the Syndics of the Fitzwilliam Museum to whom rights in this publication are assigned.

cheerful and comical dance merely highlighted the witches' perversity, their rejoicing celebration of the disorder caused by regicide.

The dramatic context for this dance provides additional clues about what the witches' antics might have meant for contemporary audiences. The witches perform for Lady Macduff (a character Davenant fleshed out to serve as an exemplar of a good woman, as opposed to the bad woman, Lady Macbeth) and her husband. Macduff is frightened by the witches' "hellish song," but Lady Macduff is too virtuous to be cowed by the "messengers of darkness." After hearing their songs, watching them dance, and hearing their "dire predictions," she declares, "He that believes ill news from such as these, / Deserves to find it true. Their words are like / Their shape; nothing but fiction" [II.v. 88–90].[79] In short, Lady Macduff implies that if one is gullible enough to believe the witches' prophecies, one deserves to have them come to pass. For the discriminating lady, these witches are full of sound and fury, but ultimately signify nothing—a significant departure from the powerful prognosticators in Shakespeare's original or even the entertaining and astonishing witches from the 1623 folio *Macbeth*.

Lady Macduff's discernment and skepticism reflects that of the Restoration audience, for whom the witches would probably have been a pleasant musical diversion, "nothing but fiction." Fear of witchcraft waned over the course of the century, and writers on witchcraft increasingly associated belief in witchcraft with the poorer, more superstitious elements of society.[80] A pathologization of witchcraft, the attempt to view it as the product of a diseased mind rather than a genuine occult phenomenon, influenced witchcraft discourses, a trend that can be seen as early as Reginald Scot's *The Discoverie of Witchcraft* (1584). As noted in the previous chapter, Scot believed that many accused of witchcraft did not actually possess supernatural abilities; they were merely deluded old women, possibly suffering from melancholy.[81] The skepticism toward witches is also evident in John Gaule's 1646 treatise quoted above, as he lambastes those who believe that all impoverished old women in ragged coats, by virtue of their ugliness, must be guilty of witchcraft. This skepticism only intensified as the century progressed. John Webster, after acknowledging the possibility that some of the accused might be witches, later claims in his 1677 treatise, *The Displaying of Supposed Witchcraft*:

> The Witch must be taken to be either a person *insanae, vel sanae mentis*; and if they be *insanae mentis*, their Confessions are no sufficient evidence, nor worthy of any credit; because there is neither Reason, Law, nor Equity that allows the testimony or confession of an Idiot, Lunatick, mad or doting person, because they are not of a right and sound understanding, and are not to be accounted as *compotes mentis*, nor governed by rationability.[82]

As science, rationalism, and empiricism gradually prevailed in England, particularly after the mid-century, prosecutions of witches became less frequent.[83] In particular, the idea that witches were lower class continued to resonate during the Restoration, permitting members of both the middle class and the aristocracy to distance the figure of the witch from themselves, and allowing them to ridicule her as a comical, lower-class bumpkin. Yet witches were still discussed and described in treatises by Protestant clergymen who sought to explain the religious, moral, and political chaos around them and found witches convenient scapegoats. Joseph Glanvill critiques the tendency of the elites to dismiss the

Example 2.5. John Eccles, "Let's Have a Dance," mm. 47–53.

power of witches in *Saducismus Triumphatus* (1681), placing sacrilege, rebellion, and witchcraft on the same footing:

> And those that know any thing of the World, know, that most of the looser *Gentry*, and the small pretenders to *Philosophy* and *Wit*, are generally deriders of the *belief of Witches* and *Apparitions*. And were this a slight and meer speculative mistake, I should not trouble my self or them about it. But I fear this errour hath a *Core* in it that is worse than *Heresie*: and therefore how little soever I care what men *believe* or *teach* in matters of *Opinion*, I think I have reason to be concern'd in an affair that toucheth so near upon the greatest interests of Religion. And really I am astonisht

Example 2.5. *Continued.*

> sometimes to think into what a kind of *Age* we are fallen, in which some of the *greatest impieties* are accounted but *Bugs*, and *terrible Names*, *invisible Tittles*, Peccadillo's, or Chimera's. The sad and greatest instances are *SACRILEDGE*, *REBELLION*, and *WITCHCRAFT*.[84]

Glanvill fought the good fight against the advancing skepticism of the educated classes, but by the early eighteenth century he and his kind had lost the battle. In 1736 the Witchcraft Act was repealed, bringing the era of witch hunting to a definitive end.[85]

Example 2.6. Richard Leveridge, "Let's Have a Dance," mm. 64–72.

Many of the same musical strategies that marked the witch as lower class continued to be used on the late Restoration stage, although the musical gestures become increasingly stylized, as composers wrote artful and sometimes elaborate approximations of rustic songs and dances, instead of using the "real" thing. We hear this gradual shift in the jigs composed for Davenant's *Macbeth*. While Locke's jig is distinctly folkish and simple in character, both Eccles's and Leveridge's dance songs are more complex, with key changes (m. 51, Eccles), linear chromaticism (mm. 51–52, Eccles) and echo effects (Leveridge). They also require ample musical re-

Example 2.6. *Continued.*

sources as they feature choruses, string orchestras, and continuo. (See examples 2.5[86] and 2.6.[87])

One certainly cannot imagine Geilles Duncane or her compatriots performing these songs as part of their rituals. Of course, there are many reasons for the stylistic changes seen in these pieces. Late seventeenth-century English theatrical composers embraced lavish spectacle and the operatic innovations of their French and Italian counterparts. While it is impossible to pin down the reasons for a specific musical stylistic change, in practical terms Eccles's

Example 2.6. *Continued.*

and Leveridge's settings of "Let's Have a Dance" sound significantly different from the witches' music heard earlier in the century. In these elaborate songs the rustic onstage musical practices of witches have been severed from the lived experience of the folk, transmuting their singing and dancing into entertaining theatrical fictions.

Political, Sexual, and Spiritual Transgression

Although Lady Macduff is skeptical of the witches' magic, their treason is less easily dismissed, as they celebrate the death of kings.

Davenant was not being particularly innovative in accentuating the political subversion of his witches; instead he drew upon a long-standing tradition that associated witchcraft with all sorts of political, sexual, and religious transgressions. In particular, Catholics were frequently accused of being witches. Even Reginald Scot's relatively enlightened treatise on witchcraft is rife with diatribes against popery, and Samuel Harsnett's description of witchcraft practices is entitled *A Declaration of Egregious Popish Impostures* (1603). These anti-Catholic sentiments, while certainly present, did not consistently inflect Jacobean and Caroline onstage portrayals of witchcraft.[88] After the Restoration of Charles II to the English throne in 1660, this changed, as anti-Catholic rhetoric intensified both on- and offstage. The associations among witchcraft, subversive female behavior, sexual profligacy, deformity, rebellion, and treason facilitated the association of witchcraft with Catholicism, the most feared religion in late seventeenth-century England. After the Restoration of Charles Stuart and the Anglican Church in 1660, many viewed Catholicism as a serious threat to the Protestant state of England.[89] This anxiety may have been heightened because Charles II, James, Duke of York (later James II), and other Royalist exiles had enjoyed the hospitality of Catholic countries on the Continent during the Interregnum.

Perhaps as a result of his own Catholic sympathies, Charles II tried to soften government policy toward the Church of Rome.[90] Although he fought against a recalcitrant Parliament for more religious toleration of Dissenters (Protestants who were not a part of the Church of England) and Roman Catholics, Parliament instituted the Test Acts of 1673 and 1678, which required all public servants to openly take communion in the Anglican Church. Anti-Catholic sentiment increased after the Popish Plot scare of 1678, which played on fears about the weakness of the body politic; Titus Oates, a former Anglican clergyman, and Israel Tonge, a clergyman and former schoolmaster, accused English Catholics of plotting with the Pope. According to the story, England would be attacked from Ireland and France, and England's new rulers would suppress individual freedom and liberty, installing an absolutist regime after the manner of Louis XIV.[91] The Exclusion Crisis of 1679–81 followed, as Parliament attempted to block Charles's Catholic brother, James, from succeeding to the throne. James II was crowned in 1685, but because of his ill-advised policies and overt Catholicism, his reign was short. The Glorious Revolution of 1688 paved the way for the joint rule of William III (Prince of Orange) and Mary II in 1689, reestablishing the Protestant monarchy. But this action caused a conflict in the line of succession between Catholic James II and his descendents and foreign-born monarchs such as William who had a more distant claim to the throne but were safely Protestant.[92]

Protestant writers detailed the connection between witchcraft and this most feared religion—Catholicism—demonstrating that Catholics, constructed as being sexually suspect, feminine, and treasonous, were also versed in the black arts. Anti-Catholic writers regularly resorted to the same rhetoric of misogyny and sexual deviance found in witchcraft treatises, as they compared the Church of Rome to "a foul, filthy, old withered harlot . . . the great Strumpet of all Strumpets, the Mother of Whoredom."[93] According to Protestant tracts, practicing Catholicism was heresy, and this heretical church was constructed as a deformed, sexually inconstant female, implying that the true Church (the Church of England) was its opposite: pure and male. Such anti-witchcraft, anti-Catholic discourses served as policing mechanisms, effectively drawing a line between moral, loyal Englishmen and deviant, rebellious witches, between a healthy, masculine, Protestant England and a diseased, feminine, Catholic state. For example, Titus Oates, one of the instigators of the Popish Plot panic, connected witchcraft, Catholicism, treason, and female sexual excess in *The Witch of Endor, or the Witchcrafts of the Roman Jesebel* of 1679:

> *We have again detected the Contrivances of the* Romish *Interest against our Religion and Liberties, therefore, my Lord, I humbly conceive, That those that appear for a* Popish Successor, *are for* Popery *by wholesale, let their Pretences be what they will against it by retail, and would at once betray our Land to* Rome's *Tyranny and Witchcrafts, and are content for the Gust of a sweet Morsel to sell all, even God, their King, Religion, and everything that may conduce to the Peace, Welfare and Advantage of King and Kingdom: all which appears by their slighting, nay opposing the kindness of God our Saviour in this great Discovery of their intended Malice against us, and by their fawning and flattering with* Jesebel, *whose Whoredoms and Witchcrafts are many: they incourage and abet the devilish Interest both of* Rome *and* France, *to the great Confusion of Prince and People.*[94]

For Oates, the Catholic Church was a "Jesebel," a "whore," and a "witch," a woman who did not submit to her "Prince," the head of state and the Church of England, instead providing illicit favors to a corrupt and evil authority figure, the Pope.

Thomas Shadwell explicitly connects contemporary religious and political debates and musical witchcraft practices in his *The Lancashire Witches* (1681), as the playwright draws analogies between Catholic ritual and witchcraft. Written during the aftershocks of the Popish Plot and the tumult of the Exclusion Crisis, this play features a less-than-celibate Irish Catholic priest, Tegue O'Dively, who has sex with one of the witches. But Catholics aren't the only ones indicted for foolishness in the play. Shadwell, reflecting the skepticism of his time, censures the actions of Sir Jeffrey Shacklehead, a deluded witch-hunting justice, suggesting that many of the women who were persecuted were not deserving of punishment. Indeed, Shadwell comments in his preface that the only reason he gave the witches "real" power onstage instead of showing "the ignorance, fear, melancholy, malice, confederacy, and imposture that contribute to the belief of Witchcraft" was because it would not have been as "divert[ing]" for the public and there might have "been another clamor against it, it would have been call'd Atheistical."[95]

The witches' music for this play articulates both their power and their spiritual corruption. In act 1 the witches' song, "Come Sisters, Come, Why Do You Stay?" while textually related to other witchcraft songs (beckoning the sisters to "come," mentioning nocturnal creatures such as owls, referring to spindles and mandrake), evokes the language of a perverted black Mass, as Mother Demdike requests "a flood of Black Lambs blood":[96] the inverse of the blood of the white Lamb of God (Christ), whose actual blood Catholics imbibed through the miracle of transubstantiation. This was a considered move on Shadwell's part, a continuation of the connection between witchcraft and Catholicism that he makes explicit in his preface:

> *I have but one thing more to observe, which is, that Witchcraft, being a Religion to the Devil, (for so it is), their charms upon several occasions being so many offices of the Witches Liturgy to him,) and attended with as many Ceremonies as even the Popish Religion is, 'tis remarkable that the Church of the Devil (if I may catachrestically call it so) has continued almost the same, from their first writers on this subject to the last.*[97]

The witches' use of "Black Lambs blood" during their musical conjuration would have been understood to represent the perceived foolishness (or even wickedness) of Catholic ritual. Shadwell high-

Example 2.7. Richard Leveridge, "Speak, Sister, Speak," mm. 112–19.
GB-Cfm. Mu MS 87. By permission of the Syndics of the Fitzwilliam
Museum to whom rights in this publication are assigned.

lights the horror of this ritualized bloodletting, as his witches slaughter the black lamb onstage, tearing it into pieces and "pour[ing] the Blood into [a] hole," a potential parody of the part of the Mass where the Host (representing the Agnus Dei—the Lamb of God) is broken into pieces.[98]

Although Shadwell blatantly connects Catholicism and witchcraft, not all entertainments were so specific. The music for William Davenant's revision of *Macbeth* points toward a generalized spiritual corruption instead of associating a particular religious group with witchcraft. As we have seen, in Davenant's reworking of *Macbeth*, witches sing a treasonous jig, a dance with longstanding

Example 2.7. *Continued.*

sexual connotations ("Let's Have a Dance"). Elsewhere in the play, they celebrate the murder of King Duncan with music that sounds uncomfortably sacred, a conflation of treason with spiritual deviance. In their first musical appearance onstage, "Speak, Sister, Speak," they describe their gleeful reaction to regicide. Leveridge's setting of "Speak, Sister, Speak" features an alternation between the solo, "What then, when monarchs perish shou'd we do?" followed by the elaborately imitative and melismatic chorus, "rejoyce"—a structure that is uncomfortably reminiscent of a verse anthem. (See example 2.7.[99])

Eccles's "Speak sister, speak" features the witches celebrating

Example 2.8. John Eccles, "Speak, Sister, Speak," mm. 66–74. GB-Lbl. Add. MS 12219. By permission of the British Library.

regicide in a fashion that recalls numerous sacred pieces that contrapuntally "rejoice" in God's greatness. (See example 2.8.[100])

By setting treasonous texts with sacred-sounding music, Eccles and Leveridge link political and religious subversion. The witches' murderous impulses are made repugnantly transgressive, or, if the witches were understood to be Catholics, understandable, through their bastardization of sacred genres.

The Summation of a Tradition: The Case of Dido

Stylized rusticity, the association of witches with disordered noise, and the use of sacred-sounding music: all of these elements can be found in the scenes for the Sorceress and her cackling coven in Henry Purcell's miniature masterpiece, *Dido and Aeneas* (ca. 1687). Because of problems with dating the work and the ambiguity of

Example 2.8. *Continued.*

the text, the musical witches of *Dido* have proved somewhat resistant to exegesis. Jack Westrup comments, "the choruses are jolly rather than frightening."[101] Wilfred Mellers claims, "on no account should the Sorceress be treated grotesquely."[102] More recently, Steven Plank wonders about Restoration witches: "Are their grotesqueries more comic than bizarre? Is their magic impressive?"[103] If we read the witches in the context of long-standing conventions associated with musical witchcraft, it becomes possible to ascertain a range of potential meanings *Dido*'s "wayward sisters" would have held for their original audiences.

The witches were creatures of Tate's invention, as he replaced the meddling deities Venus, Juno, Jupiter, and even Dido's rejected suitor, Iarbus from Virgil's *Aeneid*, book 4, with the malicious Sorceress and her coven. Tate's witches are directly opposed to order, love, and the power of the sovereign within the opera, and certainly

Example 2.8. *Continued.*

represent a treasonous threat to the body politic. During the Restoration, the relationship between monarch and subject was often constructed as a loving relationship between husband and wife.[104] The witches in *Dido* are directly, and as several commentators have pointed out, senselessly undermining the "true love" that exists between Dido and Aeneas, and therefore, symbolically are trying to disrupt the relationship between subject and monarch.[105]

Tate may have gotten the idea for inserting the Sorceress into *Dido and Aeneas* from several sources. In Tate's own earlier play, *Brutus of Alba* (1678), a thinly veiled reworking of Virgil's *Aeneid*, book 4, the witch Ragusa, like her operatic counterpart, has an irrational hatred of the Queen. Virgil's original mentions a "Massylian priestess,"[106] sometimes erroneously translated during the seventeenth century as "great Sorceresse,"[107] "Witch,"[108] and "Inchantresse."[109] As Andrew Pinnock has recently shown, travesty translations of Virgil often inserted a debased witch character in place of the priestess.[110] Despite such translations, the travesty Massylian priestess is not analogous to the Sorceress in *Dido and Aeneas*. In the original Virgil, in the travesty translations, and in the seventeenth-century translations by Richard Fanshawe and John Dryden, Dido *willingly* visits the priestess and even partici- pates in what Dryden called "the Rites obscene."[111] She and the Massylian priestess are allies. As Restoration audiences often alle- gorically interpreted entertainments, Tate might have thought it unseemly for Queen Dido (who might have been thought to rep- resent "a real-life queen") to participate onstage in such infernal rites; perhaps in order to preserve the correct ideological message, it was necessary for Tate to make the Sorceress Dido's enemy.

Many scholars have claimed that the witches in *Dido and Aeneas* not only represented generalized disorder and chaos, but were spe- cific representations of the Catholic threat to the kingdom of En- gland.[112] Certainly, as we have seen, there was a longstanding as- sociation between witches and Catholics, particularly during the Restoration era. Keeping with the anti-Catholic mood of the time, Thomas D'Urfey's epilogue for the 1689 performance of *Dido* at Josias Priest's boarding school asserts the girls' chastity and their Protestantism in opposition to Rome's "strange Tricks."

> Besides to show we live with strictest rules,
> Our Nunnery-Door, is charm'd to shut out Fools;
> No Love-toy here can pass to private view,
> Nor *China* Orange cram'd with Billet dew,
> *Rome* may allow strange Tricks to please her Sons,
> But we are Protestants and *English* Nuns,
> Like nimble Fawns, and Birds that bless the Spring
> Unscar'd by turning Times we dance and sing.[113]

This epilogue is full of the ambiguity and ambivalence that makes the opera so difficult to interpret. While D'Urfey indicts Rome's "strange Tricks," the good Protestant girls perform charms to shut out their suitors, potentially tainting them with witchcraft. Other statements in the epilogue seem sexually precocious. In particular, the fact that a supposedly naïve young girl knows about China oranges "cram'd with Billet dew" (*billets doux*, or love notes) implies a lack of innocence. Sex was for sale in the public theaters, and the modus operandi for this activity was to pay the girls who sold or- anges to carry messages back and forth between those engaged in illicit sexual activities.[114] This information should not have been readily available to a chaste schoolgirl unless D'Urfey put the words in her mouth.

D'Urfey may have chosen to include the anti-Catholic and sexual content in his epilogue as a sly reference to the Catholic background of the student who spoke the text, Lady Dorothy Burk. Her father, the Catholic Eighth Earl of Clanricarde, fled to Ireland in 1689 with James II. In spite of her Catholic parents' vehement opposition, Lady Dorothy, a staunch Protestant, chose to continue her English education and was allowed to remain at Priest's school with funding from Queen Mary.[115] The fact that Burk, a Protestant "nun" personally funded by the queen, spoke this anti-Catholic epilogue explains the slippages in the text and potentially supports an anti-Catholic reading of the opera. Just as Burk was struggling against her Catholic parents, D'Urfey's text implies that she was struggling against urges (witchcraft and illicit sexual knowledge) that, according to Protestant polemicists, were the earmarks of popery. Ultimately, Burk prevailed: she was "Unscar'd by turning Times" thanks to the aid of the benevolent Protestant Queen Mary.

Following the standard trope, which conflated the spiritual deviance of witchcraft and/or Catholicism with political discord, the witches in *Dido*, like their counterparts in Jonson's *Masque of Queens*, or even Davenant's *Macbeth*, have a pure, unprovoked hatred for their betters. Unlike Jonson's masque, however, where the hags are easily dispersed by Fame's loud music, or even Tate's *Brutus of Alba*, where a spirit tells Ragusa that she will lose her powers, within the opera the wayward sisters' malevolent plans are successful; the witches disappear from the stage, but they leave a dying queen in their wake. In short, their disorder triumphs, plunging the kingdom into chaos. If Tate and Purcell were sending some kind of allegorical message, it was an unpleasant, dangerous one.

Beyond their potential allegorical role as representatives of the Catholic threat, the witches in *Dido* are similar in many other respects to their theatrical contemporaries and predecessors, although Purcell accords his Sorceress more musico-rhetorical power than other witches.[116] Accompanied by hovering strings (a texture later adopted by Eccles and Leveridge in their settings for *Macbeth*), the Sorceress beckons to her sisters in the key of F minor—a significant change from the jolly major keys favored in many other scenes of seventeenth-century musical witchcraft. Despite the Sorceress's departure from musical witchcraft traditions, her language is undeniably indebted to earlier models, as she mentions ravens (a bird recently mentioned in Davenant's "Let's Have a Dance"), and encourages her coven-mates to "appear" in a fashion similar to "Hecate, Come Away" from Middleton's *The Witch*, a text that also appears in the musical reworking of *Macbeth*.[117] Even on these stock texts, Purcell subtly shows the Sorceress's skill as a musical orator, with tangy dissonances on "dismal ravens crying." Her hubris, her confidence in her own mischief-making abilities, is made clear as she vividly illustrates, with a descending minor seventh on the word "all," how complete her victory over the hated queen will be. Hearing such musical rhetoric, we believe her when she tells us that she will "make *all* Carthage flame."

Why does the Sorceress sound different from other seventeenth-century witches? The answer, perhaps, is simple. While the other witches considered in this chapter fall squarely within the hag/witch tradition, Tate and Purcell, given the source of the opera, imbued the Sorceress with a classical regality that her counterparts lack. Furthermore, Roger Savage has suggested that the Sorceress represents the dark side of Dido within the opera: "a formidable anti-self embodying all her [Dido's] insecurities and apprehensions of disaster contingent on her involving herself in any deep personal relationship."[118] If the Sorceress is Dido's "anti-self," then she would need to match the musical gravitas of her queenly inverse.

When her coven responds to her desire to see "Carthage flame," the difference between the imperious Sorceress and her rustic minions is put into sharp relief. The key turns to a far more cheerful B♭ major (a key frequently used by Purcell in pastoral scenes!) as the coven sings a celebratory manifesto: "Harm's Our Delight and Mischief All Our Skill," a lilting, exuberant four-part chorus. Purcell's coven, like Eccles's and Leveridge's witches, are one step removed from the folk tradition. Their English rusticity has been transmuted by Purcell's art into a stylization that echoes, but does not completely replicate, the jigs of the past.

Purcell highlights again the difference between the Sorceress's music and that of her coven in the musical sequence that follows the celebratory "Harm's Our Delight." Upon the chorus's final cadence, the Sorceress immediately brings the proceedings back to a more gloomy F minor as she reveals her plan and her unrelenting hatred for those who possess wealth and power: "The Queen of Carthage, whom we hate, / As we do all in prosp'rous state, / Ere sunset shall most wretched prove, / Depriv'd of fame, of life and love." The Sorceress, once again, the master musical rhetorician, uses dissonance on the word "wretched," making aurally manifest the pain she wants the doomed queen to experience. Her moral inversion is foregrounded, as she uses an ascending melisma and a turn to C major to illustrate her joy at the prospect of Dido's betrayal and death. Her minions are also pleased as they take her C major cue, breaking out into a nonsensical, imitative chorus, which consists entirely of the word, "ho." Her servants, her coven-mates, now play upon another musical witchcraft trope, as they sing a stylized version of noise: their mistress may be extraordinary, but they are typical hags. Tate's antecedent for the cackling chorus is his own *Brutus of Alba*, where a coven responds to Ragusa with similar sounds of approval, although their cackles are not set to music. Other textual antecedents may also be found in Shadwell's *The Lancashire Witches* (1681) and even Heywood and Brome's *The Late Lancashire Witches* (1634), which had included such cackling witches. Going back even further, Jonson suggests in his copious documentation to *The Masque of Queens* that such sounds as "Har" and "Hoo" were particular to witches, and were noises in honor of the Devil. Whether audiences would have heard the witchly cackling in *Dido* as humorous or threatening noises in honor of the Devil is unclear.

In the chorus "In Our Deep Vaulted Cell" another familiar strategy is adopted to place the coven within the established boundaries of musical witchcraft. The homophonic, mostly homorhythmic texture, as well as the solemnity of the D minor setting, invites the comparison to a hymn (albeit a demonic one). Strangely, this type of setting is more similar to that used in Protestant services, given its simplicity. Perhaps these witches are Puritans, not Catholics! Nevertheless, the witches' sacred-sounding music is rendered frightening and grotesque by the use of echo, which subverts its perfection while simultaneously suggesting the echoing acoustical properties of the "deep vaulted cell" where the witches perform their dreadful rites.

In act 3, as the Sorceress's plan to destroy Dido comes to fruition, she begins to laugh maniacally and sing with unbridled glee—an indication of her extreme emotionalism and perhaps even her lack of rationality. Ironically, as she triumphs, the Sorceress loses some of her classical dignity and rhetorical control. Her vocal line is suffused with sixteenth-note and thirty-second-note flourishes, and an upward thrusting melisma is reserved for Dido's other name, Elissa. Finally, the Sorceress descends into giggles with her coven-mate, singing "noise" with the best of them. The song that follows, "Our Next Motion," continues in the same vein, sounding grotesque and irregular because of the strangely awkward text setting. The Sorceress, despite all her power, and her eventual triumph, reveals herself to be an imperfect speaker after all. In her malevolent exuberance she reveals her true nature: she can never truly be noble.

Transgression as Entertainment

During the seventeenth century, distinct musical conventions for the portrayal of witches emerged. Playwrights and composers chose genres that musically represented the witches' transgressions and their cultural marginalization. Sometimes they accomplished this by assigning theatrical witches music associated with lower-class festive unruliness (the round, the morris, the jig). Sometimes they focused on the witches' ability to provoke societal discord by associating them with noisiness and dissonance (*The Masque of Queens, The Witch of Edmonton, The Late Lancashire Witches, The Lancashire Witches, Dido and Aeneas*). Other musical choices connected political, sexual, and spiritual transgression (the jigging and pseudo-religious choral celebrations of regicide in Eccles and Leveridge's *Macbeth;* the hymnal quality of "In Our Deep Vaulted Cell" sung by *Dido*'s treasonous witches).

But how effective was this musical vilification of witches? How can one explain their frequent presence, if they were so culturally dangerous? Would it not have been more effective to simply silence them, instead of parading them forth for the delectation and delight of the theatergoing public? Of course, this last point was at the heart of critiques made by anti-theatrical polemicists who warned of the power of vice to seduce and enchant.[119] While we may cringe at the anti-theatricalists' intolerance, they made an important argument: the magical musical rituals performed in the theater were not simply empty spectacle; they worked their own magic, both upon audiences and even upon those who created them.

Jonson's extensive commentary to his *Masque of Queens* provides one of the most interesting examples of the ambivalence that marked seventeenth-century attitudes toward witches, and, as this book demonstrates, that also characterized attitudes toward all disorderly characters. Despite Jonson's obvious distaste for the rag-clad hags, his description of their onstage ceremonies and music is more meticulous than his description of the other musical portions of the masque. It would seem that Jonson and the courtly spectators were bewitched by the hags' disorderly feminine vice, a vice directly opposed to what he called "masculine virtue." Even as Jonson and the composer of the witches' dances attempted to mark them as the debased Other, in the end their innovative music and dancing was probably even more memorable than the procession of Queens, led by Queen Anna herself. Indeed, as we have seen, the musical, terpsichorean, and dramatic tropes established in *The Masque of Queens* bewitched later playwrights and composers, who used similar strategies for portraying theatrical witchcraft. The conventions established in *The Masque of Queens* continued to resonate throughout the century, as sonic deviance proved tremendously entertaining. While witches' music and dance represented their deformity, it also, ironically, increased their popularity.

3

"Remember Me, But Ah, Forget My Fate"

"Remember me," lovesick Dido sings, voice soaring despite her impending demise. "But ah, forget my fate," she continues, as she sinks into abjection and death. Dido's final cry presents the listener with a double bind. She is asked to remember Dido, but also to forget—to forget the less pleasant aspects of her tale (her illicit affair with Aeneas, her rejection by him, her death). Once again, the portrayal of musical disorder, in this case a lovesick lament, presents us with ambiguity and a lack of easy answers; here an inexorably repeating ground bass sets the boundaries for Dido's emotional outpouring. Dido may request that we forget her fate, but this is impossible because it is memorialized by her evocative music. In singing, Dido ensures her immortality. No one can forget her, nor will they, judging from the continued popularity of her swan song.

Recently Janet Schmalfeldt and Wendy Heller have compellingly claimed that this operatic Dido is a highly sympathetic figure, not the fallen, abandoned woman found in Virgil. Although they acknowledge the ambiguities of Virgil, both authors strongly argue that Nahum Tate, *Dido*'s librettist, and Henry Purcell, the composer, erased any lingering questions about the Carthaginian queen's character, as her final aria imbues her death with an undeniable dignity.[1] So why do I claim that Dido's voice is one of ambiguity, even at her tragic end? How can we contextualize her musical language? Why does she ask us to forget at all? In order to understand this aria, and indeed, the songs of other suffering women on the English stage, I argue that one must first understand lovesickness. Perhaps Dido exhorts her auditors to forget because she and other lovesick women are rendered memorable by transgressions, their rejection of the patriarchal dictums of silence and chastity. Her disorderly femininity fascinates, and, as with the other characters discussed in this book, her music titillates and entertains, using innovative compositional practices that challenge performers with the unexpected. I agree with Schmalfeldt's and Heller's assessment that audience sympathies are exclusively with Dido in the opera; however, I would argue that Dido's character appeals to us (and appealed to seventeenth-century audiences) because her illicit passion for Aeneas simultaneously intrigues us and causes us to sympathize with her plight through her emotional outbursts. She is neither the transgressive Dido of Virgil's epic nor the virtuously repentant Dido extolled in recent scholarship; she is a hybrid of the two.

If we put the sheer musical ravishment of Purcell's lament aside, Dido is not unique. Deserted women poured out their laments with great frequency, or, to maintain propriety, had a servant sing them instead. Others went mad before they died, unleashing a tirade of semi-lucid commentary about the world that had done them wrong. Just as lamenting, deserted women employed a special musical language, so did madwomen. And these lovesick women had power of a sort, albeit a power granted through their musical replication of the symptoms of their disorder. Particularly after 1660, when the roles of lovesick women were taken by actresses instead of boys, their musical performances held an intensified erotic appeal; this can be verified when we consider the careers of Moll Davis and Anne Bracegirdle, two women who increased their popularity through their performance of lovesickness.

Lovesickness: The Medical Tradition

Most of the women who lamented or ran mad on the English stage suffered from "erotic melancholy," or lovesickness, giving playwrights and composers the opportunity to create titillating displays of excessive, "lascivious" emotion as they represented the common symptoms of the affliction.[2] These women appeared in various states of disarray (both onstage and off), singing and speaking in a voluble, disjointed manner that violated the code of proper conduct. The behavior of both actual and theatrical lovesick woman subverted the notion that they were chaste and decorous helpmates to men. Lasciviousness was frequently a symptom of the ailment— a particular problem in a patriarchal society in which female chastity was fundamental.[3] Furthermore, the rambling, excessive, obsessive speech that characterized madness and melancholy was considered particularly unseemly for women. In 1641 Richard Brathwaite's *The English Gentlewoman* advised, "Silence in a *Woman* is a moving Rhetoricke, winning most, when in words it wooeth least . . . More shall wee see fall into sinne by Speech then Silence."[4] Richard Allestree's conduct book from later in the century, *The Ladies' Calling* (1673), similarly defines the ideal woman's speech, although he uses musical terms to set boundaries:

> Nor do's she only refine the Language, but she tunes it too, modulates the tone and accent, admits no unhandsom earnestness, or loudness of Discourse . . . A Womans tongue should indeed be like the imaginary Music of the Spheres, sweet and charming; but not to be heard at distance.[5]

As one might imagine, given Brathwaite's and particularly Allestree's descriptions, a woman who sang in public would have been heard as transgressive. Perhaps as a marker of this transgression, mad and lamenting women on the seventeenth-century stage frequently sang in situations that were acknowledged as being inappropriate. Indeed, as with other transgressive characters, conventions developed that critiqued and bracketed the conduct of these sufferers of "erotic melancholy": the display of these characters was carefully mediated and framed by the responses of those around them and by the meanings associated with their conventionalized musical gestures.[6] Composers assigned music to lovesick women aesthetically marked as emotionally excessive and created laments using devices that focused attention on the spectacularly obsessive, overly passionate quality of female love, accentuating the misogynist notion that women were irrational and emotionally volatile. While allowed some degree of license within the generic frame of the lament and mad song, such female characters, like other transgressive women, were eventually silenced, often dying at the end of the play or opera.

While conduct book writers praised chastity and silence, few females were thought to live up to those ideals. The typical, flawed woman was thought to be prone to mental disorder and lovesickness in particular. Ruled by her emotions, her reason was weak. As Laurent Joubert commented at the end of the sixteenth century:

> Women especially take it [love] to an excess that is unbearable and upsets the patient more than the others do. This is due to a natural condition that drives them to overstep the limits of common sense and always to be excessive, more so than men, in their affections and actions.[7]

Jacques Ferrand, in his influential *Erotomania* (translated into English in 1640) explains:

> Without a doubt a Woman is in her Loves more Passionate, and more furious in her follies, then a man is. . . . Women are Naturally of meaner Spirits and lesse courage, then Men; neither is their reason so strong as theirs: and therefore are they lesse able to make resistance against so strong a Passion, as *Galen* saies. . . . This opinion is confirmed also by daily experience, which affords us Examples great store of Women, that are ready to run Mad for Love; but seldome any Men, whom we never see brought to that Extremity: unlesse they be some effeminate weake spirited fellowes, that have been alwaies brought up in Lascivious courses, and in Ladies Laps.[8]

Ferrand emphasized the tendency of women—who were naturally passionate, cowardly, and irrational—to "run mad for love." Ferrand might have been drawing on his own experience as a physician, as during the seventeenth century mental disorders were not just female ailments in theory, they were also female ailments in practice. Contemporary statistics indicate that female sufferers outnumbered male sufferers two to one.[9] For Ferrand, lovesickness was so thoroughly associated with women that if a man did suffer from it he was transgressing the implied masculine norms of stoicism, courage, and rationality—as the following chapter demonstrates, only "effeminate" and "weake spirited fellowes" went mad for love. So, in some respects, a disorderly woman was simply conforming to the behavior expected from the "weaker sex." However, a good woman was supposed to reject her true nature, remaining chaste, silent, and obedient, even though her instincts encouraged her to descend into irrationality and sin.

As detailed in the following chapter, melancholy and its related afflictions were caused by an excess of black bile (melancholy) or by an overheating of the body, which caused one of the other three humors to blacken, producing a damaging humor adust. For women, who were often excluded from the positive intellectual tradition associated with melancholy, their mental problems were almost always pathological, but usually black bile wasn't thought to be the cause of their suffering.[10] A woman's wandering womb or noxious vapors emanating from the unruly organ were frequently blamed for her malady.[11]

According to Ferrand, Burton, and others, females fell into mental disorder because their humoral composition and their wombs made them more prone to unbridled lust.[12] In particular, young girls were thought to be at risk because of their susceptibility to sexual intemperance:

> Those that in their first puberty give themselves to the immoderate use of venery, in them, those vessels that serve for generation grow larger, and attract the greater store of blood unto them: so that this meanes the desire of copulation growes the stronger.[13]

It was necessary for girls suffering from the so-called greensickness to get married posthaste, containing their insatiable sexual behavior within an acceptable, patriarchally sanctioned institution.[14]

The denial of desire, whether by choice or by circumstance, also caused lovesick melancholy and madness. Burton pointed to abstinence from sexual relations, especially in women, as one of the reasons for the development of these afflictions:

> Venus omitted produceth like effects [lovesickness], Mathiolus, *epist. 5., lib. penult.*, avoucheth of his knowledge, "that some through bashfulness abstained from venery, and thereupon became very heavy and dull; and some others that were very timorous, melancholy, and beyond all measure sad." . . . And so doth Galen himself hold, "that if this natural seed be over-long kept

(in some parties) it turns to poison . . . Lodovicus Mercatus, *lib. 2 de mulierum affect. cap. 4*, and Rodericus à Castro, *de morbis mulier. lib. 2. cap. 3*, treat largely of this subject, and will have it produce a peculiar kind of melancholy in stale maids, nuns, and widows . . . they are melancholy in the highest degree, all for want of husbands.[15]

Many of the women we will encounter in this chapter suffer from textbook cases of erotic melancholy. They are either maids who have descended into lovesickness because of an unwanted separation from the object of their desire or mature women whose desires have been thwarted by fate or circumstance. Almost without fail, their ending is unhappy, their ravings and laments silenced by the tomb—the ultimate vessel of containment. As Burton notes, "It is so well known in every village, how many have either died for love, or voluntarily made away themselves, that I need not much labour to prove it."[16] Yet, while these women live, they sing and allure the senses of the listener: one can imagine a seventeenth-century auditor being torn among the conflicting emotions of sympathy, desire, and scorn for these disorderly women.

Suffering, Deserted Women

Whether they were rejected by their lovers, separated from them by death, or unfairly suspected of being unchaste, suffering and deserted women were a frequent, unhappy presence on the seventeenth-century stage. Playwrights and composers crafted a textual and musical language associated with this specific feminine brand of grief. As Ellen Rosand notes in her groundbreaking study of the origins of the lament in opera, the lament featured strongly metered and rhymed texts that set it apart from its dramatic context. Particularly affective lines (or words) were repeated or enhanced through their musical setting, using melodic sequencing and dissonance.[17] One of the most influential continental models was Claudio Monteverdi's lament for Arianna (1608), taken from his now-lost opera of the same name. Arianna's lament features a highly reactive musical language in which Monteverdi musically responds to every nuance of the meaning of the text. English examples of the lament from this period are more restrained; nevertheless, they too feature a highly mimetic musical language and repetition, particularly of affective words. And in England, laments are automatically set apart from the rest of the drama, as they often provide an opportunity for music in otherwise spoken plays.

By the 1630s and '40s a new type of lament emerged in Italy, one that featured a descending tetrachord ground bass, usually in a minor key. Again, Monteverdi was at the vanguard of this generic shift: his "Lament of the Nymph" from book 8 of his madrigals (1638) featured this innovation. As Rosand notes, the repeating bass line afforded new affective possibilities as it "increased the opportunities for conflict with the voice."[18] Indeed, Monteverdi and those who followed him relished the opportunity to thwart the tonal implications of the repeating bass line, with suspensions and unpredictable vocal entrances. In addition, the inexorably descending tetrachord was a perfect musical representation of obsession.[19] The ground bass pattern, so popular in mid-century Europe, did not really take hold in the English lament until the late seventeenth century, when composers, such as Purcell, who were influenced by the Italians picked it up, reformulating it to serve their own dramatic ends. These composers also incorporated other effects from the Italians' bag of tricks: later English laments were sometimes cast in a triple meter with string accompaniment.

But what did these musical gestures signify for contemporary audiences, given the discourses surrounding women, emotionality, and lovesickness? In her article on Arianna's lament, Suzanne Cusick wonders how the Italian ladies listening might have responded to the deserted, lovesick woman. She cites Federico Follino's eyewitness account of the first performance of *Arianna*—that "there was not one lady who failed to shed a tear" and claims that women were moved because Arianna "was recognizable as an early modern woman."[20] In other words, Arianna's lament was not just entertainment, a harmless musical fiction: it represented something very powerful and true for those that heard it. For some women, it reinforced the indoctrination of dominant notions of proper female behavior, warning against the dire consequences of succumbing to passion. As Wendy Heller notes in a recent study of women and opera in *seicento* Venice, Arianna, in her lament, actually censors herself:

> with a curious schizophrenia, she regrets her curses as soon as they are uttered. . . . At Arianna's greatest moment of eloquence,

she breaks with her own myth, adhering to the female virtue of silence.[21]

On the other hand, for some men, Arianna's lament provided a potentially salacious display of female emotion. As Cusick puts it:

> Because women's speech was ineluctably associated with sexual expression, the very fact that Arianna was granted such a long and self-expressive lament scene constituted a display of licentiousness. Her licentiousness is not simply represented by her words, however; the fact of her speech's musical expressiveness, which had the power to elicit tenderness from the men in the audience, heightens her characterization as not only incontinent but seductive.[22]

What might the deserted lamenting woman have signified for audiences in early seventeenth-century England on a stage where these songs were featured in otherwise spoken plays and ostensibly "female" roles were played by young boys? We can begin to consider these questions with Ben Jonson's early comedy, *Cynthia's Revels* (1600), performed by the Children of Queen Elizabeth's Chapel. From the start, Jonson overturns the notion of the idealized chaste and silent female, retracting the legendary punishment of the mythological Echo, who had been silenced for her loquaciousness. Mercury, acting on Jove's command, returns Echo's body and her own voice to her. According to the myth, Juno silenced Echo, and she was doomed to lament her beloved Narcissus by repeating others' phrases—an erasure of her own subjectivity and agency. Acknowledging the classical sources, Mercury excuses the reformulation of the familiar tale, implying that Echo had been punished long enough:

> Now (after three thousand yeeres,
> Which have beene exercis'd in JUNOES spight)
> Thou take a corporall figure, and ascend,
> Enricht with vocall, and articulate power. [I.ii.8–11][23]

Why did Jonson empower Echo in this way? Perhaps he wanted to exploit the entertainment value of a "what if" scenario. What if the Echo of legend had been able to sufficiently express her grief? What if she had been "[e]nricht with vocall, and articulate power"? What would it sound like? Apparently, like music. Upon her return, Echo first takes the opportunity to decry the death of her beloved and his folly at loving himself too much, bewitched by his own image instead of looking in a "truer glasse" and embracing Echo's love, seeing "his beauties by more kind reflection." After giving a lengthy speech, Mercury cautions that her time is short; she must be brief in order to escape the wrath of Juno. Echo agrees and requests music, so she may "sing some mourning straine / over his watrie hearse." Mercury assents to her request.

> The humorous aire shall mixe her solemne tunes,
> With thy sad words: strike musicque from the spheares,
> And with your golden raptures swell our eares. [I.ii.61–64]

Here the humorous (humor-filled) air (which had a double meaning, referring to a musical genre and to the air around Echo) shall combine its music with Echo's sad lament, causing "golden raptures" in the auditors. In this passage it is made clear that female lamenting could cause extreme pleasure in the listener. This is a trope that will be revisited again and again in the lament and mad song. Viewing and hearing female grief, even its theatrical simulacrum, seduces and entertains.

Echo's lament is musical not only because of the obvious fact that it is sung; it is musical also because her grief is compared to musical features. The first line makes clear the tempo: "Slow, slow, fresh fount, keepe time with my salt teares." The tempo must be slow, she tells us, to match her weeping. The choice of tempo then, in this and other laments, is not arbitrary. It matches the lugubrious travel of tears down the lamenter's cheeks. After establishing the tempo, Echo acknowledges the listener, again bringing to the forefront the relationship between the singing lamenter and her eager audience: "List to the heavy part the musique beares." The music that supports her also supports her grief and, in doing so, allows the auditor to partake of it as well, voyeuristically reveling in her emotion. "Woe weepes out her division, when shee sings": Echo then anthropomorphizes woe itself, gendering it female. But woe is also musical, like Echo, the nymph who gives the emotion a voice. She weeps out her division—again a symptom of grief is converted into music, as a division was a method of improvisation in which longer notes were divided into shorter ones or intervals were divided into step-wise passages, demonstrating the talents of the performer. Thus, weeping is transformed into a virtuosic musical act.

The only extant musical setting of this text is a three-part madrigal, found in Henry Youll's *Canzonets to Three Voices* (1608). It is appropriately elaborate for a virtuosic display of grief, but it is unclear whether it was ever used in the theater or if the composer simply took a fancy to Jonson's evocative poem and decided to set it to music. It is also possible that Youll simply wrote a multivoice arrangement of a popular playhouse tune.[24] Regardless of what music was actually performed, Mercury surprisingly remains unmoved by Echo's plaint (he callously responds, "now, ha' you done?"). Mercury's response suggests that Echo, whose voice had been restored specifically so she could express her grief, had somehow overstepped her bounds with her musical outpouring. Mercury cautioned her to be brief, but her natural female loquaciousness got the better of her. Although Mercury is annoyed, Echo's behavior also confirms typical ideas about emotionally volatile women: they cannot hold their tongues. Thus, in this brief scene we see the tensions among notions of *proper* female behavior (chaste, silent, and obedient), notions about *actual* female behavior (women are loquacious), and the concomitant anxieties about the power of the unbridled female voice—a voice that Mercury would silence.

I suspect Elizabethan audiences did not share Mercury's callous reaction to Echo's grief. In fact, one literary scholar suggests that they would have been more moved than ever, by virtue of Echo's performance by a young boy. Mario Digangi claims, "Given the extended banter about the attractiveness of the boy actors or 'fine ingles' in the Induction, Jonson's audience might have been led to an even sharper aesthetic appreciation of Echo, the first female character to appear in the play."[25] It is entirely possible that some would have been enchanted by the alluring combination of a young boy singing in female garb. Linda Austern has written about the seductive qualities of the boy's high-pitched voice and Stephen Orgel has provided ample contemporary evidence to suggest that male spectators found boy actors to be extremely alluring.[26] Of course, the charms of these boys were not unproblematic. As Austern, Orgel, and Laura Levine observe, early seventeenth-century anti-theatricalists frequently complained about the corrupting quality of these young female impersonators, as men were tricked into believing them women, falling in love with a simulacrum of womanhood instead of the "real" thing.[27]

In fact, Jonson does not seem to view the attractiveness of the boy actors as being harmless. Indeed, the anxiety over sodomy is present in Jonson's description of the boy actors: an "ingle" was slang for a boy favorite or a catamite.[28] In the Induction to *Cynthia's Revels*, the attractions of boy actors are both celebrated and mocked. Their beauty is praised, but they are also called "sir cracke" which could refer to their cracking voices, to their roguish demeanor, or to something bawdier—crack was slang for a female prostitute.[29] And Echo, as we've already seen, was not an unproblematic female figure, regardless of who embodied her. Mercury allows her musical lament, but, in "typical" female fashion, she cannot quiet her tongue. She continues her spoken lamenting, even after her sung lament has faded into memory. Mercury sharply admonishes her,

Stint thy babbling tongue;
Fond ECCHO, thou prophan'st the grace is done thee:
So idle worlding (Meerely made of voice)
Censure the powers above them. Come, away,
JOVE calls thee hence, and his will brookes no stay. [I.ii.92–96]

In response to Mercury's chastisement, Echo now indicts those above her, which propels her into increasing unruliness, until, in violation of Jove's decree, she continues to speak, cursing the "Fountayne of Self-Love" the pool in which Narcissus saw his reflection. After this, eschewing the authority of the gods, she makes the decision to leave. "Now, HERMES, I have finisht," she tells him, and Mercury returns her to her previous disembodied state. Although Echo is "contained" in the end, her insubordinate tone resonates throughout the larger play, which is a critique of the aristocratic manners at court.[30]

Despite Echo's ignominious exit in *Cynthia's Revels*, the musical and dramatic spectacle of a woman (or boy actor) out of control, at the prey of her emotions, critiquing her unfair treatment at the hands of men, proved to be remarkably potent. Indeed, the most famous lamenting woman on the Jacobean stage, Desdemona, in William Shakespeare's *Othello* (1604), bears several similarities to Echo, particularly in her use of music. Desdemona resorts to a musical lament because her beloved husband, Othello, with prompting from the evil Iago, has become insanely jealous, as he believes his wife to be unfaithful. Desdemona, still stinging from her husband's public humiliation and his ominous dictate that she dismiss her servant before she goes to bed, has a premonition of her own death: "If I do die before [thee]," she instructs her maid Emilia, "prithee shroud me in one of these same sheets" [IV.iii.24–25]. She then reminisces about an old song of "Willow" that her mother's maid, Barbary, sang, lamenting the fact that "She was in love, and he she lov'd prov'd mad" [IV.iii.27]. Desdemona then informs us that the unfortunate Barbary died singing the song. As Emilia prepares her for bed, Desdemona begins to remember the song (albeit imperfectly) and begins to sing. Although other versions of the "Willow Song" exist, the most famous version is in GB-Lbl. Add. MS 15117, a manuscript that dates from around 1614–16. As Frederick Sternfeld comments, "The London Book [GB-Lbl. Add. MS 15117] is justly famous, for it combines an extended text with an instrumental accompaniment."[31] Although this tune may not have been sung by Desdemona (she may have used an earlier tune, found in lute sources from the sixteenth century), the lyrics found in this manuscript are close enough to Shakespeare's that one can assume that the playwright was familiar with a version of this text.[32] He undoubtedly adapted the ballad to suit his dramatic purpose, and the changes he made are quite significant, as they give Desdemona's performance an air of authentic spontaneity and applicability to the situation at hand.[33] (See example 3.1.[34])

Desdemona's plaint changes the gender of the lovesick protagonist (in the ballad reproduced in example 3.1, a lovesick man is the sufferer), opening with an image familiar from contemporary illustrations of lovesickness: her "hand [is] on her bosom, her head on her knee."[35] As performed by Desdemona, the refrain, "Sing willow, willow, willow," represents the obsessive thoughts of the lovesick singer, as she pours out her soul to the natural world, that, unlike her hard-hearted lover, responds to her sadness with moans from the water and stones made soft by her tears. Adding to the dolorous tone, in the musical refrain of GB-Lbl. Add. MS 15117 the vocal line frequently starts phrases on a high note, before sinking rapidly downward (see particularly mm. 7–8). If Desdemona sang this version in the Jacobean theater (and this, as John Ward and Frederick Sternfeld point out, we can never know), the despairing melodic trajectory would have neatly imitated the falling of her tears.

Abruptly taking us out of the world of song, Desdemona interrupts her music with a spoken request that Emilia "Lay by these," "these" being bits of her costume that have been removed as she disrobes. Desdemona then resumes the repetitive chorus,

Example 3.1. "Willow Song" ballad, GB-Lbl. Add. MS 15117,
verse 1 (lute part omitted). By permission of the British Library.

"willow, willow," before breaking off, instructing Emilia to leave before Othello arrives. When Desdemona begins to sing again, she misremembers the ballad: "Let nobody blame him, his scorn I approve," a text not found in GB-Lbl. Add. MS 15117. Quickly, she acknowledges her mistake: "Nay, that's not next." Of course, Desdemona's interjection has a double meaning. First, she acknowledges her imperfect remembrance of the "Willow Song." Secondly, her reaction indicates that she rejects the implications of the line: she *doesn't* approve the scorn that has been heaped upon her. We *should* blame "him" (Othello) for his actions and unjust behavior. She is not simply a despondent victim at this point—she realizes that she does not deserve her husband's abuse.

Desdemona continues altering the song, but now she takes a turn into the bawdy that seems strangely out of character for this woman, who thus far has been a model of propriety. Indeed, the tragedy of *Othello* doesn't work unless the audience believes in Desdemona's absolute innocence. The tragic fatal flaw must belong to her husband. Yet, according to Desdemona's version of the song, her "false love" tells her that "If I court moe women, you'll couch with moe men"—in short infidelity breeds infidelity. The use of the word, "couch" (to lay down) undoubtedly had lascivious connotations that seem out of tune with the rest of Desdemona's lover's complaint. But if we diagnose Desdemona as suffering from lovesickness as a result of her husband's cruel treatment, her behavior becomes more legible. Sufferers often lapsed into bawdy talk, as it was thought to be a common symptom of the disorder. Indeed, at least one critic has noted the similarity between Desdemona and Dido from Virgil's *Aeneid*, one of western culture's prototypical lovesick women.[36]

The fact that Desdemona sings at all may also explain the seemingly out-of-character bawdy talk that infects the end of her lover's complaint. As Linda Austern and Rochelle Smith have shown, the act of female singing on the Jacobean stage was consistently associated with their sexuality.[37] In play after play, courtesans sang songs of seduction to please the audience and their onstage prospective lovers. Perhaps, as Smith suggests, Desdemona's musical performance would have been read through the lens of these musical courtesans, although according to Smith, the "Willow Song," instead of indicting Desdemona's sexuality, celebrates it. Smith claims that Desdemona's singing "becomes an expression of her love for Othello, the fullest expression of her chaste and mature sexuality."[38] This statement is puzzling, as the "Willow Song" obviously shows the dangers of love (it leads to death). Desdemona's bawdy editorializing about "couching" and her rejection of the line she sings about accepting a lover's scorn also call Smith's reading into question, as male authority is rejected and female (and male) constancy is called into question. I do not, however, want to suggest that contemporary audiences heard Desdemona's musical performance as a sign of her looseness, justifying Othello's misguided opinion of her. While some of what she says in her ballad is transgressive (and indeed, her musical performance itself might be read as such) it is likely that her song drew the audience in, promoting sympathy for the unhappy Desdemona as she moved the auditor's passions with her unhappy lover's complaint, a recognizable ballad that she shapes to be applicable to her situation. I suspect the audience was affected by "her" plight, especially if the boy actor who portrayed her managed to perform the song without his voice cracking.[39]

Another scorned woman, Aspatia in Francis Beaumont and John Fletcher's *The Maid's Tragedy* (1610), presents a different side of musical lovesickness. Although she sings a willow song like Desdemona, her presentation is quite different from that of her grief-stricken predecessor. Unlike Desdemona, Aspatia is not married, but she wishes she were. Aspatia's beloved, the fickle Amintor, has cast her aside in favor of the king's secret mistress, Evadne. Amintor is first elated by the prospect of possessing the beautiful Evadne on his wedding night, but his enthusiasm soon turns to horror as he discovers the marriage is a sham, not to be consummated. He is merely a cover so that the king may continue his illicit relationship with Evadne. Aspatia is, unfortunately, unaware that Amintor's marriage to Evadne is merely one of convenience. Believing her beloved to be sexually unfaithful, she quickly descends into lovesickness, her thwarted desires festering within her.

While Desdemona's lament takes place in a private space with only her maid as onstage audience, Aspatia's musical outpourings are all too public, as a male spectator describes them in loving detail. Although Aspatia has not experienced the pleasures of carnal love, her affliction has rendered her inappropriately available to men in a way that Desdemona certainly was not, as her musical grief spills into the public sphere. When the audience first encounters Aspatia, a nuptial masque is about to be celebrated. Melantius, Evadne's brother, has just returned from war and unfortunately mistakes Aspatia for the happy bride. Aspatia informs him of his error and hastily departs, allowing Melantius and his companion Lysippus to discuss Aspatia in her absence, framing her affliction from a male perspective. Lysippus's description of Aspatia's plight focuses on both her overflowing, ornamented appearance (the tears that leak from her eyes, her flower-strewn body) and the disordered and discontented sounds she makes (sighing, weeping, mournful singing):

> Yes, but this lady
> Walks discontented, with her wat'ry eyes
> Bent on the earth. The unfrequented woods
> Are her delight, and when she sees a bank
> Stuck full of flowers she with a sigh will tell
> Her servants what a pretty place it were
> To bury lovers in, and make her maids
> Pluck 'em and strow her over like a corse.
> She carries with her an infectious grief

That strikes all her beholders; she will sing
The mournfull'st things that ever ear hath heard,
And sigh, and sing again; and when the rest
Of our young ladies in their wanton blood
Tell mirthful tales in course that fill the room
With laughter, she will with so sad a look
Bring forth a story of the silent death
Of some forsaken virgin, which her grief
Will put in such a phrase that ere she end
She'll send them weeping one by one away. [I.i.89–107][40]

While Aspatia seeks solitude, ironically, she cannot escape the male gaze that consumes her grief. Her flower-strewn body, laments, and tales of silent deaths provide an entertainment of sorts, an entertainment that causes the spectator to be "infected" with sorrow. Lysippus's description allows the audience member to imagine and enjoy the plight of the blameless "forsaken virgin," making her scintillatingly available, although she is physically absent.

In act 2, Lysippus's poetic descriptions of Aspatia's musical grief become sonorous reality. She enters, willow garland in hand, with Evadne. London spectators would have undoubtedly remembered the association between a grieving, musical woman and the willow, articulated just a few short years before in Shakespeare's *Othello*, but again, Aspatia's position is quite different from that of her predecessor. While Desdemona's marriage collapsed under the weight of her husband's jealousy, the grieving Aspatia has not sampled connubial bliss. Instead, she is placed in the excruciatingly difficult position of preparing her rival, Evadne, for her wedding night with Amintor—a wedding night Aspatia longed to experience. This task soon inspires her to sing, "Lay a Garland on My Hearse."

The reference to the bedtime scene from *Othello* cannot have been accidental; Beaumont and Fletcher contrast Aspatia's virginity with Desdemona's sexual experience.[41] Aspatia sings lyrics completely beyond reproach (although she does seem to take an almost masochistic delight in her own grief), while Desdemona's "Willow Song" is considerably more ambiguous, with its turn into bawdry at the end, suggesting her lovesickness or even her greater sexual knowledge as a married woman.[42]

While the music for Aspatia's lament does not survive, its place in the drama also facilitates the comparison between Aspatia's virtue and Evadne's vice. As with the "Willow Song," Aspatia's lament is interrupted by dialogue; however, instead of Aspatia's interrupt-

ing herself, as did Desdemona, Aspatia's companion Evadne interrupts her, commenting on her "sad song." Aspatia retorts that her
tune is "very pretty" and resumes her singing, perhaps a musical
punishment to provoke her thoughtless rival. As she continues
singing, Aspatia explicitly asserts her virtue, something Evadne has
lost: "My love was false," Aspatia tells us, "but I was firm" [II.i.
76]. Finally, to stir up audience sympathies (and perhaps to provoke
Evadne's conscience), Aspatia describes the death that will be the
outcome of her affliction. She invites the maidens that bear willow
branches in mourning for her to lay "gentle earth" upon her buried
body.

Aspatia's song is not well received by the worldly Evadne, further evidence of the difference between the two women. Instead
of being impressed or moved by Aspatia's obvious grief, she reacts
with hostility: "Fie on't, madam! The words are so strange, they
are / able to make one dream of hobgoblins" [II.i.80–81]. She then
requests her bawdy nurse, Dula, to perform "I Could Never Have
the Power," a song that celebrates lasciviousness, as it details a
pretty young woman's promiscuous amorous exploits. It would appear that Beaumont and Fletcher wanted to draw a clear boundary
between the musical expression of a chaste female (Aspatia's righ-
teous lament) and a lustful one (Dula's bawdy song for Evadne).
The fact that Aspatia's musical performance of the willow plaint
fails to find favor with the promiscuous Evadne only accentuates
Aspatia's virtue.

Despite all the careful reminders of Aspatia's virtuous virginity,
this strategy cannot erase the fact that throughout the play the
symptoms of Aspatia's erotomania were displayed for the audience's
delectation and delight. From Lysippus's evocative description of
her physical and musical symptoms to the potentially alluring performance of her lament in act 2, Aspatia, while admittedly a chaste
maid, has fallen ill because she is a sexual being whose desires have
been cruelly thwarted. Further evidence that Beaumont and
Fletcher wanted to advertise Aspatia's sexual charms while promoting audience sympathy for her sad condition can be found in
the final act, as Aspatia achieves, even suicidally encourages, her
yearned-for death. She dresses up as a boy (a transgression that
would have titillated contemporary audiences, as it highlighted the
fact that Aspatia was played by a boy actor) and goads Amintor to
kill her, achieving the longed-for penetration by her lover only in
death. This act of erotically tinged violence obviously piqued the

The Maides Tragedy.

AS IT HATH BEENE

diuers times Acted at the *Blacke-friers* by
the K ɪ ɴ ɢ s Maiesties Seruants.

ASPATIA.   AMINTOR.

LONDON

Printed for *Francis Constable* and are to be sold
at the white Lyon ouer againſt the great North
doore of *Pauls Church.*   1 6 1 9.

Figure 3.1. Title Page of the First Quarto of *The Maides Tragedy*
(1619), Mal.233(1). By permission of The Bodleian Library,
University of Oxford.

imagination of playgoers, as Aspatia's murder was used to entice prospective buyers of the playtext: the scene is memorialized in the title page of the first quarto. (See figure 3.1.)

As the previous discussion suggests, musical laments, even when sung by chaste characters such as Aspatia and Desdemona, often had a sexual resonance. Perhaps to separate these already problematic women from the taint of whoredom, playwrights and composers often had them listen to laments sung by servants that ventriloquized their emotions rather than engage in questionable music-making themselves. But, as we shall see, the erotic snare of music cannot be easily escaped.

In the case of Shakespeare's *Measure for Measure* (1604), the lovesick Mariana's morality is called into question by the very fact that she is listening to music. The unfortunate girl has been deserted by her fiancé, the overly dogmatic deputy, Angelo, because she could not pay her dowry. At the beginning of act 4, scene 1, she takes refuge in melancholy music as a boy, Mariana's servant, sings "Take, O, Take Those Lips Away." As the boy sings, Duke Vincentio enters, disguised as a friar. Mariana seems embarrassed and commands her servant to "break off thy song." She then begs the "friar" to excuse finding her in the potentially compromised situation, listening to music.

> I cry you mercy, sir, and well could wish
> You had not found me here so musical.
> Let me excuse me, and believe me so,
> My mirth it much displeas'd, but pleas'd my woe." [IV.i.10–13]

In other words, she wasn't using music in a lighthearted way. The love song did not spark merriment, but rather fed her lovesickness. This is perfectly in line with medical treatises that claim certain kinds of music could actually exacerbate melancholy, rather than cure it.[43] As Burton warns in *The Anatomy of Melancholy*, "for music enchants . . . it will make such melancholy persons mad."[44] Indeed, the Duke is not comforted by Mariana's excuse. He is obviously concerned that music may not be the best medicine: " 'Tis good; though music oft hath such a charm / To make bad good, and good provoke to harm" [IV.i.14–15]. For the Duke, music is dangerous: its beauty can make evil sound sweet ("make bad good").

If the Duke heard the only extant contemporary setting of this piece, the suitably melancholic plaint by composer John Wilson, we might understand his concern about the effect the song had upon the already heartsick Mariana. Wilson probably worked for the King's Men between 1614 and 1629;[45] thus, it is probable that his setting, which survives only in manuscript copies from the 1650s, was used in a revival, not in the original 1604 production. It is also possible that Wilson's setting was for a later play that incorporated Shakespeare's song, John Fletcher's *The Bloody Brother*, as extant manuscript copies contain the setting of a second verse that appears in that play but is missing from *Measure for Measure*. The earliest manuscript copy, GB-Ob. MS. Mus. Sch. B.1, has this additional verse from *The Bloody Brother* written below the music, but the composer has not set it. Other manuscript copies also contain this second verse from *The Bloody Brother*.[46] Regardless of when Wilson's setting was used, it is a highly evocative and erotic song, the performance of which would have justified Mariana's defensive posture and the Duke's response. If we analyze the music found in GB-Ob. MS. Mus. Sch. B.1, we immediately notice the key: G minor. This is a common key for laments on the seventeenth-century stage; Curtis Price even goes so far to claim that it becomes symbolic of death.[47] The setting is completely straightforward, with an emphasis on clear text setting with little elaboration. The words are perfectly applicable to Mariana's unhappy situation, as the protagonist demands that the lips be taken away (perhaps the lips of her fiancé, Angelo). The singer acknowledges that kisses may bring seals of love, but ultimately these seals are in vain. In short, promises made in the heat of carnal passion mean nothing.

Mariana's attempt to pass herself off as a "good girl" who is embarrassed when caught listening to such a song doesn't serve the Duke's ultimate purpose: he doesn't want a "good girl." He wants to convince her to take the chaste Isabella's place in bed with the lustful Angelo, a plan to which Mariana accedes. Mariana's character is immediately called into question in this scene because she's listening to music, and although her emotions are ventriloquized by a boy, she cannot escape the melodious taint of lament. Her consumption of music suggests her lascivious tendencies.

Later plays employ similar strategies of ventriloquism as servants give air to the grief of their mistresses. But here too the lovesick noblewomen are not completely absolved: in these cases, listening to laments incites lust. In Philip Massinger's *The Renegado* (1624), Donusa, the niece of the Sultan, has fallen desperately in

love with the Christian, Vitelli. She realizes the folly of her attraction, but she is compelled to love him. Vitelli appears before her
and is ravished by the spectacle of her wealth and her beauty. Donusa commands her servant to "Sing ore the Dittie, that I last com-
posde / Upon my Love-sick passions, sute your Voice / To the
Musique thats plac'de yonder" [II.iv.1–3].[48] The music serves two
purposes (neither the song text nor the song itself survives). First,
it allows Donusa to give voice to her passion; second, her musical
composition further seduces Vitelli. Although she does not sing
herself, Donusa falls under the rubric of the musical courtesan,
charming the Christian Vitelli through her carefully crafted song.
Indeed, Vitelli succumbs completely to Donusa's musical and physical charms. After the performance, he "stands amazde" and responds: "Is not this *Tempe*, or the blessed shades, / Where innocent
Spirits reside? Or doe I dreame, / And this a heavenly vision? How-
soever / It is a sight too glorious to behold / For such a wretch as
I am" [II.iv.6–10]. Here, the music of lovesickness and the charms
of a beautiful woman go hand-in-hand as tools of seduction.

Likewise, in Robert Chamberlain's comedy, *The Swaggering
Damsel* (1640), music, sex, and lovesickness are conflated in a ventriloquized lament. Sabina and Valentine are madly in love, but her
father refuses to pay for a dowry. Nevertheless, her passion over-
whelms her, and she summons the lovesick swain to her room for
a tête-à-tête. While waiting for Valentine, she becomes restless and
impatient, so she commands her servant, Betty, to sing a pretty
love song to assuage her sadness. Betty warns that the love song
will only increase her despair, but Sabina throws caution to the
wind, claiming that she loves being melancholy and welcomes the
increase of the humor. Betty finds this strange, but she obliges her
mistress, singing "Be Not So Cruel Fairest Boy," a typical lovesick
lament that blames cruel and capricious Cupid for the pains of
lovers whilst simultaneously asking for a cure. No sooner has Betty
completed the song then a knock is heard at the door. Valentine
has arrived.

While the music for Chamberlain's comedy does not survive,
the role it played in the drama is clear. Again, a lovesick woman
of questionable morality (whose chastity is in peril) has her servant
articulate her passionate emotions through song. While the music
does not seduce Sabina's suitor, Valentine, it does whet her own
appetite for the pleasures of their interlude. Music again plays an
ambiguous role. While musical performance is foisted onto Sa-

O Let Us Howle Some Heavy Note

Example 3.2. Robert Smith, "Ah, Coridon!" in *Choice Ayres, Songs, and Dialogues* (London, 1676), verse 1.

bina's lower-class servant, Betty, Sabina is not cleared of wrong-doing. Her lovesickness (and the lustful symptoms thereof) have made her embrace the symptoms of her disease, enjoying her passionate response to Valentine even as she hopes for a cure through consummation with her beloved.

Musical ventriloquism, while still in existence, fell out of vogue somewhat after the Restoration. Singing actresses emerged who used laments and mad songs as showcases for their talents. Gone too is the automatic association between music and lasciviousness frequently found in the earlier entertainments. For example, Caelia, the unfortunate heroine of Henry Nevil Payne's *Fatal Jealousie* (1673), is wrongly accused of adultery by her pathologically jealous husband, Antonio. As the play opens, Antonio has killed one of his new wife's friends, because she met with him shortly after the wedding. These violent tendencies persist, culminating in a bloodbath in act 5. At the opening of act 4, Caelia, mourning her husband's suspicious nature, requests music from her servant, Flora, to lull her to sleep. The song her servant chooses, "Ah, Coridon!" set by Robert Smith, does not seem suitable for this purpose. A tragic lament, the text foreshadows Caelia's demise at her husband's hands in the following act. "For better 'tis your heart were lost, / Then thus suspitious prove: / You then would kill me by disdain."

To convey the sense of melancholy and unease, Smith's song is in A minor and features unsettling off-beat entrances. As it is a strophic song, Smith strives to portray a generalized affect; however, it seems particularly appropriate that, in the first verse, a descending bass line accompanies the text "You then would kill me by disdain"—a fitting musical representation of a distraught women succumbing to death, sinking to the ground as a result of her lover's scorn. (See example 3.2.)

Madness and the Bawdy Ballad

While ventriloquism sought to negotiate the sexualized aspects of female music-making, female mad songs shunned decorum and celebrated licentiousness. As seen in Desdemona's "Willow Song" and even the ventriloquized laments, bawdy language, a symptom of lovesickness, frequently crept into female articulations of grief and mental anguish. The sexual element is even more explicitly displayed by those who are driven mad by their beloved's rejection. Doomed to wander aimlessly, picking at or ripping clothing and singing and speaking in an excessive and irrational manner, these women provide a sexually charged fantasy of female transgression.

Shakespeare created the prototype for alluring female madness when fair Ophelia lost her wits in *Hamlet* (1603). Laertes, witnessing his sister's music-riddled descent into madness, exclaims: "Thought and afflictions, passion, hell itself, / She turns to favor and to prettiness" [IV.v.188–89]. Laertes' comment suggests that women do not go mad to incite horror in the audience. They go mad to entertain, turning suffering and affliction into "prettiness." The music (the aural equivalent of the flowers Ophelia adorns herself with before she drowns) aids immeasurably in this enterprise, her madness providing an excuse for the heightened discourse of song.

Much ink has been spilled about Ophelia's mad songs and their meanings. Feminist critics have adopted the unfortunate maid, reading her either as a victim of patriarchy or as an empowered female who eludes the dominant discourse of patriarchy (words) in her flowing, feminine musical madness.[49] I would suggest that it is not an either/or proposition: Ophelia is both powerful *and* a victim. She is a victim of her father and brother as they advise her to reject Hamlet, a victim of Hamlet's cruel behavior toward her as he feigns madness, and finally, a victim of madness itself—a madness caused by the twin misfortunes of Hamlet's public humiliation and her father's death.[50] Yet her memorable madness grants her authority within the drama, allowing her to say things that would otherwise be impossible. Her music imbues her mad speech with a persuasive power that renders Ophelia dangerous, making her death an ideological necessity.[51]

Through her mad performance, Ophelia makes strange otherwise familiar music—quoted ballads, ballad-like tunes, and dirges suited to her unhappy situation—imbuing her songs with a special rhetorical power. As Ross Duffin notes in his recent *Shakespeare's Songbook*, "there is frequently some extra layer of meaning or expectation created for his [Shakespeare's] audience through the use of these [ballad] references."[52] For example, Ophelia's first song, based on the ballad "Walsingham," would have held preexistent meanings for the audience (the original is a dialogue between a pilgrim from the Holy Land and a person seeking her lover), but, as did Desdemona, Ophelia shapes the textual and musical language of others to articulate her own points: another sort of musical ventriloquism.

More generally, the very act of singing grants Ophelia power, as music could alter the humoral balance of listeners. As we saw in *The Maid's Tragedy*, Aspatia's musical grief "infects" those around her. In *Hamlet*, Ophelia's brother Laertes observes that she is "a document [instruction] in madness" [IV.v.176]. This line has a double valence: the listener hearing Ophelia's rambling discourse might be instructed in mad behavior. Simultaneously, Laertes' comment suggests that Ophelia's discourse, while mad, teaches a lesson or tells an essential truth. Both these features render Ophelia's musical madness dangerous.

Beyond the possibility of being "instructed" in madness, those who bore witness to Ophelia's mad musical discourse might also fall prey to base desires. Throughout *Hamlet* (and throughout the Shakespeare canon) music is shown to be an enchanting medium. Earlier in the play, Laertes cynically describes Hamlet's love talk to Ophelia as "songs," warning against their power to seduce [I.iii.30–31]. Music's seductive qualities were heightened if performed by a woman; indeed, as noted above, early modern playwrights frequently associated female singing with sexuality and the courtesan. Public music making by women was viewed with particular suspicion. As Baldassare Castiglione advises in his influential *The Book of the Courtier* (translated into English in 1561), young noblewomen should be reluctant to perform music before the court:

> Therefore when she commeth to daunce, or to shew any kind of musicke, she ought to be brought to it with suffring her selfe somewhat to be prayed, and with a certain bashfulnesse, that may declare the noble shamefastnesse that is contrarie to headinesse.[53]

Ophelia's exuberant musical performance thus calls her nobility, her sanity, and, because she performs bawdy ballads, her chastity, into question—she is without shame.[54] Although her songs make her an object of pity, they also render her tantalizingly available in a way that Desdemona, singing in her bedchamber, was not.

The dangers of Ophelia's madness are carefully introduced through the reactions of onlookers. A male observer first frames Ophelia's distraction, as Beaumont and Fletcher later do in *The Maid's Tragedy*, preparing the audience for the spectacle that follows. And, as with Aspatia a few years later, the ability of Ophelia's lamenting speech to move the auditor is foregrounded:

> She speaks much of her father, says she hears
> There's tricks i' th' world, and hems, and beats her heart,
> Spurns enviously at straws, speaks things in doubt,

That carry but half sense. Her speech is nothing,
Yet the unshaped use of it doth move
The hearers to collection. [IV.v.4–9]

Ophelia's ability to incite sympathy for her murdered father could
have significant ramifications for the rotten state of Denmark. Horatio responds to the description of Ophelia's mad speech and cautions against the "danger" of her rambling discourse. " 'Twere good
she were spoken with, for she may strew / Dangerous conjectures
in ill-breeding minds" [IV.v.14–15].

Unlike the cases of lamenting women considered earlier in this
chapter, Ophelia's madness is dangerous (as Horatio acknowledges)
from both a social and a *political* standpoint. Socially, her behavior
is transgressive, as she indulges in bawdy speech and performs music publicly. Politically, she is also dangerous, as her madness could
be seen as emblematic of all the evils afoot in Denmark—she has
been infected by the madness of a kingdom ruled by a murderous
usurper. The twin dangers of Ophelia's mad speech are heightened
when the distracted maiden sings, "How Should I Your True Love
Know?" in which lovesick madness and political subversion circu-
late together. Ophelia sings this song, a variant of the famous
"Walsingham" ballad, and initially her words confirm a straightforward diagnosis of erotomania-induced madness: "How should I
your true love know / From another one?" she asks.[55]

Although in the first stanza, Ophelia appears to be talking
about her true love, Hamlet, by the second and third stanzas she
has moved to a description of her father ("he is dead and gone").
The mention of her father's murder is politically dangerous, as it
highlights the corruption in the kingdom. The tune that accompanies Ophelia's words is fairly simple, fitting perfectly within the
English ballad style, where the emphasis is on communication of
the text rather than on vocal virtuosity. In performance the boy
(and later the actress) playing Ophelia had (and has) plenty of
power, of control, over the delivery of this ballad. In its simplicity,
it gives the performer freedom of interpretation, imbuing it with
persuasive power: a power that was recognized as dangerous by her
auditors.

Ophelia's second song, "Tomorrow is Saint Valentine's Day,"
while symptomatic of lovesickness, also has political undertones.[56]
Initially, the words of this song are blatantly erotic. Most obviously,
Saint Valentine's Day is the traditional celebration for lovers. In

the first stanza, Ophelia describes a maid (possibly herself) standing at the window, waiting for her suitor. The final lines of the first stanza "Let in the maid that out a maid / Never departed more" places a morsel of doubt in the auditor's mind. Did Ophelia give herself to Hamlet? Or has she run mad for love because this consummation was never achieved?

The second stanza is far bawdier than the first and here we find a potent combination of lovesickness and political subversion. While the sane Ophelia appeared to be a paragon of virtue, the mad Ophelia rejects chastity, mimicking a dialogue between a young man and his paramour, who protests that "Before you tumbled me, / You promis'd me to wed." The man responds that he would have married her "And thou hadst not come to my bed" [IV.v.62–66]. Whether this dialogue is the product of Ophelia's fevered brain or is the mad recollection of actual events is unclear. Regardless of the veracity of Ophelia's mock lover's quarrel, upon hearing this ballad, Claudius's sympathy for Ophelia evaporates. He asks, "How long hath she been thus?" perhaps worrying whether others may have heard versions of this inflammatory song that suggests his nephew despoiled Ophelia: an accusation with political and moral ramifications. Claudius then instructs Horatio to follow Ophelia, watching her actions (and perhaps monitoring her musical speech).

Upon Ophelia's exit, we learn how completely Ophelia's madness has unsettled Claudius. He turns to Gertrude and gives an emotional response to Ophelia's songs, but completely glosses over the bawdry in her utterance, focusing instead on her troubling grief over her father's death. He is primarily concerned that Ophelia's madness will stir the "thick and unwholesome . . . thoughts and whispers" of the people and is anxious about Laertes' reaction to Ophelia's utterances and the news of Polonius's death.

In confirmation of Claudius's fears, he learns that Laertes has arrived and is being touted by the people as the true successor to the throne of Denmark. Suddenly, Laertes himself bursts in upon Claudius and Gertrude, demanding answers about his father's death. Claudius is obtuse in his response, but then Ophelia, the dangerous purveyor of truth, enters, singing a snippet of a tune, "They bore him bare-faced on the bier / Hey non nonny, nonny, hey nonny," a mix, as before, of grief for her father's death with lovesick bawdry: the refrain, "hey nonny" and its variants was a frequent substitute for obscenities in early seventeenth-century songs.[57] Laertes' response demonstrates the power of her musical utterance: "Hadst thou thy wits, and didst persuade revenge, / It could not move thus" [IV.v.169–70]. In other words, Ophelia's mad song is more effective at goading him into action than any rational speech could be.

Ophelia's last extended musical outburst also combines bawdry and politically loaded speech. She begins with "For Bonny Sweet Robin." This snippet may have been sung to a tune "Bonny Sweet Robin," also known as "Robin is to the Greenwood Gone," which exists in thirty contemporary sources.[58] While not immediately apparent to a modern audience, Elizabethan audiences would have readily understood the bawdiness of Ophelia's text. "Robin" was a common term of endearment but it was also a euphemism for the male sex organ.[59] But Ophelia, as in her previous songs, quickly leaves "Robin" behind. Yet for an Elizabethan audience, the rest of one of the various "Robin" ballads would have perhaps played in their minds. As Sternfeld notes, this class of ballad typically deals with "lovers, unfaithfulness and extra-marital affairs."[60]

As before, Ophelia fluidly shifts from the typical eroticism symptomatic of a lovesick maiden to the lament of a daughter: "And Will A Not Come Again?"[61] The constant substitution of father for lover in her diseased fancy perhaps tells an emotional truth about Ophelia's feelings toward Polonius, who, along with Laertes, discouraged her relationship with Hamlet, as they were suspicious of the Prince's motivations. Then her father, the man for whom she sacrificed her relationship, dies at Hamlet's hands. It's not surprising that in her madness she would oscillate between two men she loved: one who limited her passions and who would, or—depending on the reading of *Hamlet*—did, relieve her of her maidenhead. As before, Ophelia lingers over the sad finality of her father's death: "No, no, he is dead, / Go to thy death-bed, / He never will come again" [IV.v.192–94]. Upon singing this final dirge, Ophelia departs, leaving Laertes and Claudius to react (and to frame the audience's reaction). Their discourse moves quickly from Ophelia's madness to the murdered father. Like Ophelia herself, Laertes and Claudius focus on the death of Polonius. In this, perhaps, Ophelia's disruptive and fluid musical language has served its purpose. Whether we read her as a lovesick maid, a lamenting daughter, or both, her madness foregrounds the death of Polonius and prompts Laertes to act. Her mad music is simultaneously disturbing and persuasive. After being a passive tool of her father and brother, ironically, she achieves political agency by losing her wits.

As her fluid madness—moving between thoughts of her father and her erstwhile lover, between speech and song—had given her a modicum of power, it is disturbingly fitting that Ophelia would die a fluid death. Drowning was associated with the feminine, as women were considered particularly liquid. Their eyes flowed with tears, their blood flowed during their monthly menstrual cycle, and when pregnant, they possessed the watery amniotic fluid that supported new life.[62] Ophelia's death by water, by the feminine, ironically drowns the fluidity of her musical discourse: her excessive femininity is terminated by excessive femininity. As Elaine Showalter observes, "The mad Ophelia's bawdy songs and verbal license, while they give her access to 'an entirely different range of experience' from what she is allowed as the dutiful daughter, seem to be her one sanctioned form of self-assertion as a woman, quickly followed, as if in retribution, by her death."[63]

Although Ophelia's watery end occurs offstage, Gertrude's evocative description of her suicide holds Ophelia's victimhood and her power in exquisite tension. While the girl is pitiful, hurling herself into death, she is also dangerously sexual and alluring to the very last, adorning herself with phallic flowers, "long purples." She takes the masculine power, and bedecks herself with it, even as it kills her. Her fluidity is also emphasized in Gertrude's description. Ophelia sang "snatches of old lauds" (reminding us of her fluid, feminine musical discourse) and although her clothing initially bore her weight, "mermaid-like" (a fluid creature, neither fish nor woman) she ultimately sank to her death. Laertes responds appropriately, eulogizing her most prominent (and most excessive) feature: "Too much of water hast thou, poor Ophelia, / And therefore, I forbid my tears" [IV.vii.185–86]. Laertes' response is multivalent. Naturally, "too much water" refers to Ophelia's unhappy drowning, but there is also another resonance to this line. Laertes recognizes that Ophelia's fluid femininity was excessive, and it might seduce him into a womanish display of grief ("tears"). He would stay dry and masculine, untainted by her madness, but he cannot help but succumb to weeping, with the excuse that "When these are gone, / The woman will be out" [IV.vii.188–89]. Just as Laertes would shun effeminate weeping, Ophelia's watery voice must also be silenced, even as she behaves to the last, in Gertrude's words, "like a creature native and indued / Unto that element" [IV.vii.179–80].

Other madwomen followed Ophelia's sad example, singing their mad ballads to sympathetic onlookers: a spectacle of fluidly excessive femininity. In John Fletcher and William Shakespeare's *The Two Noble Kinsmen* (1613), the lovesick Jailer's Daughter is the direct descendent of Ophelia. Like Ophelia, she loves her social better, in this case a noble prisoner in her father's jail, Palamon (admittedly, the class disparity is greater than that between Hamlet and Ophelia). While Laertes refers to Hamlet's love-talk as "songs," the Jailer's Daughter is ensnared by Palamon's literal performance of melancholic music. As she exclaims, "To hear him / Sing in an evening, what a heaven it is!" [II.v.18–19]. And, like Ophelia, the Jailer's Daughter is associated with water—she maintains contact with the object of her affections by bringing the noble prisoner water every morning, and later in the play she wanders by a lake.

Like Ophelia, the Jailer's Daughter is preoccupied with thoughts of both her father and her lover, although the political resonance found in *Hamlet* is not present. The Jailer's Daughter falls prey to erotomania after allowing Palamon to escape. She becomes increasingly distraught and lovesick as she realizes that her beloved has left her behind. She wanders the woods (perhaps the return to the natural world symbolizing her return to her "natural" feminine state of irrationality) searching for Palamon, her wits scattering like leaves beneath her feet. She is concerned that her father will be hanged for letting Palamon escape, and she worries about the fate of her beloved, imagining him torn to bits by wild beasts. Finally, her reason fractures completely and she begins to sing—a conclusive sign that she has succumbed to madness.[64]

The use of music in *Two Noble Kinsmen* demonstrates how certain songs and snippets of songs became associated with female lovesickness on the early modern stage. The Jailer's Daughter sings "Willow, Willow, Willow," a direct reference to the unhappy Desdemona's lament. And she has even more in common with the unfortunate Ophelia. The Daughter's "For I'll Cut My Green Coat a Foot above My Knee," like Ophelia's "They Bore Him Bare-Faced on the Bier," includes the suggestive refrain "Hey, nonny, nonny." Other specific musical allusions also connect the Daughter with Ophelia. Upon her appearance, she brags of her singing abilities and claims that she can sing many songs, including "Bonny Robin," a ballad snippet also quoted by Ophelia. Her subsequent scene (IV.iii) contains further musical allusions to Ophelia's madness, as the Daughter refers to a song with the burden "down-a, down-a"—a refrain quoted by Ophelia in her mad ramblings. Admittedly, this was a common refrain; however, given the other musical and textual similarities to Ophelia, the choice of this particular turn of phrase was certainly not coincidental.

The musical and dramatic relationship between the two characters is further confirmed when the Wooer, who hoped to procure her hand in marriage, tells the Jailer about his daughter's unhappy state. In a speech that bears more than a passing resemblance to Gertrude's description of Ophelia's suicide, he describes the Jailer's Daughter, wandering by a lake, singing. Like Ophelia, she sings much, but the Wooer denies she made any sense. And like Ophelia, the watery Daughter sings her fluid discourse, weeps, and then seeks death in water. Luckily, the Wooer is able to rescue her from drowning, saving the Daughter from her predecessor's fate.

As in the case of *Hamlet*, *Two Noble Kinsmen* highlights the attractiveness of female madness. The Wooer's friend, upon hearing his description of the Jailer's Daughter's musical madness, exclaims "pretty soul," confirming female madness as titillating and seductive. The Doctor who observes her behavior comments, "How prettily she's amiss!" [IV.iii.28–29]. The seductive eroticism of female madness becomes even more important in the latter half of the century, when women appear on the public stage, using musical distraction to highlight their considerable charms.

Actresses and Musical Disorder

In part because of the increased public role taken by women during the Civil War, women's speech had become slightly more acceptable in the second half of the seventeenth century, as was evinced by the introduction of actresses onto the London stage and the rise of female playwrights. However, as Richard Allestree and other conduct book writers indicated, it was considered subversive for a woman to speak too loudly or too often (they should be silent, like the music of the spheres). Even the proto-feminist Sarah Fyge acknowledged the association between chastity and female silence in *The Female Advocate* of 1686 as she apologized for her own verbosity:

> For as one great Commendation of our Sex, is, to know much
> and speak little, so my Virgin-Modesty hath put a Period to the

intended Length of the ensuing Lines, lest censuring Criticks should measure my Tongue by my Pen, and condemn me for a Talkative, by the length of my Poem.[65]

Despite the lip service paid to the professed ideal of the chaste and silent woman, as we have seen, transgression appealed to seventeenth-century audiences, and the introduction of actresses to the English stage allowed the female mad song, the excessive musical genre par excellence, to flourish. Both Bedlam (Bethlehem Hospital in London) and the theater were relatively "safe" places to display these antic figures of disorder, as they clearly separated the audience from the spectacle, whether with cells at Bedlam or the proscenium stage.[66] Voyeurism was an integral part of the experience at the London theaters, just as it was at Bedlam. Mad songs advertised the charms of the actresses, who appeared in disheveled, emotionally vulnerable states, often singing sexually suggestive texts, symptomatic of their lovesick grief. Their music was unpredictable, defying logic as they shifted rapidly from recitative to aria, from bawdy ballad to lament to furious melismatic raging. These songs enhanced the actresses' popularity and increased their demand as mistresses.[67] In 1708 prompter John Downes described the effect that Celania's mad songs, performed by the actress Moll Davis in *The Rivals* (for the 1667 revival),[68] had on the most important audience member of all, Charles II:

> *The Rivals*, a Play, Wrote by Sir *William Davenant*; having a very Fine Interlude in it, of Vocal and Instrumental Musick, mixt with very Diverting Dances . . . And all the Womens Parts admirably Acted; chiefly *Celia* [Celania], a shepherdess being Mad for Love; especially in singing several Wild and Mad Songs. *My Lodging it is on the Cold Ground, &c.* She perform'd that so Charmingly, that not long after, it Rais'd her [actress Moll Davis] from her Bed on the Cold Ground, to a Bed Royal.[69]

Moll Davis's performance of these "Wild and Mad Songs,"[70] her display of irrational yet irresistible femininity, exercised such erotic appeal that it seduced the monarch. While an actress's status could be raised, and a powerful benefactor might be captivated by her erotically charged performance, ultimately these actresses performed fantasies of female transgression written and composed by men.[71] While these scenes gave actresses the opportunity to show off their dramatic and musical prowess, their power to captivate audiences was gained at a price, as their performances supported misogynist notions of female irrationality and emotional excessiveness.

The mad songs composed for the actress-singer Anne Bracegirdle reveal the ways in which femininity, madness, and music resonated together on the Restoration stage.[72] In the 1690s Bracegirdle became known for her portrayals of mad characters. She proclaimed her chastity, a quality that most actresses during this period did not share (consider the example of Moll Davis),[73] but her protestations of virtue were ignored by numerous suitors who pestered her, sometimes violently trying to break her resolve.[74] While Bracegirdle sought to maintain at least the appearance of virtue in her offstage life, rumors circulated about her supposed liaisons, and composers and playwrights frequently made her a victim of erotic melancholy onstage, allowing the audience to indulge their fantasies as they viewed the spectacle of Mrs. Bracegirdle "in love."[75]

Elements of Bracegirdle's biography combine with theatrical fantasy in her most famous mad song, John Eccles's "I Burn, I Burn" from Thomas D'Urfey's comedy *Don Quixote, Part II* (1694). While Bracegirdle's performance was powerful, inspiring passionate responses from her admirers, her character, Marcella, is a pitiful victim of unrequited love. Details in the play encouraged the audience to connect tragic events in Bracegirdle's personal life with Marcella's situation, heightening the delicious titillation. In *Don Quixote, Part I*, Marcella is described in the *Dramatis Personae* as "a young beautiful Shepherdess that hates Mankind."[76] This hatred led her to reject her suitor, Chrysostome, and he has pined to death for her. While the character of Chrysostome is only mentioned and is thus spared the embarrassment of dying for love onstage, his demise may have referred to the recent death of William Mountfort, an actor suspected to be Bracegirdle's lover, who perished in the aftermath of Captain Hill and Lord Mohun's attempt to kidnap the actress.[77] Curtis Price claims that D'Urfey "provides [Bracegirdle] with a public forum from which to reply to rumours and accusations."[78] Yet Marcella's portrayal is considerably more complex than Price's statement allows. Marcella was not Chrysostome's lover (just as Bracegirdle was not Mountfort's), so in that regard both the character and the actress were blameless. However, the shepherdess's cold-hearted attitude about Chrysostome's demise and her inappropriate behavior at his funeral do not speak well of her character, and perhaps, by intimation, do not speak well of Bracegirdle's. She appears at the funeral, she tells Chrysostome's friend Ambrosio, to clear her name. But when pressed, she resorts to criticizing the dead, telling Ambrosio callously that Chrysostome's "Death was caused by his obstinate folly."[79] While Chrysostome may have been a fool for love, Marcella's behavior provokes hostility in Ambrosio and the shepherds who hear her diatribe, although the knight errant Don Quixote vows to defend her.

In *Don Quixote, Part II*, Marcella (and possibly, by extension, also Bracegirdle) gets her comeuppance. In *Part II* D'Urfey allows Bracegirdle to purge any residual animosity the audience may have felt toward her in the wake of the Mountfort affair, as Marcella falls desperately but fruitlessly in love with Ambrosio, Chrysostome's friend, who, because of Marcella's harsh behavior, has become an "inveterate enemy to women."[80] Marcella's lovesickness is humiliating; she follows Ambrosio, who actively scorns and loathes her. Occasionally, she responds to his verbal parries, but eventually she completely submits herself to him, speaking the lines:

> All stubborn Maids, let my Example guide,
> Henceforth ne're sacrifice your Love to Pride:
> Take whilst you can the kind deserving he,
> Lest in Refusing, you Repent like me.[81]

Such verse encouraged the audience to equate the repentant Marcella with the steadfastly chaste Bracegirdle, who, speaking the lines D'Urfey wrote for her, urged the "stubborn Maids" in the audience to accept the "kind deserving he." Thus, Bracegirdle enacted a male fantasy that ended in her own (onstage) capitulation. In fact, D'Urfey's preface makes clear that the punishment of Marcella, and perhaps of Bracegirdle, was his invention, designed for the delight of the public:

> *I think I have given some additional Diversion in the continuance of the Character of* Marcella; *which is wholly new in this Part, and my own Invention; the design finishing with more pleasure to Audience, by punishing that coy Creature by an extravagant Passion here, that was so inexorable and cruel in the first Part.*[82]

By act 5, scene 2, Marcella has completely succumbed to madness, allowing the audience to relish Bracegirdle's considerable erotic charms as a performer. She enters the scene and mistakes an entertainment of St. George and the Genius of England for reality. Disturbed that a man seems to have been turned into a dragon, she imagines his breath burning her. Her irrational display moves the other spectators to chastise Ambrosio for his harsh treatment of Marcella, but he continues to scorn her, calling her a "Devil."[83] Marcella then tries to seduce the unwilling Ambrosio more blatantly, showing signs of the lasciviousness typical of female victims of lovesickness:

> All Female Arts and Tricks begone, avaunt, and let the passion of my heart lye open: Turn, turn thou dearest pleasure of my Soul, and I will bathe thee with my Eyes fond Tears; lay thee upon my Breast panting with Love, and speak the softest words into thy Ears that ere were spoke by a kind yielding Maid; kiss thee with eager Joy, and press thee close, close to my heart till I am lost in transport, and am for that short time a Deity.[84]

Marcella offers to sacrifice her chastity in the most passionate terms, displaying the excessive emotion that was believed to be a common feature of the female constitution while perpetuating the fantasy that Bracegirdle was somehow sexually available—that she too might "kiss thee with eager Joy." Marcella's madness eventually boils over in the song that follows: "I Burn, I Burn."

The text to this song paints a vivid (and sympathetic) portrait of lovesick madness, while faulting Marcella for her own downfall:

> From Love's awful Throne, a curst Angel I fell
> And mourn now the Fate,
> Which my self did create.[85]

Marcella's music, composed by John Eccles, displays many of the features of musical excess found in other late seventeenth-century mad songs. A high degree of word repetition (mm. 1–7) and an extremely mimetic style (florid melismas, for example, to represent flashing and blowing) were conventionalized musical representations of mental unrest. Just as Marcella's thoughts fly from one subject to the next, so does her music. Her song becomes more declamatory as she speaks of her sinful nature. Each word is meant to be heard as she explains how "Pride, hot as Hell" has brought her low (mm. 32–45), potentially an admonishment for those ladies in the audience who might consider following Marcella's disastrous example. At the close of this piece Marcella becomes extremely agitated (represented musically by rapid figuration in the voice and bass lines). She shuns the "fantastick toyes" that dressed her "Face and Body to allure" and then expresses suicidal tendencies, as she requests "Daggers, Poyson, Fire"; however, the audience doesn't learn Marcella's fate in *Don Quixote, Part II*. As D'Urfey was writing a comedy, it would have been inappropriate for a main character to kill herself onstage. (See example 3.3.)

The reaction to Bracegirdle's "I Burn, I Burn" demonstrates her considerable powers as an actress-singer: her performance was a cultural phenomenon. Thomas D'Urfey, perhaps self-servingly perpetuating the legend of Bracegirdle, composed a laudatory poem about the actress's performance in his play. Two composers, Gottfried Finger and Henry Purcell, set versions of this text. Finger's setting, "While I with Wounding Grief Did Look," is published in the fourth book of *Thesaurus Musicus* (1695). Purcell's version, sung in a 1695 revival of John Dryden's *The Spanish Fryar*, was published in a single-sheet edition as "*A New Song in the Play call'd the Spanish Fryer . . . Sung by a Boy.*"[86] It was printed without any mention of its theatrical context in *Deliciae Musicae*, book 1, and *Orpheus Britannicus*, book 1, where it is called "A Song on Mrs. *Bracegirdle's* Singing (*I Burn &c.*) in the 2 Part of *Don-Quixote.*"[87] Finger and Purcell's songs give us a rare opportunity to gauge (male) audience response to the spectacle of female madness. Just as Charles II was seduced by Moll Davis, the text composed by D'Urfey suggests that he was seduced by Bracegirdle's/Marcella's madness. But it was more than seduction. By listening to her siren song, he was actually transformed, his humoral balance altered, rendering him lovesick as well:

> While I with wounding grief did look,
> When Love had turn'd your brain;
> From you the dire Disease I took,
> And bore my self your pain.
>
> *Marcella* then your Lover prize,
> And be not too severe;
> Use well the conquests of your Eyes,
> For Pride has lost your Deare.
>
> *Ambrosio* treats your flames with scorn,
> And rakes your tender mind;

Example 3.3. John Eccles, "I Burn, I Burn" in *The Songs to the New Play of DON QUIXOTE . . . Part the Second* (London, 1694).

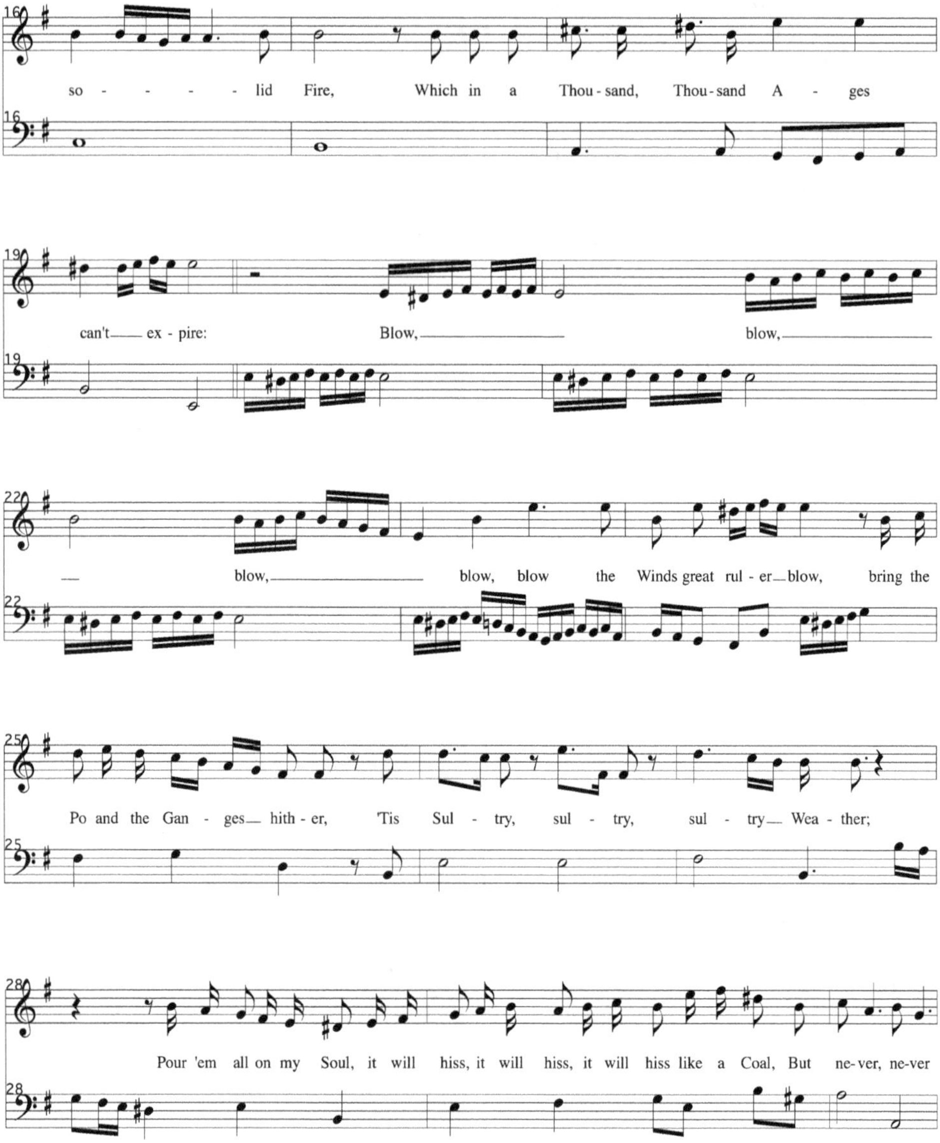

Example 3.3. *Continued.*

be——— the— cool - er. 'Twas Pride, hot as Hell, that first

made— me Re-bell, from Love's awe - full Throne, a Curst An - gel I fell;

And mourn now the Fate which my self did cre - ate, Fool,——

Fool that con - si - der'd not when— I was well; And mourn— now the Fate which my

self— did cre - ate, Fool, Fool that con - si - der'd not when— I was well.

Example 3.3. *Continued.*

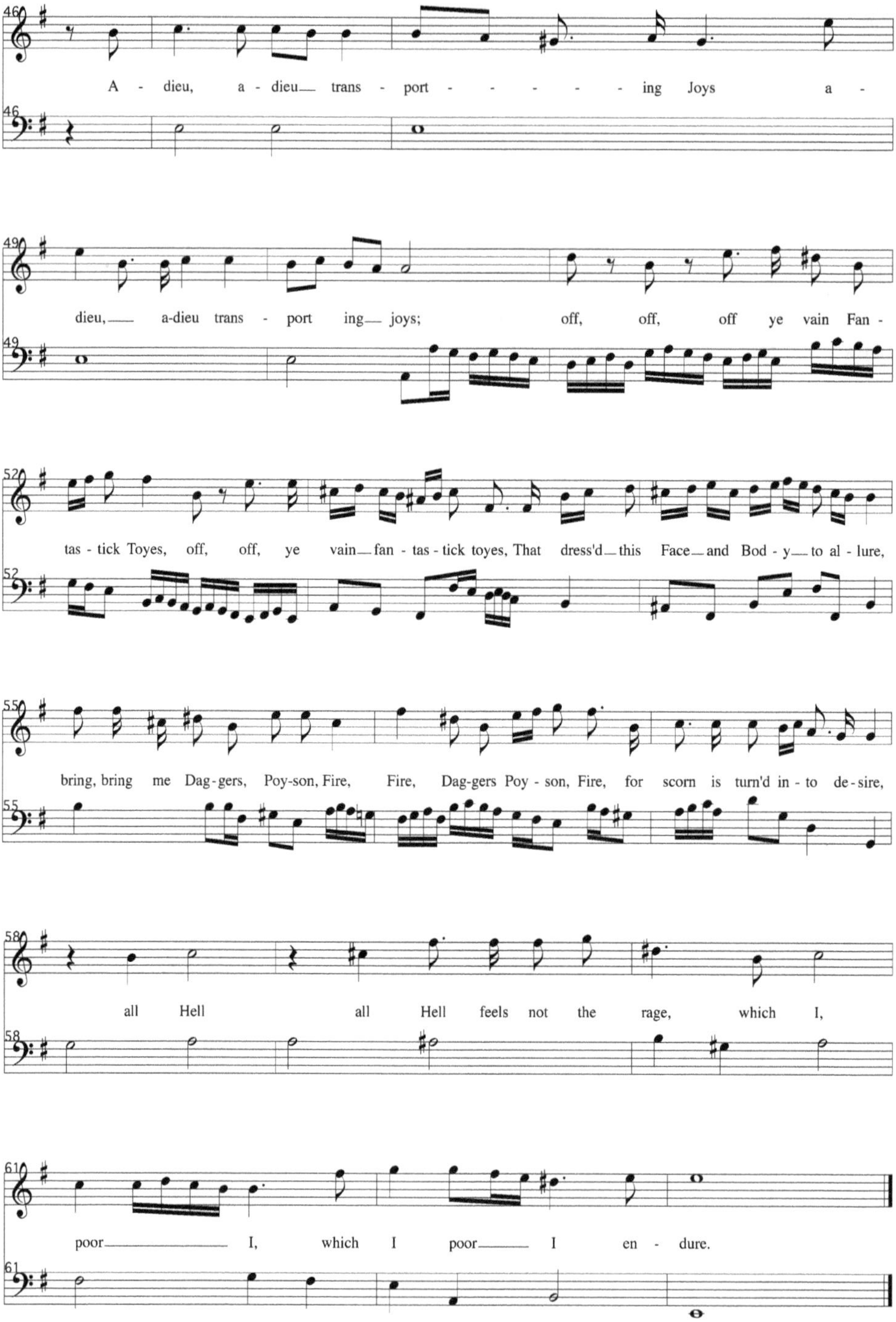

Example 3.3. *Continued.*

Withdraw your Frowns, and Smiles return,
And pay him in his kind.

Yet smiles again where Smiles are due,
And my true Love esteem:
For I much more doe rage for you
Than you can burn for him.

Finger's setting of the poem is strophic and straightforwardly syllabic, typical of his vocal style. Perhaps the Moravian Finger did not fully understand the implications of the text. Nevertheless, he sets all the stanzas of the original poem, in which the auditor admits to being infected by Marcella's disease (lovesickness), begging her to esteem his "true Love" and finally claiming, "For I much more doe rage for you / Than you can burn for him [Ambrosio]."

Although Purcell does not set the final four lines in which the auditor claims that his raging madness surpasses that of Marcella, he, being a superior composer to Finger, picks up on the unsettling insinuation of the text: by listening to a mad song, the auditor has literally gone mad. The first line, "Whilst I with grief did on you look, when Love had turn'd your Brain," is set as a lament: the key is G minor (a typical lament key) and the bass line mostly progresses downward, traveling from G to D. Florid melismas, typical of the raging music of lovesickness, are used to set words that highlight the infection: Marcella's "turn'd" brain, the "contagion" (which replaces the "Disease" of D'Urfey's original) and the pain the protagonist "bore" for Marcella. Repetition is also used, a typical musical device to signify urgency and passion, a convention used to great affect at the beginning of "I Burn." As Curtis Price notes, "All but one of the opening four lines . . . are immediately repeated at different pitch levels, thereby giving considerable weight to what at first hearing might be interpreted as mere graces."[88] (See example 3.4.)

Given the musical language Purcell assigns to him, it would appear that that auditor has fully succumbed to Marcella's disease. Of course, his portrayal of the lovesick swain's passionate reaction to Bracegirdle's fictional madness undermines the notion that the theater was a safe space in which audiences could enjoy transgression without any personal repercussions. At the very least, such musical responses highlight the considerable power Bracegirdle had over her audience. Indeed, the lovesick and delusional Captain Hill, just a few years earlier, had been inspired by her onstage

Example 3.4. Henry Purcell, "Whilst I with Grief Did on You Look," *Deliciae Musicae*, Book 1 (London, 1695), mm. 1–18.

persona to commit the twin atrocities of attempted kidnapping and murder. While one may read D'Urfey's, Finger's, and Purcell's responses to her performance as fictional artistry, the song can also be understood as a representation of the actual feelings of some of Bracegirdle's more passionate fans. In the end, Bracegirdle's performance of "I Burn, I Burn," encouraged her audience to confuse fact and fiction, biography and drama—a practice that might have sold tickets and heightened the actress's fame, but could also have disastrous, even violent, consequences. Luckily for Bracegirdle, "I Burn, I Burn" was a calculated risk that paid off. Weaving together the actress's offstage life and her onstage character of Marcella in ways that simultaneously perpetuated misogynist notions of unbridled feminine emotionalism and ideas about the seductive power of female musical speech, her performance of lovesick madness only heightened her fame.

Operatic Lovesickness in Dido and Aeneas

And so we end where we began, with another woman whose music ensnares and enraptures: the unhappy Queen Dido. Perhaps the other lovesick women who sang and died on the English stage can give us insight into Dido's portrayal. She was not an anomaly, but rather was part of an ongoing tradition of female musical representation that began many years before her appearance, and lived on after her death in the lovesick songs of Bracegirdle and others. Modern commentators have offered numerous interpretations of Dido's behavior. Should she have indulged her baser passions, succumbing to Aeneas's considerable charms? Is she a stoic heroine, an exemplar for women?[89] Does her musical power erase her victimization at the hands of Aeneas and the witches? And how (and why) does she die?

The Dido with whom many seventeenth-century audiences would have been familiar appears in book 4 of Virgil's *Aeneid*. She is a widow who made a vow of chastity after her husband's death, yet she succumbs to Aeneas's advances. After Jove commands Aeneas to leave, she descends into furious irrationality, lambasting her lover and calling upon the services of a Massylian priestess to either exact revenge upon Aeneas or cure her of her passion for the feckless prince. When this last-ditch effort is unsuccessful, Dido resolves to end her life, plunging Aeneas's sword into her breast.[90]

As both Heller and Schmalfeldt have recently argued, Tate's

reworking of Dido's tale makes the queen more sympathetic.[91] She does not consort with a Massylian priestess; she does not vow revenge. She does not commit suicide, stabbing herself with Aeneas's sword. All of these changes would render the queen more palatable for late seventeenth-century audiences: in her final lament, the audience would have been persuaded to remember her dignity, her sacrifice, and her repentance.

But perhaps the situation is a bit more complicated. Would Tate and Purcell's sympathetic portrait have completely erased the cultural baggage Dido brought to the table? Would her music have consistently been heard as stoic and virtuous? During the sixteenth and seventeenth centuries, Dido was thought to be a silly woman, completely overcome by her passions (she is described as such in the popular ballad "The Wandering Prince of Troy").[92] Thomas Phaer and Thomas Twyne also leave no doubt that Dido was "silly" in their Elizabethan translation of Virgil. Dido is compared with a stricken deer, a beast, dashing irrationally through the woods in a futile attempt to escape her pain.

> So silly *Dido* burnes, and through the towne with raging cheere
> Astray she wanders wide, as doth sometime the stricken Deere,
> Whome ranging through the chase, some hunter shooting far
>   by chance
> All unaware hath smit and in her side hath left his lance,
> She fast to wildernesse and woods doth drain, and there com-
>   plaines
> Alone, but underneath her ribs the deadly dart remaines.[93]

Frequently, seventeenth-century authors portray Dido in a more complicated fashion, not simply as a silly women or a deer wounded by love's penetrating dart, but as a victim of her own overly passionate nature and the machinations of the gods.[94] This first point, her overly passionate nature, was particularly important, as early modern writers frequently diagnosed the queen as suffering from a particularly acute version of erotic melancholy.

Jacques Ferrand, in his treatise *Erotomania*, claims that Dido exhibits the typical behavior of one afflicted by lovesickness:

> And if the Lovers eyes be thus discomposed and out of order; how much more thinke you is his heart? For you shall see him now very jocund and laughing; and presently within a moment he falls a weeping, and is extreame sad: then by and by againe he

entertaines himselfe with some pleasant merry conceipts, or other; and within a short space againe is altogether as sad, pensive, and dejected as before.

This Passion you may observe drawn out to the life by *Virgill*, in his *Dido Aeneid*.4.[95]

Similarly, in his *Anatomy of Melancholy*, Robert Burton diagnoses Dido as suffering from a classic case of lovesickness.[96] The widespread association between Virgil's Dido and erotic melancholy suggests that some audience members during Purcell's time would have read the operatic Dido's behavior through this interpretative lens.

Purcell's evocative music and Tate's libretto support the impression that Queen Dido is suffering from lovesickness. Act 1 begins with Belinda, Dido's companion, singing a cheerful, rhythmically energetic tune, "Shake the Cloud from Off Your Brow" in an attempt to rouse Dido's sluggish spirits. Belinda is on the right track with her rhythmically active song, but Dido's cure, as Belinda tells us, requires more than cheerful music.[97] Lovesickness had one very effective cure: sexual intercourse with the beloved. Burton tells us, "The last refuge and surest remedy, to be put in practice in the utmost place, when no other means will take effect, is to let them go together, and enjoy one another."[98] Indeed, Belinda seems to realize the importance of this for her queen, although, in keeping with the fairly restrained language of Tate's libretto, she alludes to the cure, rather than crudely advising her to act. She tells Dido that "fate" would allow her "wishes" (i.e., her union with Aeneas) and encourages her to focus on a growing empire (facilitated by union with the Trojan prince) and "flowing pleasures." A group of courtiers confirm Belinda's advice, telling their monarch to "banish sorrow." From these opening musical moments, we get the sense that Dido is grief stricken but that her courtiers and even her closest attendant do not understand her discomfiture, as Aeneas would gladly return her affections. Thus, according to the voices of her courtiers, Dido is needlessly suffering when she should simply succumb to the pleasures of love.

The reason for Dido's reluctance to succumb to Aeneas's charms is inexplicable, unless Tate and Purcell assumed that their audience would know their Virgil: the Queen made a vow of chastity after her husband died, and her desire for Aeneas has weakened her resolve.[99] Belinda's impression that her queen is lovesick is con-

firmed in Dido's opening aria, "Ah, Belinda, I am Pressed with
Torment." As in her famous final aria, "When I Am Laid in Earth,"
Dido occupies a confused rhetorical space. She first tells us that
she doesn't want to confess her torment (which is, ironically, the
raison d'être of her song) yet she will "languish" until her grief is
known. She wants to relieve her grief, but she doesn't want the
pain of her torment to be "guessed": a truly ambivalent position.
Why, one might ask, is she reluctant to reveal the source of her
grief? Might she be embarrassed by her passion? Might she realize
that it is inappropriate? "Ah! Ah! Ah!" she sighs over an oscillating
ground bass figure, "Belinda, I am press'd with torment." The four-
measure ground bass (mm. 1–4) that underpins her exclamations
of woe is perfectly chosen, simultaneously representing Dido's obsessive passion and her being trapped, like a fly in amber, by her
indecision (or perhaps by her vow of chastity). Furthermore, the
C–B♮ semitone heard in the first measure of the ground foreshadows the first few notes of her final recitative, "Thy Hand, Belinda,"
which features the same figure. Of course, Dido's sighs and the
persistent downward trajectory of her opening measures could also
be understood as musical replications of the torment that presses
her, making it difficult to breathe. Furthermore, these despondent
musical gestures, as we have seen, are characteristic of laments sung
by other lovesick characters. In short, for a seventeenth-century
audience her music fully revealed (and accurately diagnosed) the
source of her affliction. It tells the audience what she would not
(or could not) through her text.

Other musical features contribute to the portrait of passionate
urgency and perhaps a lack of emotional discipline. When Dido
repeats her exclamation of grief, "Ah, Belinda, I am press'd with
torment" she "jumps the gun"; her musical sigh "Ah" appears a
measure earlier than expected (m. 9). In the first iteration of her
plaint, the ground bass began a measure before the vocal entrance.
Dido's premature entrance, coinciding with the first measure of the
ground bass pattern instead of the second measure, catches the
listener off guard. It also forces a slight adjustment of her vocal
line to accommodate the underlying harmonies. The element of
surprise, coupled with the heightened tessitura on the second iteration of "Ah! Belinda, I am press'd / With torment" ratchets up
the musical tension, which isn't fully released in the final cadence
of the first section, as the restless oscillation of the ground bass

continues unabated and Dido's vocal line rests on a G, the fifth scale degree rather than the tonic of C minor (m. 17).

In the second section of Dido's song her obsession is further revealed. Again, her vocal line enters unexpectedly against the bass line, as "Peace," her opening text, coincides with the final measure of the bass pattern: a dotted half-note C. The dotted half-note C may be read as a resting place, a sign of the hoped-for "peace" that has proved so elusive. The oscillating figure, first heard in measure 1 of the ground bass, now migrates to the vocal line (m. 20) and the voice and the bass imitate each other. But alas, the musical unity between voice and bass is brief. As the imitation is quickly discontinued, the careful listener might acknowledge that "peace" will prove elusive for Dido.

After Dido laments her alienation from peace, the ground bass modulates, heightening the sense of instability. This harmonic shift underpins Dido's vocal exclamation, "I languish till my grief is known." The musical gesture that Purcell uses on "languish" further emphasizes Dido's torment. "Languish" is first set with a descending figure. The second time "languish" begins on d", eventually resting a full octave below on "known" (mm. 33–39). This downward moving gesture incorporates modal mixture, oscillating in its descent between A♮ and A♭, B♭ and B♮, other potential signifiers of Dido's irrational mental state as she refuses to be bound by the limits of major or minor. Furthermore, her octave descent is reminiscent of her octave descent at the beginning of the piece (mm. 2–8), a figure that replicated the weight of torment pressing her.

Dido then defiantly leaps up from her d' nadir to an f" as she claims that although she is suffering, she would not have the cause of her torment known—possibly because the source of her torment, lovesickness, is an embarrassment to her (mm. 39–40). Her resolve to keep counsel only with herself is musically confirmed as she sings, "would not have it [the cause of her grief] guessed" with "guessed" being held for a full eleven beats. Despite the resolve of her vocal line, the oscillating ground bass continues to churn, suggesting that her torment will be so acute that all will be able to discern the source of her pain.

Indeed, in the exchange with Belinda that directly follows Dido's aria and in the subsequent interactions with her courtiers, it quickly becomes evident that Dido's companions have easily diagnosed the source of her discomfiture, even though she wants to conceal it: Dido is lovesick over the handsome Aeneas. Belinda, after encouraging her queen to unburden herself, makes it clear how transparent Dido's behavior actually is, baldly stating, "Then let me speak; The Trojan guest / Into your tender thoughts has press'd." What ensues is a short air, "The Greatest Blessing Fate Can Give," sung by a courtier, and a chorus, "When Monarchs Unite," both of which encourage Dido to pursue a relationship with Aeneas. These inducements seem to work, as we now see the other side of Dido's lovesick affliction: unbridled desire.

In a remarkable section of recitative, Dido praises Aeneas's considerable charms, demonstrating her fevered passion by elaborating upon each word of the warrior's exploits with an evocative musical gesture (an octave burst upward on "storms," a dotted, warlike melisma on "valor" as she celebrates Aeneas's bravery, sighing figures on "soft" and a further melisma on "fierce" as she praises the unique mixture of warrior and lover that exists in Aeneas). Dido's musical language stands in stark contrast to her handmaiden Belinda's and a courtier's mostly syllabic replies, suggesting, by contrast, the Queen's passionate attachment to Aeneas. There is also, perhaps, a hint of incipient madness (or at the very least a lack of emotional restraint) in Dido's recitative, as the highly responsive musical language she uses is akin to that of a mad song, where every word is responded to individually, shunning overall musical sense. The result here, as in a mad song, is a musical discourse that is somewhat fractured. Shortly after Dido's outburst, Aeneas appears, smooth-tongued, seductive, and passionate in his own right, offering to defy destiny. (See chapter 4.)

Dido seems to resist Aeneas, but by act 2 her relationship with him has been consummated. Aeneas's crass allusion to penetration ("behold, upon my bending spear / A monster's head stands bleeding") confirms his prowess, both in hunting and in sexual conquest.[100] Shortly thereafter, their pastoral idyll is interrupted by a witch-conjured storm, and the Sorceress's false Mercury waylays Aeneas, advising him to leave Carthage. Aeneas further confirms the sexual consummation with Dido, asking, "How can so hard a fate be took? / One night enjoy'd, the next forsook." The lovers' fate is sealed, and Aeneas will desert Dido, who only just availed herself of Aeneas's cure. By the time Dido appears with Belinda in act 3, she has fallen back into a profound depression, believing that Aeneas is preparing to leave her. Belinda protests that the Prince

will stay, but Dido has convinced herself of her imminent aban-
donment. She proves to be a remarkably astute woman; when the
sad Aeneas appears, it is to tell her that they must part. But, upon
seeing how distraught Dido is, he offers to defy the gods and stay.
Strangely, she rejects his offer: "No, faithless man, thy course pursue. . . . / For 'tis enough, whate'er you now decree, / That you had
once a thought of leaving me." Dido rejects the only thing that
could cure her lovesickness and embraces death.

How should we read Dido's actions here, especially as she acknowledges that her refusal of Aeneas's love has condemned her to
the grave ("death must come when he is gone")? Is she an example
of stoic feminine virtue as Heller would argue, or is she silly to
turn her back on love? Or is she perhaps a highly sympathetic
heroine who, in a fit of pique, sends away her only hope of hap-
piness? The chorus that follows Dido and Aeneas's argument confirms the latter view of the heroine. "Great minds against themselves conspire," the chorus observes, "And shun the cure they
most desire." The lovesick Dido, incapable of rational thought, has
shunned the only thing that can cure her lovesickness: union with
Aeneas.

So why does Dido die? There's no sword piercing her breast,
as it did her Virgilian counterpart, but she is mortally wounded,
nevertheless. As early modern writers observed, melancholy could
lead to extreme weakness and even death. According to the astrol-
oger John Maplet, melancholics

> be also for the most part shorte lifed, because the exceeding cold
> in them is a shortner of their Dayes, as we see it cometh to passe
> in old men, which through coldnes of nature are chopte up of a
> sodaine: for old men as they grown on toward death becom very
> colde and dry, all heate and moysture whych are the preservatives
> of Lyfe then forsakyng them and bidding them farewel.[101]

Given such opinions, it is possible that Dido's vital heat and mois-
ture simply dried up, a victim of the erotic melancholy that infected
her body. As Burton proclaims, "Death is the common catastrophe
to such persons [the lovesick]."[102] No sword was necessary. Love
was enough.

Dido's final utterance, the affecting lament, "When I Am Laid
in Earth," takes all the acknowledged markers of musical lovesickness and folds them into a tremendously effective package. But
again, ambivalence rears its head. As I noted at the beginning of

this chapter, we (the listeners and her companion, Belinda) are asked both to remember and to forget. Similarly, we (the listeners, both modern and contemporary) are faced with musical features that diagnose Dido as being a "typical" suffering woman, irrational, obsessed by love. On the other hand, these same musical features invite us to sympathize with her, drawing us into her plight. Just as Gottfried Finger and Henry Purcell responded to Anne Brace-girdle's spectacular performance of erotic melancholy, so we, the audience have reacted to Dido's pain. If she had simply delivered a spoken soliloquy, it wouldn't have been nearly as effective. As she declaims the final words of her closing recitative "Death is now a welcome guest" (Dido has given up all desire to live—like Ophelia and Desdemona and the other women who die, victimized by un-happy love), the inexorable ground bass, the famous chromatic oc-tave descent, begins. Just as the oscillating ground bass in her first air reveals Dido's indecision and ambivalence, in death, her music tells us she has found her true purpose: martyrdom. The ground bass is inexorable, always leading downward, always leading to the hoped-for condition of oblivion and the tomb (mm. 1–6). As be-fore, Purcell (and Dido) throws the listener off balance, with vocal entrances against the ground bass that subvert previously estab-lished expectations. At the beginning of her aria, Dido enters on the downbeat, on the last measure of the ground bass pattern. In the second half of her aria, she unpredictably enters too soon (and on a weak beat) on "Remember me," giving her plea an additional dose of urgency. This sense of urgency is heightened as, after a few rests, she repeats herself, again entering on a weak beat, a pattern that continues as she advises the listener, "but ah! Forget my fate." As Heller, Price, and others have noted, Dido's fate is sealed on the repetition of this cry, "Remember me!" (ascending to a high g") "but ah, forget my fate": she finally, for the first time, cadences with the ground bass, a clear indication that the lure of the grave can't be avoided. Heller claims, "her fate is sealed in this ultimate act of submission."[103] But again, I would suggest that am-bivalence is the order of the day. Dido may succumb to inexorable fate (and arguably this is the moral of the opera: fate cannot be circumvented), but she asks us to *forget* this. She would not have us celebrate her death. While listeners may sympathize with her female suffering, she does not go quietly. She continually avoids closure until her final utterance, when she asks us not to celebrate her sacrifice, but to forget it. In the ambivalence of her discourse, in its musical unpredictability, despite the rigor of the ground bass, she is a watery creature, just like Ophelia.

Further confirming her fluidity, her lamenting is carried into the orchestra, even after her collapse, with sobbing, sighing figures featured prominently in the strings. Even the instruments are not immune to Dido's grief, her sorry plight. Perhaps we are meant to sympathize with Dido, but I do not know if seventeenth-century listeners, in this impassioned outburst (complete with weeping strings), would have heard a woman stoically submitting to death. Rather, given contemporary discourses about Dido and lovesickness, audiences would have experienced a sensitive musical depiction of a woman, victimized by lovesick grief, deserted by her faithless lover, mournfully accepting death and asking forgiveness for her "sins."

Dido and the other musical women in this chapter are powerful and affecting, both for us and for the original audiences who heard their songs. Their musical language and their onstage behavior make them tremendously seductive and sometimes heartbreakingly sympathetic. Their fractured musical discourse, as Susan McClary and Ellen Rosand have observed, frequently pushes the limits of convention.[104] But at what cost? These women simultaneously subvert notions of proper female behavior (chaste, silent, and obedient) and confirm early modern notions of the overly emotional, irrational female. And, more so than any other disorderly character in this book, these characters consistently pay a very steep price for their transgressions. Almost always their brilliant musical discourse is drowned in the silence of death.

4

"O Let Us Howle Some Heavy Note"

In John Webster's tragedy, *The Duchess of Malfi* (1614), the eponymous Duchess has married beneath her station and against her brothers' wishes. In retribution, her brothers imprison her. The Duchess's mistreatment reaches its peak as Ferdinand, her cruel twin, sends musical madmen to torture his sister. The madmen enter and one of them sings "O Let Us Howle Some Heavy Note," a song that makes disorder aurally manifest; here an irrational man is transmuted into a howling beast.

The scene in *The Duchess of Malfi* in which the madman howls his "heavy notes" shows how profoundly problematic male mental disorder was for those in the seventeenth century: the madman has sunk so low that he has become bestial. Although the lovesick women discussed in the previous chapter were transgressive, violating ideal notions of womanhood with their unruly musical speech, their behavior actually, in some respects, reinforced misogynist ideas about the "typical" overemotional, irrational female. Men, on the other hand, were *supposed* to be rational, courageous, and stoic. Therefore, when they suffered from mental distress far more was at stake, as their behavior violated societal norms about appropriate male gender performance.[1]

Although the unruly womb was frequently blamed in cases of female mental disorders, male maladies had a different origin— melancholy—a humor that held both negative and positive connotations for those in the seventeenth century. To simplify an exceedingly complex matter, melancholy was thought to be of two primary types: natural melancholy and unnatural melancholy. Natural melancholy was, quite simply, the naturally occurring humor. But even natural melancholy was viewed with suspicion. It was base and excremental, and was thought to have potentially deleterious effects. As physician Timothy Bright describes it in his *Treatise of Melancholie* (1586):

> Naturall is either the grosser part of the bloud ordained for nourishment, which either by abundance or immoderate hotenesse, passing measure, surchargeth the bodie, and yeeldeth up to the braine certaine vapors, whereby the understanding is obscured; or else is an excrement ordained to be avoyded out of the bodie, through so manie alterations of naturall heate, and varietie of concoction, having not a drop of nourishing juyce remaining, whereby the bodie, either in power or substance may be relieved.[2]

These natural melancholics had dark complexions and were usually sad, fearful, "cold, heavy, dull, solitary, and sluggish."[3] Robert Burton in his *Anatomy of Melancholy* quotes Hippocrates' description of the common symptoms of melancholia:

> That they are "lean, withered, hollow-eyed, look old, wrinkled, harsh, much troubled with wind, and a griping in their bellies, or belly-ache, belch often, dry bellies and hard, dejected looks, flaggy beards, singing of the ears, vertigo, light-headed, little or no sleep, and that interrupt, terrible and fearful dreams."[4]

Unnatural melancholy, the second primary type, resulted from the corrupted blackened (adust) version of one of the four humors. As with natural melancholy, diet, insomnia, excess wine, and unbridled passions—all of these and more could cause the humors to overheat, overthrowing reason. According to Bright:

> The unnaturall is an humour rising of melancholie before mentioned, or else from bloud or choler, whollie changed into an other nature by an unkindly heate, which turneth these humours,

which before were raunged under natures government, and kept
in order, into a qualitie wholly repugnant.[5]

This sort of melancholy was extremely serious. Complete madness
was frequently the end result if melancholy was caused by humors
adust.[6]

Indeed, early modern writings frequently blurred the boundary
between melancholy and madness. Jacques Ferrand noted this fluidity in *Erotomania*, stating that madness was often "confounded"
with melancholy as they differed only in degrees, melancholy being
the milder form of the disease.[7] This notion that melancholy and
madness were on a continuum was common, and the causes and
symptoms of the two ailments were thought to be interchangeable,
although the symptoms of madness were more acute: ranting, delusions of grandeur (frequently mythologically based), complete in-
coherence, unbridled lust, and singing and dancing.[8]

Despite the obvious deleterious effects of melancholy and madness upon the body, some types of melancholy and madness had
positive connotations. In fact, melancholy was believed to enhance
a man's cognitive abilities. Marsilio Ficino and his followers had
promulgated the notion of the melancholic genius during the fif-
teenth and sixteenth centuries, after reading Aristotle's *Problemata*,
which begins, "Why is it that all those who have become eminent
in philosophy or politics or poetry or the arts are clearly melancholics?"[9] The French physician Andreas Laurentius notes that if
blood is mixed with melancholy, then it "maketh men witty, and
causeth them to excel others."[10] And Robert Burton describes both
the bad and the good qualities of melancholy:

> And although they be commonly lean, hirsute, uncheerful in
> countenance, withered, and not so pleasant to behold, by reason
> of those continual fears, griefs, and vexations, dull, heavy, lazy,
> restless, unapt to go about any business; yet their memories are
> most part good, they have happy wits and excellent apprehen-
> sions.[11]

We can see the trope of the scholarly melancholic given visual and
poetic form in Henry Peacham's emblem, *Melancholia*, from his
Minerva Britanna (1612). The melancholic sits alone, with only the
nocturnal owl and a "melancholly Pusse" for company. "Pale
visag'd" with a "cold and drie" complexion, he uses his good memory and "happy wits" to study. (See figure 4.1.)

H EERE *Melancholly* muſing in his fits,
Pale viſag'd, of complexion cold and drie,
Allſolitarie, at his ſtudie ſits,
Within a wood, devoid of companie:
  Saue Madge the Owle, and melancholly Puſſe,
  Light-loathing Creatures, hatefull, ominous.

His mouth, in ſigne of ſilence, vp is bound,
For *Melancholly* loues not many wordes:
One foote on Cube is fixt vpon the ground,
The which him plodding *Conſtancie* affordes :
  A ſealed Purſe he beares, to ſhew no vice,
  So proper is to him, as *Avarice*.

T I. 　　　　　　　　　　 *Sanguis*

Figure 4.1. Henry Peacham, "Melancholia," *Minerva Britanna*
(1612). By Permission of the Folger Shakespeare Library.

Even madness had some positive connotations within early modern culture. According to Laurentius, when the melancholic humor is heated by

> the vapours of blood, it causeth as it were, a kinde of divine ravishment, commonly called *Enthousiasma*, which stirreth men up to plaie the Philosophers, Poets, and also to prophesie: in such maner, as that it may seeme to containe in it some divine parts.[12]

Enthusiasm or "furor" allowed the sufferer to circumvent reason, to create great works of art, or even to communicate with the divine.

Because melancholy was a mark of the sensitive, the refined, and the intellectual, it was a disease of upper-class men; the lower sorts afflicted with mental disorders of this kind were labeled "mopish."[13] In the early seventeenth century, many English court-iers affected melancholy, donning black hats, befriending ravens and owls (night's black birds, associated with the darkened humor), and the like in the hopes that their compatriots might consider them tortured geniuses. The courtly melancholic lute songs of John Dowland are the most famous musical articulations both of the cult of melancholy that existed among the aristocracy and of the inspiration that mental disorders could provide. However, elements of this aristocratic obsession with melancholy were also presented seriously and lampooned in early seventeenth-century theatrical music.[14]

Both the positive and the negative connotations of male mel-ancholy and madness circulated in the seventeenth-century theater, affecting the sorts of music assigned such characters. Early seven-teenth-century plays and masques frequently associate discordant music and inappropriate musical performance with melancholy and madness. The madman or melancholic in such works often takes the role of social critic; his illness simultaneously allows him to see things that those around him cannot while reflecting the decay of the society at large.

But even in works that acknowledge the intellectual acumen or creativity fostered by melancholy and madness, playwrights and composers treat melancholy and madness as a problem. While male laments and mad songs share many musical features with those genres performed by their female counterparts, these gestures res-onated quite differently in a culture that frowned upon male emotionalism, irrationality, and public music making. In several studies, Linda Austern has shown that male music making was associated with effeminacy in early modern England.[15] Effeminacy did not, at this point, have an automatic association with homosexuality; rather, it often was used to refer to the behavior of men who desired women too much and, thus, became like them.[16] And like a beautiful woman, music could cause a man to degenerate into vice. In the late sixteenth century, the puritanical Phillip Stubbes, in his typical, overheated fashion, warns against the effects of male musical performance:

> If you wold have your sonne softe, womannishe, uncleane, smoth mouthed, affected to bawdrie, scurrilitie, filthie rimes, and unsemely talking: brifly, if you wold have hym, as it weare transnatured into a woman, or worse, and inclyned to all kind of whordome and abhomination, set him . . . to learn musicke, and than shall you not faile of your purpose.[17]

Specific musical features, too, were considered to be effeminate, by composers, music theorists, and Puritan reformers alike. Thomas Morley in his treatise *A Plaine and Easie Introduction to Practicall Musicke* (1597), stated:

> The naturall motions are those which are naturallie made betwixt the keyes without the mixture of any accidentall signe or corde, be it either flat or sharpe, and these motions be more masculine causing in the song more virilitie then those accidentall cords which are marked with these signes. x.b. which be in deede accidentall, and make the song as it were more effeminate & languishing then the other motions which make the song rude and sounding: so that those naturall motions may serve to expresse those effectes of crueltie, tyrannie, bitternesse and such others, and those accidentall motions may fitlie expresse the passions of griefe, weeping, sighes, sorrowes, sobbes, and such like.[18]

In 1636, Charles Butler recapitulated Morley's scheme, writing in his guide to composition and singing:

> A manly, hard, angry, or cruel matter is to bee exprest by hard and harsh short tones, qik Bindings, and concording Cadences; and that with the ordinari or unaltered Notes of the Scale: but words of effeminate lamentations, sorrowful passions, and complaints ar fitly exprest by the inordinate half-notes, (such as ar

the smal keys of the Virginals) which change the direct order of the Scale; flatting the Notes naturally sharp, and sharping them which are naturally flat: and those in longer time; with slow Bindings, and discording Cadences.[19]

For Morley and Butler, masculine music (using modern theoretical terminology) was diatonic, consonant, used smaller note values, and was appropriate for expressing masculine attributes such as heroism, the virile aggression of war, or anger. Effeminate music, defined as the opposite of masculine music, contained sighing figures and chromaticism, used slower note values, and was suited to express the "female" or "effeminate" emotions of love, lament, or seduction. These ideas resonated throughout the seventeenth century as John Playford, Thomas Mace, and Henry Purcell each made distinctions between warlike or aggressive types of music and lamenting, sensuous, or seductive music, assigning these categories the same musical attributes as Morley and Butler.[20]

While composers used "effeminate" music to accurately portray the emotions of lamenting women and men, anti-theatrical polemicists criticized these musical properties, using powerful rhetoric to discredit effeminate music and its deleterious effects. As William Prynne stated in 1633:

Modest and chaste harmonies are to be admitted, by removing as farre as may be all soft, effeminate musicke from our strong and valiant cogitation, which using a dishonest art of warbling the voyce, do lead to a delicate and slothful kind of life. Therefore Chromaticall harmonies are to be left to impudent malapertnesse in wine, to whorish musicke crowned with flowers.[21]

Such sentiments proved remarkably persistent. In 1698 Jeremy Collier, taking a page from Prynne's playbook, also lambasted the effects of certain kinds of music—music Prynne would have recognized as "effeminate." Collier claims that "when the Musick is soft, exquisite, and airy, 'tis dangerous and ensnaring."[22] While the music discussed below serves multivalent dramatic purposes—as a social critique, a representation of macrocosmic disharmony, or a portrayal of the various symptoms of lovesickness—to fully understand this music one must always bear in mind the profoundly transgressive qualities these melancholics and madmen possessed for those who listened in the seventeenth century.

Microcosmic and Macrocosmic (Musical) Dissonance

As noted in chapter 1, the notion that the microcosm and macrocosm affected each other pervaded early seventeenth-century culture, and this had a direct effect on musical production. The early modern conception of the body politic, as Jonathan Gil Harris elegantly states in a recent study, "was not simply a heuristic device; it was imbued with a cosmic significance, participating within a system of correspondences between the body of man, or microcosm, and the larger body of the universe, or macrocosm."[23] Bright's description of unnatural melancholy, cited above, participates in this analogic notion of the body politic, as he claims that the humors in a healthy body are "raunged under natures government and kept in order," but in the melancholic body are transmuted "into a qualitie wholly repugnant." According to Bright's formulation, the well-regulated body is analogous to the well-regulated subjects under a good ruler—he does not choose the word "government" arbitrarily. The body in which reason has been overthrown by the passions was analogous to a government overthrown by disorderly, rebellious subjects.[24] Bright's model of illness represents one way that mental disorder and politics were represented on the early modern stage: the diseased body of man—with all its transgressive qualities—reflected the diseased body politic. But there was also a more positive way that melancholy, madness, and politics coalesced on the early modern stage: the melancholic and the madman, unlike their female counterparts, could also be touched by genius, giving them a uniquely enlightened perspective.

The positive and negative attributes of melancholy (and their concomitant political implications) are held together in musical tension in John Marston's *The Malcontent* (1603), which features a melancholic character who is at odds with his society.[25] Giovanni Altofronto, having had his dukedom usurped by Pietro Jacomo, returns to Genoa, disguised as the malcontent Malevole in hopes of regaining his rightful place. As he plots, his antic persona allows him to comment scathingly upon the dissolute court: in this respect he is the enlightened melancholic, who, with his special insight, perceives societal ills others cannot.

We can hear in *The Malcontent*'s music elements of the melancholic as social critic and as transgressive. The play opens with the stage direction, "*The vilest out-of-tune music being heard.*" Upon hearing this "vile" music, one of the auditors confronts the musi-

cians: "Why, how now! Are ye mad? or drunk? or both? or what?"
[I.i.1–2].[26] But the musicians are none of these things. Seventeenth-
century audiences would have understood the discordant music
emanating from Malevole's room as an aural manifestation of his
inner turmoil, reflecting a commonplace in contemporary literature, which, as elucidated in chapter 1, compared musical harmony
with a healthy body and dissonance with disease.[27] The discordant
strains also represented the disharmony within the kingdom—a
musical version of Malevole's astute social commentary. The microcosmic disorder of Malevole's internal struggle is writ large
within the dissolute macrocosm of the court—a court that has deposed him from his rightful place as Duke. Indeed, the melancholic
and madman's internal disorder often paralleled the breakdown or
erosion of political and social hierarchies, particularly during the
sixteenth and early seventeenth centuries.[28]

As *The Malcontent* features a disorderly state, a dukedom in
which the natural governance of the true ruler has been subverted,
it would follow that Malevole's musicians would produce music that
represented this overthrow, this transgression of courtly hierarchy:
inharmonious music for those who live in a society that shuns the
natural order. Yet, while the courtiers who hear Malevole's discordant music are responsible for the decay of their kingdom, they do
not embrace the lack of harmony. They recognize the music's lack
of decorum and express their displeasure, commenting that the
musicians' noisy strains are better suited to Babylon or a tavern
than court. This suggests that the auditors understand Malevole's
and his musicians' conduct to be subversive and inappropriate (and
perhaps, in turn, they are made uncomfortable by music that points
to their own transgressions).

But any social criticism intended by the discordant music is
ambivalent. Although Malevole wants to indict the immorality and
unnaturalness of the court by creating this "noise," he and his musicians run the risk of actually becoming infected with melancholy.
As chapters 1 and 2 describe, the power of music to affect the body
and soul was explained in terms of sympathy—musical harmony
(or disharmony) affected the harmony within the listener. As we
have seen in the previous chapter, such music (like Ophelia's mad
ballads or even Bracegirdle's "I Burn, I Burn") could negatively
affect a body's humoral state, causing internal discord. Judging
from the dialogue (one auditor asks "Where breathes that music?")
the music performed by Malevole's musicians was vocal, and vocal

music was considered to be particularly efficacious for affecting the body of the listener. As the Renaissance magician and philosopher Heinrich Cornelius Agrippa noted:

> Singing can do more then the sound of an Instrument, in as much as it arising by an Harmonial consent, from the conceit of the minde, and imperious affection of the phantasie and heart, easily penetrateth by motion, with the refracted and well tempered Air, the aerious spirit of the hearer, which is the bond of soul and body; and transferring the affection and minde of the Singer with it, It moveth the affection of the hearer by his affection and the hearers phantasie by his phantasie, and minde by his minde, and striketh the minde, and striketh the heart, and pierceth even to the inwards of the soul, and by little and little, infuseth even dispositions: moreover, it moveth and stoppeth the members and the humors of the body.[29]

Thus, in performing their discordant music, Malevole's musicians may not simply infect their courtly auditors with their disharmony—they may also infect Malevole and themselves. Contemporary audiences would have recognized this musical perpetuation of melancholy as an "abuse" of music, an art form that ideally should have been used for higher purposes than perpetuating that blackest of humors.[30]

Indeed, one of Malevole's comments to his musicians suggests their humoral balance has been affected. Malevole requests that they "Howl again!"—a noise that would have been understood by early moderns as symptomatic of mental disorder. Of course, the musician could just have been playacting, but noisy howling was expected from those with corrupted reason.[31] As Philip Barrough's *The Method of Physick* notes, "also they that be melancholious have strange imaginations: for some thinke themselves brute beasts, & do counterfeit their voice & noise."[32] Given contemporary notions about the power of music, even playing at melancholy could be dangerous.

Other musical evidence suggests that Altofronto's act as Malevole has gone too far: later in the play, he indulges in improper musical performance, singing two ballads—lower-class music—a distinctly inappropriate genre for a gentleman. The inappropriate singing of ballads by the mad was a theatrical commonplace, as seen in the previous chapter with Ophelia and the Jailer's Daughter. As with that of his female counterparts, a man's improper musical performance called both his sanity and his status into question.[33] Writers and moralists scorned noblemen who performed music publicly. As Castiglione states in his influential *The Book of the Courtier*: "Therefore let our Courtier come to show his musicke as a thing to pass the time withall, and as he were enforced to doe it, and not in the presence of noble men, nor of any great multitude."[34]

Instead of behaving in this genteel manner, Malevole publicly sings the ballad "When Arthur First in Court Began," which was also sung by Shakespeare's clown, Falstaff, a character known for his low humor and debauchery.[35] The second ballad is a duet with the court panderess: doubly transgressive, both by the lowness of the musical discourse and by his choice of singing companion. Trading lines, they sing:

> The Dutchman for a drunkard,
> The Dane for golden locks;
> The Irishman for usquebaugh,
> The Frenchman for the [pox]. [V.i.1–4][36]

Music, which establishes Malevole's malcontent nature and the dissolute court's discord, plays a pivotal role articulating the return to harmony and legitimate rule of Altofronto. As Altofronto prepares to take his place as the legitimate Duke of Genoa, he enters the stage with his allies as part of a courtly masque. He performs measured dance steps to the accompaniment of cornets, behaving the way a courtier should—no howling, no bawdy songs. Within the course of the play, Altofronto has moved from his antic disposition as Malevole, accompanied by disordered music, to the ordered strains of the courtly masque. He has transformed himself from the melancholic malcontent Malevole to the judicious nobleman Altofronto. His return to musical health corresponds to his return to power and signals a return of harmony to the kingdom.

Likewise, in *The Duchess of Malfi* (1614), the play that opens this chapter, John Webster associates madness with musical and political discord, although *Malfi* presents the purely negative side of male mental disorder. Webster indicts the Duchess's warped and power-hungry brothers for their desire to control their sister: their unnatural behavior, torturing the Duchess and eventually having her killed, creates madness in the world. Like Bright's disorderly humors, the Duchess's brothers have shunned "natures government." As Antonio, the Duchess's future husband, warns at the beginning of the play:

> A prince's court
> Is like a common fountain, whence should flow
> Pure silver drops in general, but if't chance
> Some cursed example poson't near the head,
> Death and diseases through the whole land spread. [I.i.11–15][37]

The musical mad scene heightens audience sympathy for the Duchess, making clear her brothers' villainy. Because of her inappropriate marriage, the Duchess has been cruelly imprisoned. To add insult to injury, Ferdinand, her twin brother, sends madmen to torment her. A servant appears, introducing the masque:

> I am come to tell you
> Your brother hath intended you some sport:
> A great physician, when the Pope was sick
> Of a deep melancholy, presented him
> With several sorts of madmen, which wild object,
> Being full of change and sport, forced him to laugh,
> And so th'imposthume broke; the self-same cure
> The Duke intends on you. [IV.ii.37–44]

Duke Ferdinand's desire to "cure" the Duchess is, of course, disingenuous. He has no intention of helping his unfortunate sister purge her melancholy. He wishes to perpetuate it. Discord produces discord, so his discordant masque of madness should do the trick. Yet the Duchess proves remarkably resistant to her brother's pestilent, infecting music. In fact, she embraces the disorderly sounds: "Nothing but noise and folly / Can keep me in my right wits, whereas reason / And silence make me stark mad" [IV.ii.5–7]. In a world run mad, the Duchess tells us, discord is the only appropriate music—the only music that can adequately give voice to her torment.[38]

Given the rich dramatic context, the mad music in *Malfi* resonates in multiple microcosmic and macrocosmic ways. The mad song performed during this scene, "O Let Us Howle Some Heavy Note," survives, although the fluidity of its musical text complicates the hermeneutical process. Four different versions of "O Let Us Howle" exist, dating from ca. 1620–1704. Three of them are variants of the same tune, attributed to King's Men composer Robert Johnson, but the 1704 version is a completely new setting by John

Example 4.1. Robert Johnson, "O Let Us Howle Some Heavy Note," US-NYp. Drexel MS 4175, mm. 1–6 (lute tablature realized). Music Division, The New York Public Library for the Performing Arts, Astor, Tilden and Lenox Foundations.

Eccles. This setting was used in an early eighteenth-century revival—the play apparently continued to appeal to Augustan audiences.

The first setting, found in US-NYp. Drexel MS 4175, a manuscript compiled ca. 1620, literally replicates howling, harshly portraying the horrible spectacle of a man separated from his reason.[39] The piece begins with an ascending semitone gesture in the vocal line on the word "howle" and a modal disruption as the harmony shifts suddenly from G minor to G major. There is nothing abstract about this madman's music—he literally howls. The text then elaborates upon the specific nature of the howl (a "deadly dogged howle") and the semitone musical gesture returns, musically suggesting the unbridled noise flowing from the madman's throat. (See example 4.1.)

The version found in GB-Lbl. Add. MS 29481 calls attention

to the irrationality of the madman in a more subtle way. The melodic outline of US-NYp. Drexel MS 4175 exists, but the howling is laced with melismas. The first "howle" is softened somewhat, as the initial ascending semitone replication of howling is omitted, although the second semitone "howle" is retained. The madman further proves himself incapable of elegant musical rhetoric, singing melismas on words that have no particular importance ("as," "of," "and"). It is possible that the British Library manuscript is a transcription of how the piece was later performed by singers in the theater. Augustus Hughes-Hughes dates this manuscript to ca. 1630 in his catalogue of British Library manuscripts, meaning this version may be a representation of how the piece was performed several decades after the play's conception.[40] If a singer performed the GB-Lbl. Add. MS 29481 version in the playhouse (*The Duchess of Malfi* was revived at the Cockpit in Court in 1630), then Caroline audiences would have heard a madman, full of sound, fury, and ornamental excess.[41]

The third version of Johnson's song, found in US-NYp. Drexel MS 4041, a manuscript that dates from ca. 1640–49, looks rather insipid when compared with the other two versions.[42] The musical howls have been omitted, and there is no trace of the ornamentation found in the British Library version. The second half of the piece is a duet between bass and tenor, subverting the stage direction that "a madman" (singular) sings. As no revival of *The Duchess of Malfi* is recorded for the 1640s, it is possible that this version was never performed on the public stage.

Although the differences among the versions of "O Let Us Howle" may have been a result of the peculiarities of the individual manuscript compilers, they stand as a record, nevertheless, of how male musical madness was represented at specific moments in time. It is impossible to know which setting of "O Let Us Howle" is the most authentic; indeed, the very question of "authenticity" is a fraught one in the theater, as productions were often altered in response to changing audience tastes as well as performance concerns. Each setting indicts the dissonance of madness to varying degrees, although the first two versions are more mimetically bestial than the third. The first version literally replicates the howls of a madman; the second laces the madman's music with ornamentation on insignificant words, indicating his lack of control over his own musical rhetoric; but the third version omits the howling altogether. In these three settings, it seems that musical madness is becoming progressively less visceral. As we shall see at the end of the chapter, the fourth setting continues this trend toward abstraction.

Despite their differences, each setting of "O Let Us Howle" represents the internal bodily dissonance of madness and makes it aurally manifest to the Duchess and the audience, providing a sounding simulacrum of mental disorder and, indeed, of the disorder of the world in which her cruel and corrupt brothers control her fate. This display of disorder continues after the song, as the madmen dance, physically embodying the discord envoiced by "O Let Us Howle." The stage directions for the dance are maddeningly vague: "Here the dance of eight madmen, with music answerable thereunto." What kind of dance? What kind of music? Literary critics have provided divergent explanations. For distinguished Renaissance literary scholar Inga-Stina Ekeblad, the madmen's song and dance can be read as a charivari, sponsored by the Duchess's brother, to mock her inappropriate marriage.[43] Frederick Kiefer, drawing on early seventeenth-century depictions of mad dancing in the visual arts, claims that the madmen probably performed a morris, a dance, as shown in chapter 2, that had negative and unruly connotations. Kiefer suggests that contemporary audiences would have understood the morris as an amusing indictment of the world's folly.[44] Indeed, the whole mad masque is a twisted inversion of a typical masque, which usually culminates in the ceremonial overthrow of discord and the ritualized restoration of harmony. Rather than presenting order, the madman's song and dance winds up the madness of the world. The aural and terpsichorean disorder of the madmen is then transformed into physical violence, as the masque scene in *The Duchess of Malfi* culminates with the Duchess's onstage strangling: a mad world, indeed.

With both the mad song and dance in *Malfi*, it is impossible to recover precisely how the madmen performed. And, as I mentioned above, the rich dramatic context invites multiple readings of the mad masque. On the individual level, the mad song might represent the Duchess's own disordered state of mind. Or perhaps the musical howling foreshadows her brother Ferdinand's fate—later in the play he descends into the howling madness of lycanthropy, a well-known form of lunacy, described by Burton as "when men run howling about graves and fields in the night, and will not be persuaded but that they are wolves, or some such beasts."[45] Alternatively, the song represents the complete collapse of the world into madness. Or perhaps—and this is the wonderful thing about music—it signified all of these things at once. Context helps us delimit meaning, but we must acknowledge the interpretive fluidity inherent in sounded music, particularly when multiple versions of the same tune exist.

While *The Malcontent* and *The Duchess of Malfi* use music to critique male irrationality and to represent the disharmony of their respective imaginary kingdoms, other early seventeenth-century productions drew analogies between musical and bodily dishar-mony and the real-life contemporary political situation, particu-larly in the years leading up to the Civil War. Charles I ruled absolutely, enjoying masques that were elaborately staged celebra-tions of the supposed harmony of his kingdom, even as faction and discord raged outside the doors of his masquing hall. The political situation invited playwrights and composers to satirize the har-mony celebrated in the court masque. In Richard Brome's *The An-tipodes* (written in 1636 but postponed until 1638 because of plague), widely understood associations among music, melancholy, and harmony function as tools of critique. As in his earlier play, *The Late Lancashire Witches*, discussed in chapter 2, the disruption of social and gender hierarchies suggests a pervasive disease in the kingdom, a disease that was creeping ever closer to the head of the body politic, the king.[46]

The connections among politics, melancholy, and music coa-lesce around the character Peregrine, who, as a result of his ob-session with a popular travelogue, *The Voyages and Travailes of Sir John Mandeville, Knight* (1625), has completely lost touch with re-ality. Peregrine is a poor specimen of manhood: his obsession is so complete that he shows absolutely no interest in consummating his marriage with his lovesick wife, Maria. As his father, Joyless, re-veals, "for though they have been three years wed, / They are yet ignorant of the marriage bed" [I.ii.60–61].[47] To cure Peregrine's disease (and perhaps, by ritual extension, the diseased kingdom of England), the Doctor feeds Peregrine's delusion. He proposes a trip to the Antipodes, or Anti-London, a place where everything is upside down, topsy-turvy, where the people rule the magistrates, the women rule the men, and servants rule their masters.[48] A play of the Antipodes perpetuates Peregrine's illusion, leading the hap-less man to crown himself king. While the Doctor's dabbling in amateur theatricals may seem unorthodox and even counterpro-ductive, in fact he is deploying a typical cure for melancholics.

Numerous physicians advise humoring the patient in his hallucinations and delusions—to contradict him could cause him to sink
deeper into his illness.[49] As Peregrine transforms from spectator to
participant (and from sickness to health), Brome reveals another
tidbit about the strange Antipodes: the king's subjects are loyal to
their sovereign and ask him to "freely use our purse for what great
sums / Your majesty will please" [III.ix.101–102]—the opposite of
the real-life rebellious subjects of Charles I.

As in *The Malcontent*, Peregrine's return to sanity is enacted
through musical performance. But there is a crucial difference between Marston's and Brome's plays. Rather than celebrating harmony, the music indicts the chaos of the real-life kingdom. Reca-
pitulating the splendid panegyric found at Whitehall in the
masques performed for Charles I and Henrietta Maria, in act 4 the
Antipodeans praise their King Peregrine with a Neoplatonically
inflected song that conflates marital bliss with the harmony of the
kingdom. The spectacle begins as "Queen" Martha, the wife ab-
jured by Peregrine, appears. Mimicking the worship of Charles
and Henrietta Maria's harmonious marital relationship so frequently and lavishly praised in the court masque, the first song
presents Peregrine with his beauteous queen, a "delicious, chaste,
and fruitful bride" [IV.xi.17].[50] The music, which unfortunately
does not survive, apparently softens Peregrine's resolve. He kisses
his wife. Still, however, he resists her charms, until he is told that
for the "safety of your kingdom, [he] must do it" [IV.xi.53]. This
admonition finally inspires Peregrine: the couple retires and
has sex, and Peregrine's sanity (and manhood) is restored. He may
not be the king of the Antipodes, but he has taken his proper place
in his marriage, and the proper hierarchical order has been restored.

The microcosm of Peregrine and Martha's now happy (and
consummated) marriage reflects the harmony restored in the macrocosm. The song that softened Peregrine's opinion of his "chaste
and fruitful bride" was the pivot point, the medium that induced
this transformation (although the true cure was the consummation
of the marriage). To transfer the cure from the microcosm (Peregrine and Martha) to the macrocosm, Brome provides a full-blown
masque: the triumph of harmony over discord. However, in true
satiric fashion, Brome's masque reveals the impossibility of harmonious music as cure, either onstage or perhaps more generally
in England itself. For Brome's masque points to the emptiness and

lack of efficacy of the Caroline masque: Charles and Henrietta Maria may have had a happy marriage, but that harmony did not extend to their subjects.

The masque begins with an antimasque celebrating disorder—a strange entertainment for the only recently cured Peregrine. Indeed, the doctor worries the antimasque could provoke a relapse: "I fear your show will but perplex him, too" [V.x.17]. Yet the show must go on, despite its lack of dramatic logic, as Brome has a political point to make. Discord, Folly, Jealousy, Melancholy, and Madness appear onstage, accompanied by "a most untunable flourish." In keeping with the doctrine of sympathy that was so important to the court masque, it is appropriate that noise accompany this distempered quintet. Discord addresses his attendants in a "Song in Untunable Notes." The song tells us that by the aid of these unruly creatures, discord may be crowned king, so that misrule may rule: "Lend me your aids, so Discord shall you crown, / And make this place a kingdom of our own" [V.xi.18–19]. Of course, such statements are equally applicable to the political situation in late 1630s England—misrule and disorder was a reality, rather than an anxious fear. England of the 1630s was already antipodean, ruled by a monarch whose absolutism, instead of inspiring fealty, provoked dissent.

Just as in the Caroline court masque, the antimasque of Discord and her faction is short-lived: Harmony and her followers, Mercury, Cupid, Bacchus, and Apollo, banish disorder, causing the unruly elements to cease their antic dancing and fall down. The song for Harmony, "Come Wit, Come Love, Come Wine, Come Health," appears to be effective, as she celebrates her curative effects. Unfortunately, Discord and her followers prove remarkably resilient. Rejecting the typical trajectory of the courtly masque, Discord refuses banishment; she instead "cheers up her factions" (perhaps a direct reference to the factions that opposed Charles's policies) and they "rise and mingle in the dance with Harmony." Thus, Discord and Harmony dangerously coexist. Although Discord soon leaves the stage, the very fact that she danced with Harmony mocks the ritual of the court masque, revealing its lack of efficacy, as Discord, once presented, can never be fully contained. The court masque, as Brome's *Antipodes* reveals, provides only an illusion of containment.[51]

While these selected plays—*The Malcontent, The Duchess of Malfi,* and *The Antipodes*—illustrate the ways stage melancholics and madmen served as metaphorical representations of a disturbed macrocosm, as we have seen, harmony cannot fully banish discord. In *The Malcontent* appropriate music cures bodies and restores hierarchies, while disordered music serves as a social critique, even as it bears the risk of perpetuating melancholic infection. In *The Duchess of Malfi*, disordered music signifies in multiple ways, simultaneously suggesting the microcosmic bestiality of the Duchess's brothers and the macrocosmic madness of the world they've created—the mad masque, rather than restoring harmony through purgation, reaffirms discord and violence. And in *The Antipodes*, Peregrine's manhood (and sanity) is restored, yet Brome's masque suggests a far darker truth. Discord and her faction dance on.

The Problem of Male Lovesickness

As we have seen in *The Antipodes*, male madness could undermine one's virility. Poor Peregrine, through his unnatural obsession with Mandeville, literally loses his ability to consummate his marriage. As damaging as melancholy and madness were, undermining the rational essence of manhood, a specific type of malady, male lovesickness, was even more disturbing for those in the seventeenth century. The female object of desire effectively enslaved a man suffering from lovesickness, thus overturning the proper gender order in which men ruled women. Early modern writers were seriously troubled by this ailment. Burton devotes a section of *The Anatomy of Melancholy* to lovesickness, and of course, as we have seen, Ferrand devoted a whole treatise, *Erotomania*, to the subject, lambasting those men who succumbed to the ailment as "effeminate weake spirited fellowes."[52] The symptoms of lovesickness reflect the erotomaniac's irrationality and effeminacy. Laurentius derisively describes how love (gendered female) conquers men in his influential and widely read treatise, *A Discourse of the Preservation of the Sight; of Melancholike Diseases; of Rheumes, and of Old Age* (1599):

> Love therefore having abused the eyes, as the proper spyes and porters of the mind, maketh a way for it selfe smoothly to glaunce along through the conducting guides . . . setteth concupiscence on fire, and beginneth by this desire all the strife and contention: but fearing her selfe too weake to incounter with reason, the

principal part of the minde, she posteth in hast to the heart, to surprise and winne the same: whereof when she is once sure, as of the strongest holde, she afterward assaileth and setteth upon reason, and all the other principall powers of the minde so fiercely, as that she subdueth them, and maketh them her vassals and slaves. Then is all spoyled, the man is quite undone and cast away . . . reason is confounded, the imagination corrupted, the talke fond and senceless; the sillie loving worme cannot anymore look upon any thing but his idol. . . . You shall finde him weeping, sobbing, sighing, and redoubling his sighes, and in continuall restlessnes, avoyding company, loving solitarines, the better to feed & follow his foolish imaginations; feare buffeteth him on the one side and oftentimes dispayre on the other . . . sometime he is as hot as fire, and upon the sudden he findeth himselfe as colde as ice: his heart doth alwaies quake, and his pulse keepeth no true course, it is little, unequall, and beating thicke, changing it selfe upon the sudden, not onely at the sight, but even at the very name of the object which he affecteth.[53]

In Laurentius's derisive description, Lady Love fights a fierce battle, and eventually is victorious. She conquers manly reason, and the afflicted becomes a base creature, a "loving worme." At the end of the passage, Laurentius mentions other symptoms of lovesickness: the changeable mood of the victim, as he experiences fear, despair, hot and cold in quick alternation, and an irregular pulse. Ferrand also mentions the changeability of the lovesick, noting that there is "no order or equality at all in their Gesture, Motions or Actions"[54] and that they are "now very jocund and laughing; and presently within a moment [they fall] a weeping."[55] Reading between the lines of Laurentius, we see that the erotomaniac's subjugation to his female beloved and his unbridled emotions—what Ferrand calls a lack of order—made him socially problematic for those who viewed the ideal man as one who was able to behave in a rational, balanced fashion, ruling the "weaker sex" with an even hand.

Composers and playwrights use two divergent strategies in their representation of this troubling affliction. Depending on the severity of the disorder, either a surrogate sings a lament or the erotomaniac's obsession and irrationality is displayed in all its disturbing musical glory, serving as an exemplar for onstage interlocutors to critique.

Ventriloquized Laments

Throughout the seventeenth century, noblemen suffering from mild erotic melancholy (the version that does not involve madness, merely sadness and pining) rarely sing. As in the case of their female counterparts, their emotions are given musical voice by a servant—perhaps in an attempt to distance the character from music making. As noted above, male music making was widely associated with effeminacy. Although the melancholic lovesick men under consideration are generally spared the humiliation of public musical performance, they do not fully escape the emasculating effects of music—as we have seen in the previous chapter, musical performance by a surrogate was not without repercussions. Seventeenth-century audiences would have understood that listening to music, particularly if sung by a boy in an alluringly high register, could actually stir up lust, befuddle the mind, and further unman the listener.[56] Indeed, treble singers, especially young boys, frequently sang songs for their masters that captured the essence of their erotomaniacal complaints. Boys were appropriate mouthpieces for such "effeminate" outbursts, as they were considered imperfect men; they had not yet achieved sexual maturity.[57] Nevertheless, their musical performance was a double-edged sword. It allowed the adult male to retain a shred of his dignity, not debasing himself with the performance of "effeminate" music; however, the boy's beautiful singing voice caused the susceptible lovesick man to succumb completely to his own unruly passions. As Ferrand warns, "To these other allurements and provocations to Love, caused by the hearing, we might adde Musicke."[58]

While the lovesick melancholic normally does not sing, he often provides his own noisy accompaniment—sighs and groans—to the boy's laments: a further sign that music, in this case, perpetuates the effeminacy of lovesickness rather than curing it. The lovesick gentleman, Lucius, in Peter Hausted's *The Rivall Friends* (1632) requests his boy's presence, specifically so he might wallow in his melancholy, anticipating that music will only intensify his sadness: "Call him in, / That hee may touch a string which may dissolve mee / Into a flood of teares."[59] After the boy enters with his lute, he asks him to "teach that hollow pensive Instrument / to give a true relation of my woes / Whilst I lye here, and with my sighes keepe time."[60] Lucius, despite being saved the indignity of singing himself, shows other signs that effeminate music has unmanned him. He languishes and wants to dissolve into tears. Indeed, Lucius's companion Anteros reacts violently to the music: "Gods, and the World! You everlasting Twanger." The boy asks, "What meanes the Gentleman?" to which Anteros replies with a diatribe against the deleterious effects of music:

> Ile tell you.
> The Gentleman does meane for to consult
> With the entrals of your breeches, boy; the Gentleman
> Does meane to whip you boy, unlesse you straight
> Avoyd the place with that *seducing Fiddle*.[61]

Similarly, the lovesick Thyrsis in Joseph Rutter's *The Shepheards Holy-day* (1635) summons a boy to sing for him.[62] The boy obliges, performing a tune that celebrates the pleasures and pains of love ("Shall I because my love is gone, / Accuse those golden darts").[63] Thyrsis cannot bear to listen, as the music increases his affliction, and like Lucius he promises to "sigh the rest out," then he will seek out "some hidden place to pine and dye."[64] Unfortunately, none of this music survives, so we cannot assess from musical evidence how successful the boys were at capturing their masters' grief, although judging from the erotomaniacs' overemotional responses we know these musical interludes perpetuated melancholy and effeminacy.

Even during the Restoration, the older tradition of boys voicing the effeminate emotions of their masters continues, and unlike the earlier examples, the music survives. In Nathaniel Lee's *Mithridates* (1678) Ziphares and his father King Mithridates have fallen in love with the same woman, Semandra. Mithridates threatens to kill Ziphares if Semandra shows him any sign of affection. Semandra behaves accordingly, and Ziphares, believing his beloved to be untrue, reacts violently to her rejection. He launches into a rant full of typical misogynist notions about women's fickleness and ability to wreck men with their physical and musical wiles:

> What Story is not full of Womans falshood!
> The Sex is all a Sea of wide destruction:
> We are the vent'rous Barks that leave our home,
> For those sure dangers which their smiles conceal:
> At first, they draw us in with flatt'ring looks
> Of Summer-Calms, and a soft gale of Sighs:
> Sometimes, like Syrens, Charm us with their Songs,
> Dance on the Waves, and show their Golden Locks:

But, when the Tempest comes, then, then they leave us,
Or rather, help the new Calamity,
And the whole Storm is one injurious Woman.
The Lightning follow'd with a Thunder-bolt
Is Marble-hearted Woman: all the Shelves
The faithless Winds, blind Rocks, and sinking Sands,
Are Women all; the wracks of wretched men. [IV.i.293–307][65]

Exhausting his verbal fury, he lies down (a decidedly passive position) and asks his young page for a "sad Song" to put him to sleep. The boy obliges, performing Louis Grabu's "One Night While All the Village Slept,"[66] a song that traces the despair of the shepherd Myrtillus, a swain who bears a remarkable resemblance to his lovesick counterpart, Ziphares. The text details Myrtillus's insomniac wandering through the woods as he bemoans his beloved's fickleness. Despite his resolve to stop weeping, by the third verse the shepherd is undone by his grief, as he lies down upon "a Cold bank," and welcomes death, never waking again.

Grabu sets these melancholic lyrics in a strophic fashion and uses G minor, a key frequently used for laments on the seventeenth-century stage.[67] However, as with many early English laments, Grabu's song lacks a ground bass: a crucial element found in the Italian operatic lament that later (and very famously in the form of Dido's lament from Henry Purcell's *Dido and Aeneas*) would find its way onto the English stage. Grabu conveys sadness in another way. The musical language of this piece is restless and unpredictable. As it is a strophic song, there is no text painting, but the overall impression conveyed by the music is one of despair and volatility, an impression reinforced by an unstable modality (the use of both G minor and G major), unexpected harmonies (mm. 20–21 are particularly striking) and hemiolas (mm. 4–5, 8–9, and 15–16), which may suggest the irregular pulse of the lovesick swain. (See example 4.2.)

While the page's lament does not inspire sleep, it reduces Ziphares to languishing and sobbing on the ground (although he does not embrace death, as did his pastoral counterpart): the sad music intensifies his lovesickness. Semandra's father discovers him in this unmanly posture, and commands Ziphares to "stand up . . . dry up this womanish grief" [IV.i.374–75]. While Ziphares doesn't sing, the lethal combination of music and unrequited love has effeminized him, prompting both sympathy and rebuke from those who observe his symptoms.

Example 4.2. Louis Grabu, "One Night While all the Village Slept," in *Choice Ayres and Songs. The Third Book* (London, 1681), verse 1.

In *The Rival Sisters* (1695) playwright Robert Gould uses music in a slightly different way, as Alonzo deploys his malady as a weapon to provoke the conscience of his beloved, but fickle, Alphanta. Gould, a playwright to whom misogynist tracts, such as the ironically titled *Female Excellence*, are attributed,[68] made his protagonist a sympathetic figure, as the blame for Alonzo's ailment rests solely on the woman who spurned him (one observer of Alonzo's behavior comments that while his dress is mad, his misogynist rants are not). Furthermore, Alonzo is not overtly criticized for being effeminate, as were others suffering from lovesickness. Alonzo retains a patina of dignity, and the songs he requests are more diatribes than laments. In particular, the song "Fair and Soft and Gay and Young," for which the music does not survive, causes Alphanta to swoon with guilt. She then returns to her correct position in the patriarchal order: with the man who chooses her. Despite the use of the ventriloquized lament as a tool of punishment, Alonzo, as we shall see, does not escape unscathed after listening to the music of lovesickness.

"Celia Has a Thousand Charms," composed by Henry Purcell, functions as a thinly veiled indictment of the fickle Alphanta, but its musical language would have been recognized as effeminate and effeminating. The first half of the piece is in G minor—the key of lamenting, death, and also the *petit mort* of lovemaking. Indeed, G minor perfectly fits the mood of the first half of the song, a florid recitative that describes a libidinous encounter with Celia: " 'Tis heaven, 'tis heaven to lie within her arms," the boy exclaims, his words accentuated with passionately effusive melismas. The second half of the song, the aria, changes to a triple meter and shifts to the key of D minor, although it eventually modulates back to G minor. Chromatic harmonies, cross-relations, and sighing figures pervade this section, and the tone of the text becomes darker, turning from the pleasures of love to the pain of discovering a lover's betrayal—just the kind of music that would have been heard as potentially insalubrious. As is frequently the case with ventriloquized laments, the boy's music stokes the flames of Alonzo's lovesickness, and after the song he rants:

> I'm cold! I starve with cold!
> My heart is turn'd to Ice with her Disdain!
> Oh! It oppresses—but I'll tear it out.[69]

Given Alonzo's response, it's obvious that music provides no relief—it is an incitement to, rather than a cure for, his malady. Thus, the portrayal of Alonzo is, in the final analysis, ambivalent. He may not be responsible for his lovesickness, but his behavior is still questionable.

Lovesick Aeneas?

Through-sung opera presented another challenge for composers seeking to portray (and critique) the deleterious effects of male lovesickness, as music in these entertainments was not marked as a special language. It was the *only* mode of discourse available. In the case of the passionate Aeneas from *Dido and Aeneas*, a frequently maligned character, some of Henry Purcell's musical choices become more legible if one reads them alongside other musical portrayals of male lovesickness on the seventeenth-century stage. Although modern critics frequently identify Aeneas as the musical and dramatic weak spot of the opera, mocking him as "a complete booby"[70] and "a glorified pawn,"[71] I believe Purcell and his librettist, Tate, knew precisely what they were doing, both musically and dramatically. Aeneas's comportment in the opera can be read as a critique of incorrect male behavior. As with other erotomaniacs, Aeneas's own passions and his love of venereal pleasures cloud his judgment. As Burton notes, sexual profligacy was just as common a cause of lovesickness as abstinence: "Intemperate Venus is all out as bad in the other extreme, Galen, *lib. 6 de morbis popular. sect. 5 text. 26*, reckons up melancholy amongst those diseases which are 'exasperated by venery.' "[72]

Although we might like to think of Aeneas as a hero, those in the seventeenth century were highly critical of his behavior in book 4 of Virgil's *Aeneid*.[73] Both in Virgil's epic and in later versions of the tale, Aeneas is a morally ambiguous character. On the one hand, he is a conquering hero, valiant warrior, and eventual founder of Rome (at least according to some traditions). Importantly for England, his descendant, Brutus, founded the island nation and its capital, Troynovant (London). On the other hand, he is the wayward son of Venus, choosing sexual pleasure over duty. The operatic Dido actually comments upon Aeneas's dual nature, remarking that he possesses his father Anchises' valor mixed with his mother Venus's charms.

In choosing to dally with his lover, in placing love over duty, his character is similar to that of Paris, the prince whose impolitic choice of Venus in a beauty contest led to the disastrous Trojan Wars.[74] Virgil himself makes a comparison between the two amorous princes. When Dido's spurned suitor, Iarbas, discovers that the queen has begun an affair with Aeneas, he appeals to his father, Jove, to break up the illicit union. In his rage, Iarbas describes his rival Aeneas thusly: "After refusing to marry me [Dido] has taken / Aeneas to be master in her realm. / And now Sir Paris [that is, Aeneas] with his men, half-men, / His chin and perfumed hair tied up / In a Maeonian bonnet, takes possession."[75] Clearly, the Aeneas described by Iarbas fits the criteria of an effeminate lover: a man so given over to lust that he transforms into that which he over-loves, complete with perfumed hair and bonnet.

Early modern English translators exploited and even amplified this association between Aeneas and lovesick effeminacy. For example, in Richard Fanshawe's translation of Book 4, Aeneas is a "*Paris*, with a quofe to stay / His Beard and powdred Locks, and's Beaver trayne / of shee-men, gluts himselfe upon the prey."[76] Sir Robert Howard's translation is similarly scathing. Iarbas describes Aeneas as "this *Paris* with his troope that scarsly are / Like men, in their soft robes and perfum'd hair."[77] Later in Howard's translation, Mercury chastises the prince for having "uxorious grown": in short, he has become overly fond of his so-called wife,[78] a vice that Robert Burton mocks in his *Anatomy of Melancholy*: " 'Tis a great fault (for some men are *uxorii* [uxorious]) to be too fond of their wives, to dote on them . . . to be too effeminate, or as some do, to be sick for their wives."[79]

Is Tate and Purcell's Aeneas "uxorious"? Certainly, the operatic Aeneas seems even more flawed than his Virgilian counterpart. False counsel sways the Aeneas of Tate's libretto. He cannot tell the difference between a real god and a false spirit conjured by the Sorceress, believing the pseudo-Mercury when he tells him to dump Dido. Then, even as he agrees to the false Mercury's request, he almost immediately changes his mind—the pull of love (or lust) is too strong. His passions sully his judgment. Indeed, twice in the opera Aeneas demonstrates a propensity to place love before duty. First, in act 1, he offers to ignore the "feeble stroke of Destiny" in favor of more pleasant activities with Dido. Later, even after receiving false Mercury's marching orders, he is still reluctant to abandon Dido's bed. He tells pseudo-Mercury that he will obey him, then immediately wavers upon seeing his mistress, Dido, again.

Purcell musically emphasizes Aeneas's amorous, indecisive nature through music. In his first entrance in act 1, Aeneas cuts a

Example 4.3. Henry Purcell (music) and Nahum Tate (libretto), "Stay, Prince, and Hear Great Jove's Command," *Dido and Aeneas*, mm. 15–18. Excerpted from Purcell Society Volume 3—Full score. Edited under the supervision of the Purcell Society by Margaret Laurie. © Copyright 1979 Novello & Company Limited. All Rights Reserved. International Copyright Secured. Reprinted by Permission.

jaunty, dashing figure, with lively dotted rhythms and strongly articulated G major and D major tonalities—V and V/V within the established key of C major ("When, when, royal fair, shall I be bless'd / With cares of love and state distress'd?"). Upon his second entrance, however, Aeneas slithers unexpectedly to E minor, as he offers to "defy the Feeble stroke of destiny," paving the way for the E minor chorus that follows: "Cupid only throws the dart / That's dreadful to a warrior's heart / And she that wounds can only cure the smart." Thus, Purcell harmonically equates Aeneas's choice, spurning duty for love, with the sickness of love provoked by Cupid's dart: a sickness that has only one very effective cure: physical consummation. Given the tonal connection Purcell draws between Aeneas's defiance of destiny and the Cupid chorus, the warrior obviously has one thing on his mind, and it isn't empire building. Later, when instructed by false Mercury to leave Carthage, Aeneas resolves to obey Jove's decree. But he soon wavers, wondering how he will break the unhappy news to his lover. "Ah!" he sings, with a melismatic figure rhythmically and melodically similar to Dido's sighs in her famous final lament: a musical gesture that specifically equates Aeneas's emotional state with that of the heartsick Dido. Furthermore, this gesture, an undulating melisma, serves as a perfect emblem of Aeneas's unsteady (womanish) emotionalism. (See examples 4.3 and 4.4.[80])

Aeneas's final moments onstage (act 3, scene 2) further demonstrate how passion has clouded his reason. Aeneas appears, "lost" and bereft because the gods (according to the false Mercury) have

Example 4.4. Henry Purcell (music) and Nahum Tate (libretto),
"When I Am Laid in Earth," *Dido and Aeneas*, mm. 24–27.
Excerpted from Purcell Society Volume 3—Full score. Edited
under the supervision of the Purcell Society by Margaret Laurie. ©
Copyright 1979 Novello & Company Limited. All Rights Reserved.
International Copyright Secured. Reprinted by Permission.

decreed that he must leave his queen. Purcell subtly conveys Aeneas's instability through modal mixture. The use of both B♭ and
B♮, E♭ and E♮ causes the listener to question if Aeneas is singing in
G minor (the actual key) or G major (mm. 18–23). His wavering
explanation for his hasty departure lacks persuasion, and Dido rejects it out of hand: "Thus on the fatal banks of Nile / Weeps the
deceitful crocodile." Aeneas further tries to explain ("By all that's
good"), but Dido interrupts him, repeating his hollow phrase and
finishing his musical entreaty before he can. As her temper flares,
Aeneas resolves to defy the gods and stay, but the imperious Dido
rejects his offer. She sends him packing, and Aeneas slinks silently
offstage, allowing Dido the final word in their musical argument.

Although Virgil's Mercury might describe women as "fickle
and forever changing," this criticism would seem more applicable
to Tate and Purcell's indecisive Aeneas, who enjoyed one night
with Dido, then resolved to obey the command of false Mercury,
then changed his mind, deciding to stay, but was eventually convinced to leave by a heartbroken queen. In this final scene with her
lover, Dido wears the metaphorical pants and has the musical upper
hand. If we read Aeneas's behavior through the lens of lovesickness,
it becomes clear that Purcell and Tate's portrayal of the supposed
hero was intentional and was perfectly in line with seventeenth-
century thought about the prince's conduct during his amorous
sojourn in Carthage. Aeneas's reason was clouded by his love for
Dido, and his weakness is conveyed through Purcell's music and
Tate's text.

Lovesick Madness and Musical Excess

As presented onstage, male lovesickness was a profoundly problematic affliction full of ambiguities. Ventriloquized laments allowed the lovesick man to distance himself from distasteful, inappropriate musical performance, even as listening to the passionate music heightened the symptoms of his malady. And although the lusty Aeneas is ostensibly a hero, Purcell's music highlights his vacillation and poor judgment, as passion clouds his brain. When a lovesick gentleman completely succumbed to erotomania, losing his reason, the lure of writing lovesick male mad songs proved too tempting for composers to resist. But these male mad songs presented another set of problems than those performed by their female counterparts. As outlined in the previous chapter, women, on some level, were inherently irrational. Their mad songs provided an opportunity for men on- and offstage to consume the spectacle of female sexual excess. Male mad songs may share the same features with those of their female counterparts, but, given the ways these songs are dramatically framed, they appear to have been heard in very different ways from Ophelia's balladry or Marcella's burning.

Early in the century, composers portrayed the madman's troubling lack of control with a series of songs using radically different affects. In John Fletcher's *The Nice Valour, or The Passionate Mad-Man* (possibly written earlier by Fletcher, then revised by Thomas Middleton, 1615–16),[81] the eponymous "Passionate Mad-man" sings a series of songs that reveal his changeable emotional state. The Passionate Mad-man or the Passionate Lord (who is never given a proper name) suffers from a surfeit of emotion, and as a result has fallen into the dissolution of lovesickness. Observers of his disorder harshly criticize him; an archetype, rather than a fully rounded character, the Passionate Mad-man is the embodiment of improper manly behavior. As the courtier Shamont comments in disgust:

> I prethee thou four Elements ill brued,
> Torment none but thy selfe; away I say
> Thou beast of passion, as the drunkard is
> The beast of wine; dishonour to thy making,
> Thou man in fragments. [I.i.237–41]

According to Shamont, the Passionate Lord, having forsaken his reason, is no better than a beast, a common trope employed when discussing madness and melancholy, as evinced by the dialogue and music in *The Malcontent* and *The Duchess of Malfi*. In addition, Sha-mont, along with many Jacobean courtiers, believes that for a man to love women too much is a great fault. He claims that "love to manhood, ownes the purer troth" [I.i.264]. Echoing objections by Laurentius, Burton, Ferrand, and others, Shamont finds repugnant the Passionate Lord's lascivious fondness for the "weaker sex."

Throughout the course of the play, music accentuates the emo-tional volatility of the Passionate Lord, as he flits through various musical genres. He first breaks into song in act 2, scene 1, crooning to Cupid, "Thou Deitie, Swift Winged Love." While the music is lost, the very fact that he has broken into the heightened (and, given his inappropriate public performance, potentially transgres-sive) discourse of song calls his reason into question. Furthermore, the exaggerated textual repetition in his final lines as he entreats Cupid to "shoot more, shoot more, shoot more," highlights the overpassionate nature that has brought him low. On cue, a Lady dressed as a Cupid enters and enthusiastically offers to shoot the Lord. Ironically, the Cupid turns out to be a Lady who was victim-ized by the madman's uncontrolled desires. She has been stung by the unhappy darts of love, as she is pregnant with the Passionate Lord's bastard child: material evidence of the Lord's carnality, a weakness of character that has culminated in his madness.

Upon his next appearance, the Passionate Lord is no longer the overeager lover, welcoming Cupid's darts. He has descended into melancholy. Strangely, he does not lament his plight; rather, he embraces it. This positive embrace of melancholia further con-firms the Passionate Mad-man's status as an archetype to be cri-tiqued. Many at the Jacobean court embraced melancholy, despite its potentially deleterious effects, for it was a sign of genius, a stance that opened them up to mockery and criticism.[82] Thus, the Passionate Mad-man's sudden embrace of melancholy as a virtue invites the audience to consider him and his song through a satir-ical lens. A long-winded, exaggerated speech celebrating the trap-pings of melancholia precedes his musical outburst—he even iron-ically claims that the black humor enhances his masculinity:

> Happy is he say I, whose window opens
> To a browne Bakers chimney, he shall be sure there
> To heare the Bird sometimes after twi-light:
> What a fine thing 'tis me thinks to have our garments
> Sit loose upon us thus, thus carelessely,

It is more manly, and more mortifying;
For w'are so much the readier for our shrouds [III.iii.9–15]

"Hence All You Vaine Delights," the Passionate Mad-man's musical tribute to melancholy, can be understood as an extension of the satire. The song exists in three manuscript sources, and in all three versions the Mad-man wallows pleasurably in his pain. The earliest manuscript, GB-Ob. MS Mus. Sch. F.575, was probably copied around ca. 1630, well after the original play performance, and it presents the first eleven lines in an anonymous setting.[83] The second, attributed to John Hilton (GB-Lbl. Egerton MS 2013), appears to have been copied before 1644, and it contains a setting of the full text, although as John Cutts observes, there is no evidence to suggest that John Hilton ever wrote music for the King's Men, the company that performed *The Nice Valour*. He claims the Egerton copy is an arrangement of the Bodleian version, although I believe the two settings are too dissimilar for this to be the case.[84] The third, GB-Och. MS Mus. 350, a late seventeenth-century manuscript copied by Richard Goodson Sr., presents the treble of the Hilton version.[85] As with the mad song in *The Duchess of Malfi*, it is impossible to say which version, if any, was performed onstage. The Bodleian manuscript provides the cleanest copy; the Egerton version (and indeed the whole Egerton manuscript) appears to have been copied by an amateur and is riddled with errors, but the version of the song found there is more expansive, setting more text. The Christ Church copy is obviously problematic because of its incompleteness and late seventeenth-century provenance.

The anonymous Bodleian setting is suitably grave. The piece begins with an abjuration of worldly pleasures: "Hence all you vaine delights," a declaration given strength through rhythmic accents on "hence" and "vaine" and a clear movement from tonic to dominant. Ascetic declarations such as this were typical of the lonely melancholic genius, who preferred to consider the fleetingness of existence in solitude, preferably in the dark of night.

The Passionate Lord continues his celebration of melancholy, suggesting, through agogic accent on "sweet" and "wise," that the learned will undoubtedly recognize the pleasures of "sweet melancholy." But, as this sentiment comes from a madman, can we believe his words of "wisdom"? Or does only a fool embrace melancholy? Indeed, we might view the Passionate Lord's adoption of ascetic melancholy with suspicion. Despite the strength of his musical declarations he occasionally indulges in ornamental flourishes that indicate he has not completely abstained from "vaine delights," although his text declares otherwise.

The conclusion of the song continues to explore this tension between the Passionate Lord's earnest textual declarations and a musical language that calls his sincerity into question. At the end of "Hence all you vaine delights" the Passionate Lord vows to adopt "folded armes & fixed eyes, / A sigh that piercing mortifyes, / A look thats fastned to the ground, / A tongue chaind up without a sound," evoking with poetic words a common image of the silent, reflective melancholic. (See example 4.5.)

The Passionate Lord's musico-rhetorical tongue is in good working order for one who declares the virtues of "a tongue chaind up without a sound." Word painting enlivens this passage: a descending fifth mimics the "sigh," an octave leap upward signifies its "piercing" quality, and an octave plummet downward mimics the melancholic's "ground fastned" look. Ultimately his vow of silence is empty, as indicated by his musical language and his subsequent loquacious behavior in the play. The auditor must question the genuineness of the Passionate Lord's embrace of the rigors of ascetic melancholy. As evinced by the appearance of the pregnant Cupid, we know that the Lord has spent too many nights in passionate folly and that this overindulgence has led to his current madness. Furthermore, the symptoms of his lovesickness preclude the possibility of his carrying through with his rejection of carnal pleasures.

The later setting, attributed to Hilton, is initially more explicit than the Bodleian manuscript version in its portrayal of the Passionate Lord's embrace of melancholy. But the Mad-man is so passionate in his declaration that, like the Bodleian setting, this setting causes the listener to question his asceticism. The initial rejection of false delights is more strongly emphasized, as the word "hence" is articulated on the first, then on the fifth, scale degree. This proclamation is followed by a descending octave leap: a musical gesture that replicates the Mad-man's contraction into himself—the eschewal of worldly delights. Further accentuating his passionate embrace of the black humor, the line "sweetest Melancholly" first outlines a G minor chord (the tonic), then is repeated a third higher, this intensification representing the Passionate Lord's

Example 4.5. "Hence All You Vaine Delights," GB-Ob. MS. Mus. Sch. F. 575, f. 7ᵛ (lute tablature realized). By permission of The Bodleian Library, University of Oxford.

increasing desire to achieve a melancholic state (m. 11). Adding to the sense of yearning for melancholy is the assignment of a special musical figure to this word. Hilton sets the word "melancholly" with a syncopated rhythm (dotted quarter–eighth–eighth–dotted quarter) and a flat, uninflected vocal line. The syncopated rhythm replicates the irregular pulse of the melancholic, while the flat vocal line suggests the despondent, cheerless tone that a sigh that pierc - ing mor - ti-fyes, A look thats fast-ned to the ground,

A tongue chaind up with - out a sound.

Example 4.5. *Continued.*

infects the melancholic's voice or perhaps even the peaceful state of solitude the Passionate Lord associates with the affliction. (See example 4.6.)

As if the musical evidence weren't enough, the Passionate Mad-man's inability to adhere to the scholarly ascetic tradition of melancholy is further confirmed in the following act (III.iv). The next time the Passionate Mad-man appears, all trace of melancholy is gone—he has cast off that humor as quickly as a courtier might discard last year's garment. Now he sings a far more earthy and choleric tune, "A Curse Upon Thee for a Slave." The music does not survive, but the text overflows with imagery descriptive of the Passionate Mad-man's raving: the "sparkles" flying from his eyes, his "foame and fire," and his "knash[ing]" teeth. He then beats his hapless companion and begins singing insults again: "Thou Nasty, Scurvie, Mongrill Toad." Although the music is lost, the text is in a highly irregular, shifting meter, a sign that his lovesick madness has not been replaced by ascetic melancholy.

The Passionate Mad-man runs through several other humoral states (and types of song) before finally being restored to health, al-

Example 4.6. John Hilton, "Hence All Yea Vaine Delights," GB-Lbl. Egerton MS 2013. By permission of The British Library.

though his return to sanity is presented ambivalently. A disgruntled soldier wounds the Passionate Mad-man with his sword and this penetration restores the Lord to reason, balancing his humors through the purgative effects of bleeding. Despite this ostensible cure, onlookers still question the Passionate Lord's rationality.[86] Fletcher's vision of male lovesickness is deeply satiric and resists resolution. As in *The Malcontent*, *The Duchess of Malfi*, and *The Antipodes*, disorder, once introduced, proves difficult to control. Just

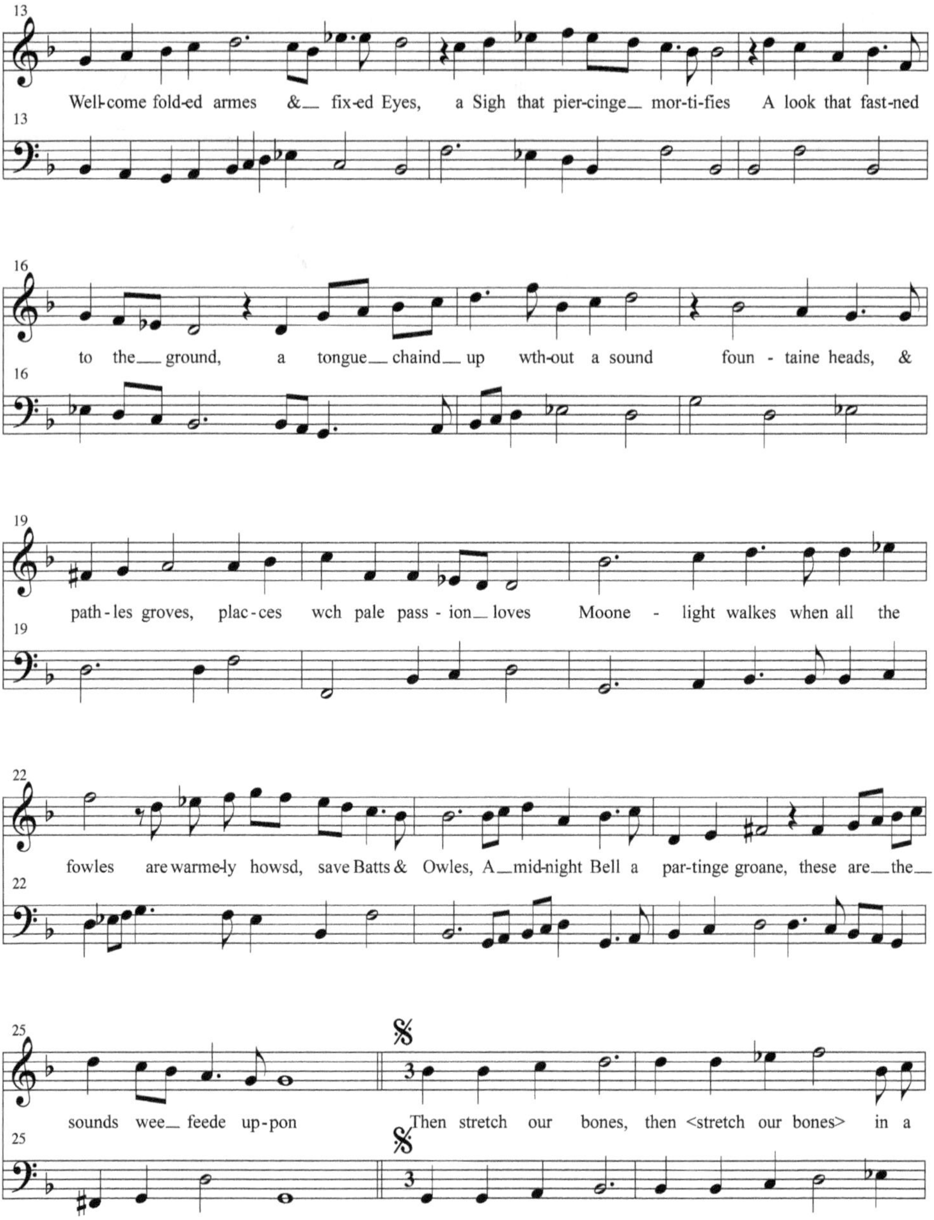

Example 4.6. *Continued.*

still gloom - y val - ly, Ther's no-thinge dain - ty sweet, ther's no-thinge dain - ty sweete

but Mel - - - an - chol - ly.

Example 4.6. *Continued.*

as the drama reinforces the troubling disorder of the Passionate Mad-man's mind, his music emphasizes the excessiveness of his behavior, as he frequently (and inappropriately) performs music that resists containment within one affective or emotional state or, as with "Hence All You Vain Delights," that subverts the textual content.

A similarly ambivalent treatment of male lovesickness can be found in Henry Purcell's mad songs for Lyonel in Thomas D'Urfey's *A Fool's Preferment; or the Three Dukes of Dunstable* (1688). Played by the accomplished actor-singer William Mountfort, Lyonel proves even more difficult to interpret than the Passionate Mad-man. D'Urfey, in a similar fashion to his contemporary Robert Gould in *The Rival Sisters*, attempts to recuperate Lyonel's questionable masculinity by having him spout misogynistic rhetoric, criticizing the behavior of the woman who allegedly did him wrong, Celia. The epilogue, spoken by Mountfort, outlines D'Urfey's intentions for Lyonel; he may be an effeminate lovesick swain, but his madness serves a "noble" purpose:

> Fond of his Act; the Poet has to day
> Mistook, and made me mad the silliest way;
> Pride, Wealth, or Wine, may Frenzy often move:
> But that's a strange Brute that runs mad for Love,
> Few now, Thank Heaven, such lewd examples find,

'Tis forfeiting the Charter of our Kind;
Shall Men have all, and Women no remorse?
Then let the Cart hereafter drage the Horse.
Let each Eve wrest the Scripture false, and swear;
She was not made for Man, but Man for Her;
No this had been a most unpardon'd Crime;
Did not the Lady here repent in time.[87]

D'Urfey makes an effort to channel Lyonel's behavior toward a moralistic end: his madness was designed to make the wayward lady Celia "repent." Judging from the defensive tone of the epilogue, D'Urfey obviously recognizes that Lyonel's behavior was problematic (and uncomfortable) for at least some of his audience.

Although D'Urfey infuses Lyonel's characterization with a misogynist edge to punish Celia, the very symptoms that render him easily identifiable as a typical erotomaniac undermine attempts to direct his behavior in a didactic, noble direction: in order to be legibly lovesick, he must be less than a man. Lyonel's effeminacy is apparent from his first appearance onstage "crown'd with Flowers, and Antickly drest, sitting on a Green Bank."[88] Lyonel languishes in a seated position, an enervated erotomaniac whose vital spirits have been sapped by lust. Furthermore, Lyonel has an Ophelia-esque fascination with flowers, as he has bedecked himself with a scented coronet. This sartorial misstep clearly calls his masculinity into question: an impression that is later confirmed by his onstage behavior. Dramatic elements also foreground Lyonel's effeminacy: his lovesickness was caused because the king took Celia from him as a gift for his favorite. That favorite, now, as Celia tells us, "is . . . in great Disgrace," so the king has sent her back to be with Lyonel. While lovesickness has surely effeminated Lyonel, his real emasculation occurred when the king took his beloved, when he ceased to have power over his amorous destiny.

We see the tension in Purcell's music between making Lyonel's affliction recognizable, by using standard musical and textual conventions for portraying lovesick madness, and recuperating Lyonel's behavior, channeling it toward a supposedly noble didactic end. While Purcell's songs showcase the more embarrassing symptoms of Lyonel's affliction, even the most effusive (and effeminate) songs serve to punish Celia, the woman Lyonel loved and lost. She must listen to her lover's rants, and all attempts to converse with him prove fruitless.

Purcell's songs cleverly combine the representation of Lyonel's effeminate pining with his misogynistic, punishing ranting. Both elements can clearly be heard in Lyonel's first song, "I Sigh'd, and I Pin'd," which begins in the tradition of a lament. Lyonel sings a musical sigh (a descending semitone) on "sigh'd" and leaps downward a fifth on "pin'd," resolving a clash of a second between the bass and voice to a consonant major third. These musical gestures evocatively suggest the pain of Lyonel's pining and its delicious release—he wallows in his affliction. He also repeats phrases: a further indication of his excessive passion and lack of self-restraint. At one point Lyonel's effeminacy is literally envoiced as he "becomes" a woman, imitating the "jilt" Celia's imagined laughter at his plight with a melismatic flourish full of dotted rhythms, singing, if only for a moment, in the voice of the cruel wench who deserted him. If these musical indications of his irrationality and effeminacy were not enough, his text diagnoses his problem, explaining that his "Passion ne'er cooled." It was commonly believed that the hot passion of love caused erotomania, which, as Laurentius and others warn, had deleterious effects upon the body, if unrequited.

In the second half of Lyonel's air he shifts from "sighing and pining" to musical ranting, changing from a lamenting D minor to D major, with racing sixteenth notes in the vocal line as well as the bass. Lyonel is now in a grandiose, expansive mood, as he believes himself as "great as a King" (echoing a line from Purcell's famous female mad song, "Bess of Bedlam") because a "dull empty Pate, soonest comes to be great." Lyonel's madness is further suggested by the high tessitura in the second half of the air, which gives "I Sigh'd, and I Pin'd" an overwrought quality. Lyonel's delusions of grandeur, which appear in many of his songs, were identifiable as symptomatic of blood adust—when the sanguine humor was burnt through the overheating produced by excess passions, it was thought to produce a specific species of high-blown melancholy.[89] According to Laurentius, such hallucinations may also reflect the character of the afflicted: "If an ambitious man become melancholike, he straightway dreameth that he is a King, an Emperour, a Monarke."[90] In Lyonel's case, his pain was caused because the king took his mistress, Celia, away, giving her as a gift to his favorite courtier. Lyonel would elevate himself in order to have the authority to take back the woman who belongs to him. He lost his manhood, and now he would recover it by becoming the king's equal. (See example 4.7.)

Example 4.7. Henry Purcell, "I Sigh'd and I Pin'd," in *New Songs Sung in The Fool's Preferment, or, the Three Dukes of Dunstable* (London, 1688).

Lyonel's second song follows closely on the first, establishing his dual musical character. In "There's Nothing so Fatal as Woman," Lyonel articulates his virulent misogyny. Purcell provides a syllabic setting for the text, which describes the lethality of women and their baseness as they use men as slaves. The high-blown, overly emotional musical rhetoric found in "I Sigh'd, and I Pin'd" is gone, replaced by a terse and precise statement of women's evils. Lyonel ends his diatribe by extolling the virtues of liquor, as it "will drive from your Head / The Delights of the Bed, / He that's Drunk, is not able to Woo."

The pattern established in act 1, Lyonel's veering between lamentation and misogyny, continues throughout the play. However, one song is an exception to this rule: the act 4 "I'le Sail Upon the

Example 4.7. *Continued.*

King,_____   so   blest__is__ the__Head that is ad-dle;__   the   dull emp-ty Pate, Soon-est

comes   to be great,   Fate   dotes   on a Fool   in the   Cra-dle,____   Fate   dotes   on a Fool   in the

cra -   -   -   dle.____

Example 4.7. *Continued.*

Dog-Star," does not use misogyny to mitigate the emasculating effects of madness; instead, the song focuses solely on Lyonel's (irrational) attempts to regain his stature—for, we must remember, it was the king's ability to arbitrarily take Lyonel's mistress, and thereby his masculine agency, that caused his madness in the first place. Although delusions of grandeur are a frequent trope in the mad song genre, considering Lyonel's particular concern with the usurpation of his power (and his mistress), it is reasonable to read "I'le Sail Upon the Dog-Star" as a mad attempt to outdo the king. Lyonel may not be a king, but in his addled brain he has godlike qualities. He can literally "chase the Moon," "coyn the Weather," "tear the Rainbow from the Sky," and "pluck [the Stars] from their Orbs." Although the exact location for this song in act 4 is not known, I find persuasive Olive Baldwin and Thelma Wilson's theory that Lyonel performed "I'le Sail Upon the Dog-Star," after imagining he is Tamberlain.[91]

The music accentuates the overblown rhetoric of the text.[92] As soon as Lyonel articulates a sentiment, he immediately repeats himself, musically and textually, sometimes more than once, giving his music an almost feverish intensity. Purcell uses imitation between the voice and the bass—a rather grand formal technique for a mad song, perhaps a musical analogue to Lyonel's grand delusions. Finally, this piece is considerably more difficult than Lyonel's other music, as it incorporates challenging melismas on "tear" and "roaring." Lyonel's performance of these vocal tricks elevates him artistically, restoring a modicum of power, although not his sanity. (See example 4.8.)

In the plays discussed earlier in this chapter, madness and lovesickness were frequently cured. *The Fool's Preferment* takes an open approach, a strange choice for a comedy in which spectators would have expected an unambiguously happy resolution. At the end of the play, Lyonel's fate is left up in the air as the doctor promises a cure and commands the onlookers to "sooth his Humour," but

Example 4.8. Henry Purcell, "I'le Sail Upon the Dog-Star," *New Songs Sung in The Fool's Preferment, or, the Three Dukes of Dunstable* (London, 1688), mm. 16–21.

there is no indication what action is taken. While Malevole/Alto-fronto achieves mental harmony through proper performance in a masque, Peregrine is cured through a theatrical ruse, and the Passionate Mad-man is cured through bloodletting, Lyonel is carried away to receive some kind of offstage treatment, and the play ends with no mention of what happens to him. This resolution is completely different from John Fletcher's *The Noble Gentleman*, the early seventeenth-century source for D'Urfey's play. In Fletcher's version the madman, Shatillion, did not sing and was cured of his ailment. In *The Fool's Preferment* madness seems an irrevocable condition. While D'Urfey attempts to negotiate the problem of male madness by having Lyonel punish the woman that did him wrong, his state is permanent. Celia tries to restore him to his senses, but she is unsuccessful—the boundary between madness and sense has become impenetrable. Although Lyonel does not die, as did many of the mentally distressed women discussed in the previous chapter, he is trapped—less than a man—within the prison of insanity. And that, perhaps, is the harshest criticism possible of his behavior.

Lyonel's musical characterization in *The Fool's Preferment*—his combination of musical ranting and lamenting, of misogynist rhetoric and womanish grief—became standard in the portrayal of male madness. By the 1690s, male erotomaniacs sang elaborate mad songs, much as did their female counterparts. While songs such as Bracegirdle's famous "I Burn, I Burn" inspired amorous devotion in those who saw her erotically charged performance as Marcella, the same musical features served quite a different function when performed by a man. Purcell's male mad song for D'Urfey's comedy *Don Quixote, Part I* (1694), "Let the Dreadfull Engines," is one of the best-known examples of the male mad song genre. An elaborate multi-sectional piece sung by the baritone, John Bowman, as the lovesick swain Cardenio, Purcell's song shifts rapidly between genres and humoral states: recitative and aria, choler and melancholy, misogynistic rant and lament.

As in the case of Lyonel, misogynist rhetoric clearly tells the audience who is to blame for Cardenio's affliction, as he calls his mistress, Luscinda, an "ingrate" and describes women as "jilts," "slatterns," "whores," and "witches." Despite such abuse directed at womankind, Cardenio cannot be heard as being blameless. Purcell's song clearly articulates Cardenio's emotional excessiveness, the fatal flaw that nourishes his lovesickness. Cardenio begins "Let the Dreadfull Engines" by singing a recitative in F major, imitating thunder with his melismas as he describes his "hot rage." Within a few measures he shifts to the darker F minor, an uncommon key on the Restoration stage, which Purcell uses to portray Cardenio's dark despair (Purcell also used this key for the prelude in *Dido and Aeneas* that introduces the dark deeds of the witches). During this section, Cardenio's rage gradually dissipates. At first, he sings a lengthy melisma on "rancour," but his focus shifts from his anger to the growing "despaire" he feels in his heart. (See example 4.9.)

After emphasis on his chilly despair with a sharply descending melisma on "cold," Cardenio's humor changes again. This time the meter shifts to 6/4 and the key returns to F major (the key of his

Example 4.9. Henry Purcell, "Let the Dreadfull Engines of Eternal Will," in *The Songs to the New Play of Don Quixote . . . Part the First* (London, 1694), mm. 17–27.

previous raging) as he wonders if anything can warm him. Finally, he remembers the one person who can do the job: his mistress, Luscinda. Just the mention of her name excites him. He repeats "yes" multiple times, and the bass line becomes extremely active in response, with restless eighth notes. Reflecting upon the beauty of her eyes, Cardenio becomes ever more impassioned, singing a rapidly ascending melisma on "mounting" as he imagines flames reaching the skies: his lust has gotten the better of him.

This humor is quickly deflated, as Cardenio reflects on his situation, filtering it through a mythological lens (he mentions Pha-

Example 4.10. Henry Purcell, "Let the Dreadfull Engines," mm. 69–91.

Example 4.10. *Continued.*

eton's fiery fall), as he beseeches the powers in a formal C major recitative, apologizing to them for invoking his beloved's name and regretting the flame-filled result of his ignited passion. This introspection leads to lament. Moving to the key of C minor and a slow triple meter, conventions typical of the lament on the operatic stage, Cardenio's grief explodes with two desperate melismatic outcries, "Ah! ah!" (See example 4.10.)

These melismas apparently rekindle his passion as Cardenio begins to "glow" with hate for "this ingrate" (i.e., Luscinda), returning to the key of F major, the key previously used for his raging opening recitative and lustful balladic ode to Luscinda's charms.

Example 4.10. *Continued.*

No sooner than he indulges his fiery passion, his humor shifts again, as he tries to calm himself with the flatted key of F minor. After a brief cooling period, Cardenio himself takes a more ironic tone, shifting to F major and indicting womankind for its cruel behavior toward men in a syllabic, matter-of-fact fashion. He closes his song with a flippant ballad, resolving to bid women, the "witches," all goodnight. Thus, in the course of one song, with its ever-shifting affects, Purcell has clearly portrayed the excessive nature of lovesickness, of the shift from rage, to utter despair, to misogynist rant. Cardenio, completely lacking reason, enslaved to a woman, is a prototypical "loving worme."

Although Purcell and D'Urfey used some of the same techniques as in their portrayal of Lyonel, there are also some significant differences. Cardenio's mad song is certainly more effusive (and difficult) than anything sung by Lyonel, yet for some reason D'Urfey doesn't feel the need to apologize for lovesick Cardenio. Perhaps an apology was unnecessary, as D'Urfey makes it abundantly clear that Cardenio is fully cured by the end of the play and is happily reunited with his mistress. He solved the problem of male madness embodied in Lyonel by making sure that Cardenio's rationality returned: he did regain the "Charter of [his] Kind."

Madness in the Age of Reason

Although most musical madmen suffered from lovesickness in the late seventeenth and early eighteenth century, an earlier, politically tinged type of madman continued to sing and dance in revivals of older plays. Such is the case in John Eccles's 1704 setting of "O Let Us Howle"—now called "Come Let Us Howle"—for a revival of *The Duchess of Malfi*. The fourth version of this mad song comes almost a century after the earlier versions, and naturally much had changed, both in terms of musical style and in the perceptions of the relationship between madness and the macrocosm. During the intervening years between the original production of *The Duchess of Malfi* and the early eighteenth-century revival, ventriloquized laments and elaborate multi-sectional mad songs had emerged, genres that, understood in their theatrical and social contexts, negotiated and critiqued the problem of male irrationality. Positive associations with melancholy and madness had disappeared by the late seventeenth century. As we have seen, male madness, with the exception of revivals of earlier plays, was almost exclusively the preserve of the effeminate lovesick. And relationships between madness and the macrocosm had mostly been relegated to the world of empty metaphors.[93]

Just as early eighteenth-century adapters of *The Duchess of Malfi* omitted some of the bawdier and more distasteful elements of the play, so does Eccles sanitize madness in his Augustan version of "Come Let Us Howle."[94] While Eccles may have been familiar with a version of Johnson's setting that incorporated the howling semitone figure (although he uses a descending semitone, rather than an ascending one), he takes radically different approach from that of his predecessor.[95] Eccles, after nodding toward the semitone howl found in earlier versions, features an elaborate Italianate melisma to represent the mad howling: it bears little resemblance to an actual animalistic howl. (See example 4.11.) The result is a distancing effect. Instead of music literally howling, giving voice to the bestiality of madness and, by intimation, the bestial discord, dissonance, and disorder of the world, madness is now an abstraction.

As explained in chapter 1, the regicide of Charles I in 1649, which severed the head of state, and the emergence of contract

Example 4.11. John Eccles, "Come Let Us Howle Some Heavy Note," *A Collection of Songs* (London, 1704), mm. 1–6.

theory, which challenged monarchical claims of divine right, undermined the old analogic model of the body politic. Just as notions of the relationship between body politic and monarch lost their mystical power, so does the musical language of madness in *The Duchess of Malfi.* In the earliest version of the song, which features a startling semitone howl and a sudden modal disruption, we hear the irrationality and unpredictability of madness, reflecting contemporary analogues drawn among political and social corruption, musical discord, and irrationality. Versions found in later manuscript copies chip away at the piece's bestial power, toning down the grinding howl or omitting it altogether. And Eccles's setting completely overthrows the old paradigm, favoring musical beauty and the progression of rational musical sequences over musical eccentricity. Of course we cannot prove that Eccles's compositional choices were directly *caused* by new ideas about madness and the relationship between the microcosm and macrocosm, but it is undeniable that his setting has a radically different effect upon the listener than the earlier versions. In Eccles's "Come Let Us Howle" we find a new musical approach to insanity—an approach that shuns the mimetic conventions of the past and embraces comforting musical filigree, an approach that suggests with its orderly melismas the desire to rationalize madness in the Age of Reason.

5

Disorder in the Eighteenth Century

Throughout this book I've discussed how theatrical music represented disorder and how portrayals of witches, the mad, and the
melancholic changed over time. Broadly speaking, the seventeenth
century saw a decline in the belief in witchcraft among the elites
and an increased suspicion of irrationality. The seventeenth century was also a time of major political upheavals (seven monarchs
in one century—if one double-counts the dual reign of William
and Mary—Civil War, the Popish Plot, the Glorious Revolution)
that had a direct effect on musical and theatrical life. The court
masque fell from grace, although its remnants lived on in the
theater music of the late seventeenth century. Actresses took
women's roles, changing the sorts of music that were composed for
female characters. Singing actors became extremely proficient, particularly in the last few decades of the century, allowing composers
such as Purcell and Eccles to create elaborate displays of musical
disorder. As the late seventeenth-century London stage was notorious for its bawdiness, a debate, led by Jeremy Collier and others,
raged about morality. But one of the largest paradigm shifts in

terms of musical and theatrical life in London was yet to come: Italian opera.

Despite the eventual dominance of Italian opera, native entertainments featuring disorderly subjects did not disappear. Witches, for example, continued to be extremely popular with eighteenth-century audiences. The attitudes toward witchcraft of people in the early eighteenth century were very similar to those of their late seventeenth-century predecessors. For some eighteenth-century spectators the witches were pure entertainment. For others, their onstage behavior was a disturbing display of heathenism. While belief in witchcraft had declined considerably, there was still unease in some quarters about the display of their supernatural activities, even in the licensed, fanciful space of the theater.

Two contemporary reactions to the witches' scenes exemplify the early eighteenth-century tension between the desire to revel in the pleasures of musical disorder and anxieties about falling prey to its questionable charms. Given the continued popularity of the musical witches, the first anecdote probably represents the dominant view. Joseph Addison, in a 1711 issue of *The Spectator*, tells of an irritating woman who talked to her friends at a performance of *Macbeth*:

> Some Years ago I was at the Tragedy of *Macbeth*, and unfortunately placed myself under a Woman of Quality that is since Dead. . . . A little before the rising of the Curtain, she broke out into a loud Soliloquy, *When will the dear Witches enter?* and immediately upon their first Appearance, asked a Lady that sat three Boxes from her, on her Right-hand, if those Witches were not charming Creatures.[1]

But what Addison's anonymous noblewoman found diverting and charming did not tickle everyone's funny bone. Arthur Bedford, an Anglican divine writing in the early eighteenth century, was upset by the lack of gravitas in the onstage representation of witches. He describes his reaction in *A Serious Remonstrance on Behalf of the Christian Religion* (1719):

> When *Witches* are concerned, the *Devil* seldom fails to act his Part for their Diversion, sometimes with the Sound of *Trumpets*, sometimes with *Martial Musick* mix'd with Instruments of Horror, and sometimes playing on Instruments of War. Sometimes they sing alone, and sometimes *Musick* is join'd with their Sing-

ing: sometimes there is a *Chorus*, and sometimes there is a *Dance* of such *infernal Spirits*. . . . When his [God's] Designs are frustrated, it is a matter of Rejoicing on the *Stage*. Accordingly, here we have *Hell* represented as a Jest, with *Tombs* and *Dungeons*, and also with Men and Women chain'd in Rows, and *Devils* for their Companions. Here we may observe them flourishing their Instruments of Horror to make Diversion, and carrying a Man to the Place of *Torments*, with a *Flourish of Musick sounding Triumph*, in direct opposition to the *Joy of Angels* at a Sinner's Conversion.[2]

While Bedford objected to the lighthearted portrayal of witches, to "*Hell* represented as a Jest," if we judge by the continuing popularity of *Macbeth*, he seems to have been in the minority. The very thing that enraged this clergyman apparently amused most theatergoers. Indeed, Bedford conceded that the audience enjoyed the witches' antics in *Macbeth*: "*the Audience were pleased to clap at an unusual length of Pleasure and Approbation*."[3]

Eventually, the sort of objections raised by Bedford fell by the wayside and the "dear Witches" lauded by the anonymous noblewoman reigned supreme. In the popular genre of the pantomime, the comical hag-type witch flourished. *Harlequin Sorcerer, with the Loves of Pluto and Proserpine* (1725) featured Richard Leveridge as the First Witch, capitalizing upon the preexistent associations between the singer/actor and Hecate, a role he had performed in his setting of *Macbeth*. The spectacle-filled pantomime also featured a witches' chorus, much to the delight of contemporary audiences, who made the show a great success.[4] The musical witches of *Macbeth* also continued to be popular with eighteenth- and even nineteenth-century audiences. Davenant's altered text was acted until the 1740s, and Leveridge's "Famous Music" (which was widely, and erroneously, believed to be by Matthew Locke or even Henry Purcell)[5] was a part of the spectacle well into the nineteenth century, even after David Garrick, the famous actor, restored the Bard's original text in 1744.[6]

Eighteenth- and nineteenth-century reactions to the musical witches reveal their complete transformation into pure entertainment, devoid of any real menace (much to the dismay of some critics). For some commentators, the witches were an embarrassment: an anomaly in an otherwise serious play. As one critic declared in the *St. James's Chronicle* of 1773, "comic actors are permitted to turn a solemn incantation into a ridiculous farce for the entertainment of the upper gallery." He then calls for the witches to be seriously represented.[7] These calls went unheeded, as the comical, musical witches continued to reign over the English stage. In 1833 Fanny Kemble remarks on the humorous quality of the travesty presentation of witchcraft: "We have three jolly-faced fellows, whom we are accustomed to laugh at . . . in every farce . . . with a due proportion of petticoats . . . jocose red faces, peaked hats, and broomsticks."[8]

While cross-dressed actors continued to sing these roles in the late eighteenth and early nineteenth centuries, theaters sometimes introduced another inducement for theatergoers: beautiful women in the roles of witches. Although women had participated in witches' choruses during the Restoration, by the nineteenth century the tendency to trade on the actresses' erotic charms had clearly run out of control. In 1864 the *Daily News* lambasted this practice: "The wild poetic grandeur of the drama [*Macbeth*] is certainly diminished by the introduction of a hundred or more pretty singing wenches, but trading managers are bound to be practical and Locke's [*sic*] music, with Middleton's words, is found to pay."[9] While customers had previously relished the travesty witches, by the late eighteenth and early nineteenth century a more alluring type of witch had replaced the hag—audiences were now titillated by the seductive spectacle and sounds of singing beauties.

Melancholy, Madness, and Gender in the Eighteenth Century

The same tension between moralistic objections to musical and theatrical disorder and the desire to be entertained can also be seen in turn-of-the-century critiques of staged madness and melancholy. Anxieties about the transgressive qualities of disordered characters were nothing new. Early seventeenth-century playwrights criticized and commented upon male unreason and lasciviousness, particularly when the man suffered from lovesickness. While onlookers were sympathetic to the ill man's plight, he was also held up as an object of ridicule (for example, the Passionate Mad-man in *The Nice Valour*). In the late seventeenth century Thomas D'Urfey had acknowledged the unacceptability of Lyonel in *The Fool's Preferment*, as he gave up "the Charter of our Kind" (masculine reason) through his mad behavior. And when John Eccles wrote his setting of "Come Let Us Howle" for a revival of *The Duchess of Malfi*, he defused madness by portraying it as a musically pleasurable abstraction rather than a bestial curse.

Why did male madness become so problematic for those at the turn of the century? The answers are complex and multiple. Some of the reasons have to do with the increasing rigidity of masculinity in the eighteenth century. The definition of effeminacy changed, causing the "effeminate" lovesick singing madman to be even more problematic. In the past effeminacy been used to describe a range of behaviors—for example, men who loved women so much that they became like them—but now the term referred to men who engaged in sex acts with other men.[10] The effeminacy of these men became an outward sign of their inner, essential deviance.[11]

Male actors and singers, who had always been sexually suspect as they occupied a social space slightly outside the margins of respectability, found themselves in a particularly precarious spot in this new gender economy. In the early seventeenth century anti-theatricalists considered boy players to be dangerously seductive, luring the audience into desiring them sexually. By the early eighteenth century, a more modern male homosexual identity had begun to emerge in the form of the molly (a man who had sex with other men), and this identity was frequently grafted onto the male actor.[12] The actor's self-display, his spectacularization, feminized him, as he was perpetually on the receiving end of the gaze. His position as object for the desiring spectator excluded him from the increasingly rigid (and homophobic) definitions of masculinity that were circulating in the early eighteenth century. Thus, it is not surprising that the display of lovesick emotion, which had always been problematic for a man during the seventeenth century, became even more so in an environment that viewed the male player as potentially homosexual and deviant. Even if the object of his onstage desire was female, his effusive, overly emotional behavior marked him as feminine, less than male, and potentially a sodomite.[13] The lines between playacting and essential effeminacy were disturbingly blurred.

Just as the boundaries of acceptable male behavior on and offstage narrowed, others sought to rationalize and more clearly delineate mad and melancholic behavior itself. Part of the problem of madness and melancholy had always been a loss of reason, but, particularly in the early seventeenth century, the mad and melancholic were thought to have increased insight (such as the malcontent who critiqued society's foibles). This positive conception of mental disorder gradually fell by the wayside over the course of the century and had virtually disappeared by the eighteenth century. Max Byrd claims, using Alexander Pope's *The Dunciad* (1728) as a point of departure, "in Pope's world of insane, nightmarish Dunces, madness is not illuminated by the possibilities of recovery. It means not punishment and insight, but only punishment."[14] Michel Foucault also makes this point about the shift in the perception of madness in *Madness and Civilization*, arguing that the mid-seventeenth century saw the definitive division of madness from truth and the separation of the madman from society, with his concurrent relegation to the asylum.[15] While Foucault marks the Age of Confinement with the founding of the Hôpital Général in France in 1656, the first laws requiring the incarceration of lunatics appeared in England at the beginning of the eighteenth century.[16] In this English Age of Reason, men might not have been afraid of witches or devils, the old supernatural causes of madness that had been mostly debunked; they were afraid of what might lurk within. As Byrd pithily remarks, "if the Devil can no longer be exorcised, at least the madman can be."[17] Thus, the urge toward confinement. And thus, perhaps, the desire to excoriate male madness and melancholy on and offstage.

These shifting notions of gender and reason also had a profound effect on female characters suffering from madness. As Kristina Straub astutely observes, in the eighteenth century male dominance became increasingly dependent on a femininity defined in opposition to masculinity. The domestic, private sphere was thought to be the woman's domain (as opposed to the public, male sphere) and the professional actress challenged this notion. As a result, discourses of the time betray an escalating need to portray the actress as "respectable" and (by extension) appropriately subservient and feminine.[18] Anxieties about the respectability and modesty of the female actress can be seen in reactions to the character of Ophelia in *Hamlet*.[19] As with the witches' music, we see a tension emerge between moral concerns and the pleasures of disorderly conduct. Some chastised Ophelia's supposed libertine discourse; others, while admitting Ophelia's disorder, expressed sympathy and argued vociferously for her chastity.

Jeremy Collier lobbed the opening salvo in this critical controversy in his *A Short View of the Immorality and Profaneness of the English Stage* (1698). Collier objected to the libertinism of female madness in general, stating:

> Women are sometimes represented *Silly* and sometimes *Mad*, to enlarge their Liberty, and screen their Impudence from Censure. . . . However, it amounts to this Confession; that Women when they have their Understandings about them ought to converse otherwise.[20]

Specific instances of female theatrical madness are also held up for ridicule and disdain as Collier negatively compares Ophelia with Phaedra. Phaedra showed remarkable restraint in her madness, and "her Frensy is not Lewd; She keeps her Modesty even after She has lost her Wits."[21] On the other hand, Shakespeare mistreated his "young Virgin *Ophelia*":

> Since he was resolv'd to drown the Lady like a Kitten, he should have set her a swimming a little sooner. To keep her alive only to sully her Reputation, and discover the Rankness of her Breath, was very Cruel.[22]

Collier's primary objection to female mad scenes was that they transgressed his notion of proper conduct for women, as "Modesty is the distinguishing Vertue of that Sex."[23] For him, Ophelia's madness presented a disturbing vision of unruly femininity, one that was unfit for public consumption. While in the past, such behavior had been considered unfortunate, but typical of the emotionally unstable female, now, for those like Collier who lauded respectability and moderation, it became abnormal.

The respondents to Collier unwittingly reinforced the moralist's point about the importance of female modesty, as they defensively emphasized Ophelia's virginity. Thomas D'Urfey, in his preface to *The Campaigners* (1698), lambastes Collier for criticizing the Bard:

> And here [in his criticism of *Hamlet*] he has no other way to shew his malice, but by ridiculously quibbling upon the prettiest Character in it, the innocent young Virgin *Ophelia*, who, because the Poet makes her run mad for the death of her Father, and less of her Lover, and consequently makes her sing and speak some idle extravagant things, as on such an occasion is natural, and at last drown her self, he very masterly tells us, the Poet, *since he was*

resolv'd to drown her like a Kitten, should have set her a swimming a
little longer; to keep her alive, only to sully her Reputation, it is very
cruel. Yes, but I would fain ask Doctor Absolution in what she
has sullied her Reputation, I am sure five hundred Audiences that
have view'd her could never find it out, tho he has.[24]

D'Urfey reinforces Ophelia's purity by calling her an "innocent
young Virgin." Furthermore, he would absolve her of lovesickness,
stating that the root cause of her madness is primarily the death
of her father; her lover's malfeasance plays less of a role. If Ophelia
is not lovesick, then she cannot be lascivious—she simply sings
"idle extravagant things." Finally, D'Urfey insinuates that Collier
simply has a dirty mind, as many audiences experienced the spectacle of Ophelia's madness and did not question her reputation.
Thus, for D'Urfey, Ophelia is appropriately chaste.

James Drake, in his response to Collier, *The Antient and Modern*
Stages Survey'd (1699), argues with equal vigor for Ophelia's virginity. While admitting that Ophelia suffered from lovesickness, a
disease that potentially stems from lasciviousness, Drake held that
her love was without fault. Hamlet's mistaken murder of her father
dismantles her hopes and naturally, given the frailty of her sex,
leads to her confusion. But she should not be faulted for this.

> Allowing the Cause of her madness to be *Purtie per Pale*, the
> death of her Father, and the loss of her Love, which is the utmost
> we can give to the latter, yet her passion is as innocent, and
> inoffensive in her distraction as before, tho not so reasonable and
> well govern'd.[25]

Drake then goes on to claim that Collier's real moral objection is
to Ophelia's mad song, and he reprints the supposedly blameless
text of "Tomorrow is St. Valentine's Day." Of course, as we've seen
in chapter 3, the text is full of double entendre, with lines such as
"By cock they are to blame. / Quoth she, before you tumbled me,
/ You promis'd me to wed." While Collier might find such lyrics
highly offensive and indicative of Ophelia's rank breath, Drake simply dismisses them as "silly . . . but very harmless and inoffen-
sive."[26] He continues with his defense of her behavior, making the
surprising claim that we cannot criticize mad Ophelia for her sexual
curiosity: "If he [Collier] pleases to consult the Records, he will
find even in the days of *Sophocles*, Maids had an itching the same
way, and longed to know, what was what, before they died."[27] For

Collier, the fact that Ophelia sings bawdy verses shows her flawed moral character and lack of modesty; for Drake, it is simply a symptom of her madness. According to him, she is still a virgin, and we should not fault her (or her classical antecedents) for wanting to relieve themselves of their maidenheads. This desire "to know what was what" was perfectly natural, and Ophelia's madness simply allows her to be honest about her sexual needs.

In the controversy over Ophelia, we see a tension between the moral objections of Collier and the defense of the fair mad maiden articulated by D'Urfey and Drake: a tension we saw before in the discourses surrounding theatrical witchcraft. With the witches, Addison's noblewoman domesticated them into "dear," harmless creatures—entertaining but hardly dangerous—even as Bedford railed against witches making "*Hell* a Jest." D'Urfey and Drake take a slightly different tack in their rebuttals to Collier's charges regarding Ophelia's immorality. For them, Ophelia is without stain. She remains a pure virgin despite her unbridled mad discourse. Even her bawdy song is perfectly understandable and merely reveals the unrequited desires of a lovesick maid.

In her study of the changing meanings ascribed to Ophelia, Elaine Showalter points out that Ophelia's madness (*pace* D'Urfey) was most frequently presented in the late seventeenth and early eighteenth centuries as being caused by erotomania—lovesickness. Actresses who had a reputation for being unhappy in love frequently performed the role, the most spectacular example being Susan Mountfort, a former actress at Lincoln's Inn Fields who went mad after being betrayed by her lover. In 1720 she escaped from her guardian and made her way to the theater where *Hamlet* was being performed. She burst onstage and gave the role of Ophelia an undeniable verisimilitude, although she died shortly thereafter. As one witness observed, "She was in truth *Ophelia* herself, to the amazement of the performers as well as of the audience."[28]

But such unbridled displays of feminine misbehavior became increasingly rare as the eighteenth century progressed. Just as the witch was relegated to a comedic role in pantomimes, was received as "dear" entertainment for the masses, or was performed in titillating fashion by "beauties," so did eighteenth-century tastes defuse the madwoman. We already can hear the rumblings of transformation in the comments of Collier, D'Urfey, and Drake. For Collier, Ophelia's disorderly conduct disturbed him and he labeled it immoral. D'Urfey takes another strategy—one that denies her sexuality—by claiming that the death of Ophelia's father, not unrequited love, set her raving, absolving her from the taint of lovesickness. Drake too defended Ophelia's virginity, and he excused her discourse as being natural for a lovesick maid. Both D'Urfey and Drake are careful to separate Ophelia's behavior from her essential, chaste nature.

This impulse to recuperate Ophelia from the taint of sexual sin turned her into a sentimentalized figure palatable for eighteenth-century viewers. Actresses began to perform Ophelia in a way that minimized the force of her female sexuality. While Ophelia's madness had always provoked sympathy, sexual titillation had been an essential component in scenes of lovesick musical madness throughout the seventeenth century (we must not forget Laertes' comment about Ophelia's madness being "pretty"). This changed over the course of the eighteenth century, and actresses such as Mrs. Lessingham in 1772 and even Mrs. Siddons in 1785 played the mad scene in a decorous way, wearing white dresses (a visual symbol of Ophelia's chastity), loose hair, and wildflowers.[29] (See figure 5.1.)

Furthering the sanitization of Ophelia, in the eighteenth century humorous or sexual lines were removed from her part. Sometimes her role was assigned to a singer instead of an actress, giving primacy to the musical aspect. This change is particularly interesting, for music had been considered one of the more dangerous elements of a madwoman's discourse in the seventeenth century: a symbol of her fluidity and unbridled nature. Perhaps, as Ophelia's sexual texts were censored and rationalized, her music, an inherently irrational medium, was foregrounded in order to convey her madness.[30] Indeed, music seems to have been particularly important in these productions, as the surviving copies of Ophelia's songs that can be directly traced to productions of *Hamlet* come from eighteenth-century productions at Drury Lane.[31] As chapter 3 argued, subversive textual elements combine with a mad style of performance to render Ophelia's music dangerous; however, if a singer were to perform censored versions of the music with carefully coiffed, flower-bedecked hair and a chaste white gown, some of the sexual power found in the seventeenth-century Ophelia would certainly have been contained.

Figure 5.1. "Sarah Siddons as Ophelia." By Permission of the Folger Shakespeare Library.

The Castrato and Disorder

While gender ideology, notions of rationality, and stricter moral standards affected the performance of eighteenth-century musical disorder, so did changing audience tastes. The popularity of Italian opera at the beginning of the eighteenth century also had a profound effect on the reception and portrayal of disorder. For early eighteenth-century English critics, the castrato became one of the most prominent symbols of disorder, of nature gone seductively awry. These singers, as with the disorderly characters discussed in this book, gained power through their vocal innovations. But in some respects the problem of the castrato was more profound than that posed by theatrical witches, melancholics, and the mad. The castrato was not playacting a fantasy of disorder. He could not discard his deviance like a costume at the end of a performance. He embodied it, on- and offstage.

London audiences had been familiar with Italian music for some time; Italian composers, singers, and instrumentalists had been working in London since the beginning of the Restoration era, and many noblemen had traveled to Italy as part of their "Grand Tour." Yet, not until the debut of Thomas Clayton's *Arsinoe Queen of Cyprus* (1705), an English opera in the Italian style using Italianate recitative, did audiences become attracted en masse to this foreign musical genre.[32] The process of persuading the English public to embrace Italian opera was a slow one, marked by occasional failures (such as Jakob Greber's disastrous *The Loves of Ergasto* [1705]), but, after the performance of an English translation of Giovanni Bononcini's *Camilla* in 1706, Italian opera began to supplant native musical entertainments on the London stage, putting many English composers out of theatrical work.[33]

Italian opera, with castrati playing heroic and amorous roles, subverted and threatened emergent notions of English masculinity, particularly among the bourgeois. *The Spectator*, the influential early eighteenth-century newspaper, ran critiques that emphasized the lack of verisimilitude in having these "unmanned" men playing heroic roles.[34] Many of these essays were written by two of the finest critics of the early eighteenth century, Joseph Addison and Richard Steele.[35] Addison rejected "eunuchs" in heroic and amorous roles. He sarcastically described the performance of the famous castrato Nicolini in Francesco Mancini's *L'Idaspe fedele* (1710):

> There is nothing that of late Years has afforded Matter of greater Amusement to the Town than Signor *Nicolini's* Combat with a Lion in the *Hay-market*, which has been very often exhibited to the general Satisfaction of most of the Nobility and Gentry in the Kingdom of *Great Britain*. . . . Many likewise were the Conjectures of the Treatment which this Lion was to meet with from the hands of Signor *Nicolini*, some supposed that he was to Subdue him in *Recitativo*, as *Orpheus* used to serve the wild Beasts in his time, and afterwards to knock him on the head, some fancied that the Lion would not pretend to lay his Paws upon the Hero, by Reason of the received Opinion that a Lion will not hurt a Virgin.[36]

In Addison's critique we see the elision of the castrato's onstage and offstage identities. His castration becomes his essence, limiting his ability to fully embody a virile lion-tamer. Even the lion, in Addison's account, recognizes that his opponent is not worthy of attack: as a virgin he is not fully a man.

Other writers concerned themselves with the seductive power of these emasculated creatures with their alluring voices, which could provoke immoral behavior in those who heard their siren song. A few critics described the influence Italian opera and castrati had upon women. John Dennis's *An Essay on the Opera's After the Italian Manner* (1706) explains that

> We can show by experience what Influence the soft and effeminate Measures of the Italian Opera has upon the Minds and Manners of Men. The Modern Italians have the very same sun and soil which the Antient Romans had, yet are their manners directly opposite; their men are neither Virtuous, nor Wise, nor Valiant, and they who have reason to know their Women, never trust them out of their sight.[37]

In short, Italian women fell into lasciviousness because they listened to Italian opera. Others more specifically expressed anxieties about women enjoying the pleasures of non-procreative sex with the castrati—sex with no strings attached. A satire published in the *British Journal* of 25 March 1727 implied a relationship between the famous soprano Faustina Bordoni and the castrato Senesino:

> To keep my Character, my Shape, my Voice
> I fix'd on Thee, cold Slave, my prudent Choice,
> Well knowing safe with Thee I might remain,
> Enjoy Loves Pleasures, yet avoid the Pain;

By Thee caress'd, continue yet a Maid,
Nor of a Tell-tale B[ab]y be afraid.[38]

Obviously, for this pseudo-Faustina, Senesino's primary attraction was non-reproductive sexual acts. The "cold slave" could not impregnate her.

Writers seemed to be more infuriated, however, by the supposed power of Italian opera and the castrato voice to emasculate men.[39] As noted above, historians mark the turn of the century as the moment when effeminacy, which formerly referred to heterosexual men who were too passionate about women, came to be exclusively associated with sodomites. Such concerns about male effeminacy haunt John Dennis's *An Essay on the Opera's After the Italian Manner* (1706), in which he warns that "*Italian Opera*, another Entertainment, which is about to be establish'd in the room of Plays, is a Diversion of more pernicious Consequence, than the most licentious Play that ever has appear'd upon the Stage."[40] The southern climes had always been associated with sexual deviance and luxury, and it was but a small step to specify the precise nature of the "pernicious consequence" of which Dennis speaks. A few years later, the author specifically connects Italian opera with homosexuality in *An Essay Upon Publick Spirit* (1711):

> The Pleasure that effeminate Musick gives, is a mere sensual Pleasure, which he who gives or he who receives in a supreme Degree must be alike unmann'd. . . . The Ladies, with humblest Submission, seem to mistake their Interest a little in encouraging Opera's: for the more the Men are enervated and emasculated by the Softness of the *Italian* Musick, the less will they care for them, and the more for one another.[41]

Effeminate music, music that must be produced by creatures who are less then men (and who thereby are potential sodomites), unmans those who listen. The essentialism of Dennis's statement is obvious. Effeminate music provokes effeminacy (sodomy) in men. Dennis, of course, uses a familiar rhetorical strategy to vilify the music of disorder: once again, musical practices on the English stage were being attacked for inciting "unnatural" lusts in male listeners. This time, however, it was a "foreign" entertainment that was the source of the offense. The danger, instead of being envoiced by an alluringly musical young boy or an actress, was attributed to the foreign bodies and unnaturally feminine voices of Italian castrati.

As was the case with the other disorderly subjects discussed in this book, political and religious issues were also at stake in the discourse surrounding the castrati. Effeminacy in the early eighteenth century had become associated, at least for the bourgeois, with the aristocracy, a class that adopted "foreign" customs, weakening essential Englishness.[42] For those who criticized the upper classes, the aristocratic love of Italian opera was simply another indication of aristocratic weakness, aristocratic effeminacy, and potentially the aristocratic embrace of Catholicism. Addison, Steele, and others created a nationalist debate drawn around lines of morality (strong, virile, Protestant English music) versus sexual deviance (lascivious, effeminate, cuckolding, Catholic Italian music).[43] Steele's epilogue for his 1705 comedy, *The Tender Husband; or the Accomplish'd Fools*, captures the essence of the polemic, as he conflates the castrato singer's Catholicism and sexual insatiability:

> *Britons*, who constant War, with factious Rage,
> For Liberty against each other wage,
> From Foreign Insult save this English Stage.
> No more th' Italian squaling Tribe admit,
> In Tongues unknown; tis Popery in Wit.
> The Songs (their selves confess) from Rome they bring;
> And 'tis High-Mass for ought you know, they Sing.
> Husbands take Care, the Danger may come nigher,
> The Women say their Eunuch is a Friar.[44]

With statements such as Steele's, we come full circle, for in his epilogue we hear the old familiar strategies used by those disturbed by musical disorder, in this case, the aural decadence of "th' Italian squaling Tribe." Fears about popery. Fears about music's seductive power. Fears about female sexual inconstancy. And, as we might expect, a strategy (an unsuccessful strategy) emerged to regulate the disorderly power of Italian opera and its castrati. In 1719 a group of aristocrats founded the Royal Academy of Music to foster the production of Italian operas on edifying, moral subjects.[45] The noble patrons of the Royal Academy chose operas with librettos that reflected their aristocratic notions of heroism and honor, although ironically, the manhood of these operatic heroes was perpetually undermined as foreign-born castrati continued to perform these roles. As we have seen, the problem of musical disorder is not easily solved.

Epilogue

Thought and afflictions, passion, hell itself,
She turns to favor and to prettiness

In *Hamlet* Laertes admits to being drawn to Ophelia's mad music, even as he is repulsed. The music performed by disorderly characters often has that effect upon the listener. Because of its innovation, its brilliance, and its unpredictability, it draws the auditor into its web, but it is these very qualities that disturb. From a moral standpoint, seventeenth-century listeners knew they should shun hell, even if it was dressed up in a sonorously seductive or provocative package—and yet they relished listening. Of course, as we have seen, disorderly characters sometimes shunned music, or only noise could exist in their presence (cf. *The Masque of Queens*, *The Malcontent*, *The Antipodes*, *The Late Lancashire Witches*, *The Witch of Edmonton*). In these cases, appropriately disordered sounds (or the complete absence of harmony) signified the chaos of the macrocosm or the disorder of the witch and the mentally ill, a theory of representation that is profitably viewed through the lens of Neoplatonism or the occult doctrine of sympathy. But more often than not actual music was used to shape these characters, and thus harmonious sounds were deployed to represent discord, and harmony to represent some of the people that most troubled seventeenth- and early eighteenth-century society—witches, the mad, and the melancholic.

Harmony representing discord: this is, perhaps, ironic? It may even be oxymoronic. And yet the music for these disorderly characters, read through the lens of contemporary religious, political, and philosophical discourses, has told us a great deal about the anxieties they provoked for those in seventeenth- and eighteenth-century England. If one might boldly presume to characterize in one word both the ways these entertaining musical purveyors of disorder were represented and their society's response to them the word might be this: ambivalence.

Because of this inherent ambivalence, the music that represents these characters invites multiple interpretations. By design it seduced and titillated and disturbed the listener. The witch dancing her backwards round to innovative, unpredictable, yet rustic music simultaneously entertained and unsettled. The listener could not fully anticipate what notes would come next and was thus kept tantalizingly off balance. In other entertainments, witches danced to cheerful music or sang in a manner that was uncomfortably close to the sacred as they celebrated regicide, clearly demonstrating their moral inversion and their religious (perhaps even Catholic) perversion, even as their music pleased the ear. Likewise, melancholics and mad people behaved in a disconcerting, yet entertaining, manner, performing when they should not, singing bawdy humorous ballads even if they were supposed to be refined gentlemen or pure maids. Later in the century onstage lunatics sang effusive, multi-sectional mad songs that clearly marked their troubling estrangement from musical reason even as it heightened their allure. Like the witches' music, their music was innovative, unpredictable, and tremendously powerful. And this music, as we have seen, could convey a substantial erotic charge when sung by a beautiful actress such as Moll Davis or Anne Bracegirdle. Indeed, erotic titillation was a hallmark of some disorderly music. Possessing many of the same qualities as the singing madwoman, the castrato brought to the early eighteenth-century London stage a new and seductive, yet disturbing, musical presence, one that challenged binary notions of gender. Their music was some of the most beautiful and difficult in the operatic repertory. Yet the possibility that one might be led into promiscuity or even sodomy by their siren songs caused profound discomfort for some in the London audience.

Although ambivalence remained a constant in the musical portrayal of disorder, other elements changed over time. This book also traces the dialogue between changing modes of representation and reception. In the case of the witches' music, listeners in the late seventeenth and early eighteenth century most likely filtered witches' songs and dances through an interpretative apparatus different from that applied by those who listened in the early seventeenth century. In the early seventeenth century, many still believed that real-life witches might possess amazing magical powers. Witches' music often had a realistic quality, reflecting the actual types of music performed by the rural poor—those most likely to be accused of witchcraft. The witches' rustic and grotesque dancing in *The Masque of Queens* might therefore have been full of magical potential for their audience, an almost journalistic representation of the way witches were thought to behave. But as witchcraft belief dissipated among the elite and anti-Catholic sentiment intensified, late seventeenth-century audiences were more likely to have heard the hags' jigs—which were now stylized and elaborate instead of rustic and raw—and their pseudo-sacred regicidal rejoicing as the deluded practices of Papists, divorced from any sort of actual magic.

Likewise, concepts of mental illness changed considerably over the course of the century, and clear lines were drawn between madness and reason. By the beginning of the eighteenth century in England, those suffering from lunacy were placed in asylums to separate them from the general population. Madness was no longer thought to be a representation of a diseased macrocosm, and the madman as sage truth-teller or social critic had largely fallen by the wayside—a relic of an earlier age. By the time we reach John Eccles's Augustan version of "Come Let Us Howle" from *The Duchess of Malfi*, a musical imitation of bestial howling that evoked the chaos of the macrocosm was no longer relevant. Now, sequential melismas represent howling in a rational, orderly fashion. Furthermore, concerns over impropriety consistently inflected discourses about theatrical madness during this period, and frequently in the Age of Reason representations of insanity were sanitized: musical filigree representing howling at one remove, Ophelia's mad songs without the disturbing bawdry.

This book has identified the conventions that composers and playwrights developed to defuse the threat of potentially controversial characters or separate them from "normal" society (witches as popish rustic bumpkins, madmen as effeminate deviants, madwomen as erotic bombshells), but, as we have constantly seen, these strategies of negotiation were never fully successful, and this, perhaps, is what troubled the anti-theatricalists and critics who derided such displays. For even in the stylized and rationalized versions of madness and witchcraft, some auditors left the theater seduced by what they saw and heard: a scrap of a memorable witches' jig hummed by a theatergoer as she left Drury Lane; a groundling at the Globe tapping his toes to Ophelia's mad balladry; a nobleman at Lincoln's Inn Fields infatuated with Bracegirdle's musical burning. In listening, the audience was infected by pleasurable, yet dangerous, sound. The allure of hell translated into harmony proved too strong. In being ravished by music's powers these listeners too became, in some sense, disorderly.

Notes

I. MUSIC AND THE MACROCOSM

1. Thomas Robinson, *The Schoole of Musicke* (London: Printed by Tho. Este for Simon Waterson, 1603), B1ʳ.

2. Samuel Rowley, *When You See Me, You Know Me* (London: Imprinted for Nathaniell Butter, 1605), H1ᵛ.

3. Maravall's book primarily concerns Spain; however, his analysis is also useful for understanding Europe as whole; on crisis see particularly chapter 1 of José Antonio Maravall's *Culture of The Baroque: Analysis of a Historical Structure*, trans. Terry Cochran, vol. 25 of *Theory and History of Literature* (Minneapolis: University of Minnesota Press, 1986). The quotation is from p. 21.

4. Reginald Scot, *The Discoverie of Witchcraft* (London: Imprinted by William Brome, 1584), 52–53.

5. Anthony Harris, *Night's Black Agents: Witchcraft and Magic in Seventeenth-Century English Drama* (Manchester: Manchester University Press, 1980), 16.

6. The useful term "melancho-like" was coined by Rebecca Wilkin in "Feminizing Imagination in France, 1563–1678" (Ph.D. diss., University of Michigan, 2000).

7. On Jorden's philosophy of womb sickness, see Edward Jorden, *A Briefe Discourse of a Disease Called the Suffocation of the Mother* (London: Printed by John Windet, 1603), 19–20; Carol Thomas Neely, " 'Documents in Madness': Reading Madness and Gender in Shakespeare's Tragedies and Early Modern Culture," *Shakespeare Quarterly* 42 (Fall 1991): 319–20 and also her more recent study, *Distracted Subjects: Madness and Gender in Shakespeare and Early Modern Culture* (Ithaca, N.Y.: Cornell University Press, 2004), 81–83; and Wilkin, "Feminizing Imagination in France, 1563–1678," 38.

8. Robert Burton, *The Anatomy of Melancholy*, ed. Holbrook Jackson (New York: New York Review Books, 2001), book 1, 415.

9. Gideon Harvey, *Morbus Anglicus: Or the Anatomy of Consumptions* (London: Printed for William Thackeray, 1672), 21.

10. Sir Thomas Overbury, the Jacobean courtier, made this comment in his influential *The Wife, with Additions of New Characters: And Many Other Witty Conceits Never Before Printed*, which went through numerous editions over the course of the seventeenth century. I consulted the 1664 edition, the "17th impression" (London: Peter Lillicrap for Philip Chetwin, 1664), G6ᵛ.

11. On changing notions of the female role in reproduction, see Wilkin, "Feminizing Imagination in France," 27.

12. On Harvey and the erosion of the one-sex model, see Thomas Laqueur, *Making Sex: Body and Gender from the Greeks to Freud* (Cambridge, Mass.: Harvard University Press, 1990), especially p. 171.

13. As medical theories of gender moved away from older humoral- and temperament-based models, the theory that women were more sensitive than men emerged. This theory distinguished women completely from men, in terms of both biology and psychology, and was largely based on new theories about the nerves; for a discussion of this change see Anthony Fletcher, *Gender, Sex and Subordination in England, 1500–1800* (New Haven, Conn.: Yale University Press, 1995), 292–93. See also Robert Martensen, "The Transformation of Eve:

Women's Bodies, Medicine and Culture in Early Modern England," in *Sexual Knowledge, Sexual Science: The History of Attitudes to Sexuality*, ed. Roy Porter and Mikulas Teich (Cambridge: Cambridge University Press, 1994), 107–133.

14. Gretchen Ludke Finney gives a useful overview of mystical ideas about music in *Musical Backgrounds for English Literature: 1580–1650* (New Brunswick, N.J.: Rutgers University Press, [1962]).

15. For an overview of humoral theory, see Stanley Jackson, *Melancholia and Depression: From Hippocratic Times to Modern Times* (New Haven, Conn.: Yale University Press, 1986), 7–12.

16. Robinson, *The Schoole of Musicke*, B1ʳ.

17. George Marcelline, *The Triumphs of King James the First* (London: Printed . . . for John Budge, 1610), 35.

18. Linda Austern, " 'Alluring the Auditorie to Effeminacy': Music and the Idea of the Feminine in Early Modern England,' " *Music and Letters* 74 (1993): 347–68; " 'Sing Againe Syren': The Female Musician and Sexual Enchantment in Elizabethan Life and Literature," *Renaissance Quarterly* 42 (Autumn 1989): 420–48.

19. Jerzy Limon, *The Masque of Stuart Culture* (Cranbury, N.J.: Associated University Presses, 1990), 55.

20. H. James Jensen, *The Muses' Concord: Literature, Music, and the Visual Arts in the Baroque Age* (Bloomington: Indiana University Press, 1976), 3.

21. Michel Foucault, *The Order of Things: An Archaeology of the Human Sciences* (New York: Vintage Books, 1994), 17.

22. Kevin Sharpe, *Criticism and Compliment: The Politics of Literature in the England of Charles I* (Cambridge: Cambridge University Press, 1987), 199.

23. Kevin Sharpe, *The Personal Rule of Charles I* (New Haven, Conn.: Yale University Press, 1992), 234.

24. Ernst H. Kantorowicz, *The King's Two Bodies: A Study in Mediaeval Political Theology* (Princeton, N.J.: Princeton University Press, 1957).

25. Jonathan Gil Harris, *Foreign Bodies and the Body Politic: Discourses of Social Pathology in Early Modern England* (Cambridge: Cambridge University Press, 1998).

26. Thomas Hobbes, *Leviathan (1651)*, ed. Richard Tuck, Cambridge Texts in the History of Political Thought (Cambridge: Cambridge University Press, 1991), 153.

27. An allegorical representation of the Stuart's whiggish enemy, Lord Shaftesbury, appears after Charles's ascension, demonstrating the persistence of disorder. Dryden and Grabu added Charles's ascension and James II's coronation by Venus at the end of the masque in response to Charles's death in 1685. On the revisions and the politics surrounding *Albion and Albanius*, see Paul Hammond, "Dryden's *Albion and Albanius:* The Apotheosis of Charles II," in *The Court Masque*, ed. David Lindley (Manchester: Manchester University Press, 1984), 169–83.

28. Many scholars have considered the reasons for this paradigm shift. One of the most cogent analyses of the problem remains Katharine Eisaman Maus, " 'Playhouse Flesh and Blood': Sexual Ideology and the Restoration Actress," *ELH* 46, no. 4 (Winter 1979): 595–617. Maus strongly argues that a shift in gender ideology allowed women to be accepted on the public stage.

29. Quoted in Elizabeth Howe, *The First English Actresses: Women and Drama 1660–1700* (Cambridge: Cambridge University Press, 1992), 25–26.

30. Roger Freitas shows how the body of the castrato was thought to be like that of a boy in his article "The Eroticism of Emasculation: Confronting the Baroque Body of the Castrato," *The Journal of Musicology* 20 (Spring 2003): 196–249.

31. William Prynne, *Histriomastix* (London: E. A. and W. I. for Michael Sparke, 1633), 211–12. Prynne cites Stubbes's authority on the matter.

32. Howe, *The First English Actresses*, 26.

33. Peter Stallybrass and Allon White, *The Politics and Poetics of Transgression* (Ithaca, N.Y.: Cornell University Press, 1986), 4–5.

34. I use ca. 1687 as a date for *Dido*, as it almost certainly had a court performance before the performance at Josias Priest's boarding school in 1689.

35. Indeed, Ian Bostridge claims that after the Restoration Catholics (associated with the "evils" of dominion by grace, absolutism, and equivocation) replaced the witch as the defining Other within English culture; *Witchcraft and its Transformations, c. 1650–c. 1750* (Oxford: Clarendon Press, 1997), 102–103.

2. "STAY, YOU IMPERFECT SPEAKERS, TELL ME MORE"

1. All Shakespeare citations in this book are taken from *The Riverside Shakespeare*, ed. G. Blakemore Evans (Boston: Houghton Mifflin Company, 1974).

2. "Imperfect," *The Oxford English Dictionary Online* (accessed 3 February 2005), http://www.oed.com.

3. Witches are frequently mocked for their ignorance of rhetoricians; see Henry Holland, *A Treatise against Witchcraft* (Cambridge: Printed by John Legatt, 1590), E3[r], "Againe, *I* cannot see *how they can be seducers, for they have no Rhetorick, nor any such acts, to seduce men by any coosenage.*"

4. On *Macbeth* and Catholicism, see Garry Wills, *Witches and Jesuits: Shakespeare's Macbeth* (New York: Oxford University Press, 1995). For contemporary treatises that connect witches' charms with Catholic formulas, see particularly Reginald Scot, *Discoverie of Witchcraft* (London: Imprinted by William Brome, 1584); Samuel Harsnett, *A Declaration of Egregious Popish Impostures* (London: Printed by James Roberts, 1603).

5. This chapter focuses exclusively on the hag-type witch. Other types of musical enchantresses are beyond the scope of this study. For the categories of musical magician on the early seventeenth-century stage, see Linda Phyllis Austern, " 'Art to Enchant': Musical Magic and Its Practitioners in English Renaissance Drama," *Journal of the Royal Musical Association* 115 (1990): 191–206.

6. Stephen Orgel, "Call Me Ganymede," in *Impersonations: The Performance of Gender in Shakespeare's England* (Cambridge: Cambridge University Press, 1996), 53–82.

7. On the male travesty performance tradition, see Anthony Harris, *Night's Black Agents*, 158–59.

8. Orgel, *Impersonations*, 110.

9. About the elderly and humoral theory, see Herbert C. Covey, *Images of Older People in Western Art and Society* (New York: Praeger, 1991), 12–13. On gender and heat, see Laqueur, *Making Sex* especially chs. 1–4; and Gail Kern Paster, *The Body Embarrassed: Drama and the Disciplines of Shame in Early Modern England* (Ithaca, N.Y.: Cornell University Press, 1993), 1–22.

10. On the one-sex model of gender, see Laqueur, *Making Sex*, especially pp. 25–26.

11. The one-sex model was the predominant theory of gender until the late seventeenth or early eighteenth century; see Laqueur, *Making Sex*, chs. 1–4. Orgel in *Impersonations*, 18–30, describes the appearance of the one-sex model in several English anatomical tracts from the early seventeenth century, and claims

that such homological arguments were used to "justify the whole range of male domination over women," 25. See also Stephen Greenblatt's discussion in *Shakespearean Negotiations: The Circulation of Social Energy in Renaissance England* (Berkeley: University of California Press, 1988), 76–86.

12. Mikhail Bakhtin, *Rabelais and His World*, trans. Hélène Iswolsky (Bloomington: Indiana University Press, 1984), particularly ch. 4.

13. Francis E. Dolan, *Dangerous Familiars: Representations of Domestic Crime in England, 1550–1700* (Ithaca, N.Y.: Cornell University Press, 1994), 191. Gail Paster analyzes the connection between the witch's teat and the early modern anxiety about maternal power in ch. 5, *The Body Embarrassed*, particularly pp. 244–60. See also Deborah Willis, *Malevolent Nurture: Witch-Hunting and Maternal Power in Early Modern England* (Ithaca, N.Y.: Cornell University Press, 1995).

14. *The Full Tryals, Examination, and Condemnation of Four Notorious Witches*, (London: n.p., 1670), 6.

15. See Natalie Zemon Davis's discussion of the anthropological sources in "Women on Top: Symbolic Sexual Inversion and Political Disorder in Early Modern Europe," in *The Reversible World: Symbolic Inversion in Art and Society*, ed. Barbara A. Babcock (Ithaca, N.Y.: Cornell University Press, 1978), 153.

16. Davis notes, "Play with the concept of the unruly woman is partly a chance for temporary release from traditional and stable hierarchy; but it is *also* a part and parcel of conflict over efforts to change the basic distribution of power within the society," ibid., 154–55.

17. Quoted in James Sharpe, *Instruments of Darkness: Witchcraft in England, 1550–1750* (London: Hamish Hamilton, 1996), 172.

18. On the transgressive power of the real-life witch's voice, see Dolan, *Dangerous Familiars*, 198–203.

19. Curtis Price and Irena Cholij, "Dido's Bass Sorceress," *Musical Times* 127 (1986): 615–18. See also my discussion of the singers for Eccles's and Leveridge's *Macbeth* in the introduction to *Music for Macbeth*, vol. 133 of Recent Researches of the Baroque Era (Middleton, Wisc.: A-R Editions, 2004), ix–x.

20. As Gary Tomlinson points out, Foucault's "magical episteme" of resemblance erroneously prioritizes the visual over the aural, as musical sound was a crucial ingredient for performing magic; see *Music in Renaissance Magic: Toward a Historiography of Others* (Chicago: University of Chicago Press, 1993), 59. On the etymology of incantation see "Incantation," *Oxford English Dictionary Online* (accessed 3 February 2005), http://www.oed.com.

21. Tomlinson discusses occult sympathy and music in *Music in Renaissance Magic*, 48–52, 129–30; see also D. P. Walker, *Spiritual and Demonic Magic from Ficino to Campanella* (University Park: Pennsylvania State University Press, 2000), 3–25; and Finney, *Musical Backgrounds for English Literature* 62–63. Sympathy is discussed at length by Michel Foucault in *The Order of Things*, as part of the premodern paradigm of "resemblance," especially pp. 23–25.

22. Henry [Heinrich] Cornelius Agrippa, *Three Books of Occult Philosophy*, trans. J. F. (London: R. W. for Gregory Moule, 1651), 156. Agrippa is actually glossing the Neoplatonist Marsilio Ficino in this passage; see Tomlinson, *Music in Renaissance Magic*, 64.

23. John Webster, *The Displaying of Supposed Witchcraft* (London: Printed by J. M., 1677), 342–43. It may seem strange that Webster disbelieves in witches yet heartily embraces natural magic and musical sympathy; however, as Thomas Jobe points out, Webster's Renaissance natural magic could provide an alternate, semi-rational explanation for magic, taking the power out of the hands of the Devil and placing it into the hands of the experimentalist; see "The Devil in Restoration Science: The Glanvill-Webster Witchcraft Debate," *ISIS* 72 (September 1981): 343–56.

24. As Linda Austern notes in her discussion of witchcraft on the Renaissance stage, "Infinite evil, then, like infinite good or any infinite desire, could be accomplished through the correct use of the proper sort of music." " 'Art to Enchant,' " 202.

25. The literature on the contrast between masque and antimasque music is vast. See, for example, discussions in David Fuller, "The Jonsonian Masque and Its Music," *Music and Letters* 54 (1973): 442–43; Skiles Howard, *The Politics of Courtly Dancing in Early Modern England*, Massachusetts Studies in Early Modern Culture (Amherst: University of Massachusetts Press, 1998), 110; Limon, *The Masque of Stuart Culture*, 62; David Lindley, "The Politics of Music in the Masque," in *The Politics of the Stuart Court Masque*, ed. David Bevington and Peter Holbrook (Cambridge: Cambridge University Press, 1998), 276; Peter Walls, *Music in the English Courtly Masque, 1604–1640* (Oxford: Clarendon Press, 1996), 132.

26. All quotations from *The Masque of Queens* come from *Ben Jonson: The Complete Masques*, ed. Stephen Orgel, The Yale Ben Jonson (New Haven, Conn.: Yale University Press, 1969).

27. Walls, *Music in the English Courtly Masque*, 78. The inability of the evil to produce music has a long tradition in the western canon. Compare, for example, Hildegard of Bingen's treatment of the Devil (who only speaks) in her medieval morality play, *Ordo Virtutum* (ca. 1151).

28. As Stuart Clark points out, the hags do not only parody religious ritual: they represent an antithetical conception of court life and values; "Inversion, Misrule and the Meaning of Witchcraft," *Past and Present* 87 (1980): 123–24. See also Peter Holbrook, "Jacobean Masques and the Jacobean Peace," in *The Politics of the Stuart Court Masque*, 80.

29. Compare the beginning of Jonson's 5th Charm: "The sticks are a-cross, there can be no loss, / The sage is rotten, the sulfur is gotten," with the witches' exchange in *The Lancashire Witches:* "Here's Sage, that under ground was rotten, / Which thus a-round me I bestow. / Sticks on the Bank a-cross are laid," *The Lancashire Witches*, vol. 4 of *The Complete Works of Thomas Shadwell*, ed. Montague Summers (London: Benjamin Blom Publishers, 1968), 116.

30. Compare this passage to the *Masque of Queens:* "Our magic feature will not rise, / Nor yet the storm! We must repeat / More direful voices far, and beat / The ground with vipers till it sweat." [lines 270–273].

31. Shadwell, *The Lancashire Witches*, 116.

32. Unfortunately, the witches' music does not survive.

33. For a contemporary source that speaks of unruly passions as a "tempest," see Walter Charlton, *A Natural History of the Passions*, 2nd enlarged edition (London: Printed for R. Wellington, 1701), 70.

34. On the significance of the courtly dancing body, see Leeds Barroll, "Inventing the Stuart Masque," in *The Politics of the Stuart Court Masque*, 121–43; Skiles Howard, *The Politics of Courtly Dancing in Early Modern England*, 39–40.

35. For an interesting discussion of the complex relationship between court and country in literature, see Leah S. Marcus, "Politics and Pastoral: Writing the Court on the Countryside," in *Culture and Politics in Early Stuart England*, ed. Kevin Sharpe and Peter Lake (Houndsmills, UK: Macmillan, 1994), 139–59.

36. For descriptions of these rituals and their "rough" music, see Davis, "Women on Top," 167–68; Jean E. Howard, *The Stage and Social Struggle in Early Modern England* (London: Routledge, 1994), 102–103; and Bruce R. Smith, *The Acoustic World of Early Modern England: Attending to the O-Factor* (Chicago: University of Chicago Press, 1999), 154–56.

37. Howard, *The Stage and Social Struggle*, 102–103.

38. Terry Eagleton, *Walter Benjamin: Towards a Revolutionary Criticism*

(London: NLB/Verso, 1981), 148–49. Stallybrass and White discuss Eagleton in *The Politics and Poetics of Transgression*, ch. 1.

39. Wallace Notestein, *A History of Witchcraft in England from 1558 to 1718* (New York: Russell and Russell, 1965); Sharpe, *Instruments of Darkness*; Dolan, *Dangerous Familiars*.

40. On *Newes from Scotland* and *Macbeth*, see Anthony Harris, *Night's Black Agents*, 40.

41. *Newes from Scotland* (1591), ed. G. B. Harrison, vol. 9 of *The Bodley Head Quartos* (London: John Lane, The Bodley Head, 1924), 13–14.

42. Geilles Duncane was the maidservant of David Seaton. Seaton, suspicious of Duncane's nocturnal activities, tortured a confession from her; ibid., 9.

43. This description from Duncane's confession is one of the earliest references to the reel in print; see Francis Collinson, "Reel," *Grove Music Online*, ed. Laura Macy (accessed 10 February 2005), http://www.grovemusic.com.

44. John Wright, "Jew's Harp," *Grove Music Online*, ed. Laura Macy (accessed 10 February 2005), http://www.grovemusic.com.

45. *Newes from Scotland*, 13–14.

46. Many witchcraft treatises ridicule the rhetorical imperfection of witches' charms, even as they grudgingly admit their power. See, for example, Holland, *A Treatise against Witchcraft*, E3ʳ.

47. On round dancing and harmony, see John Stevens, *Words and Music in the Middle Ages: Song, Narrative, Dance and Drama, 1050–1350* (Cambridge: Cambridge University Press, 1986), 159–60.

48. See Stuart Clark, *Thinking with Demons: The Idea of Witchcraft in Early Modern Europe* (Oxford: Clarendon Press, 1997).

49. On clerical objections to the carole, see Stevens, *Words and Music in the Middle Ages*, 159–71; and Christopher Page, *Discarding Images: Reflections on Music and Culture in Medieval France* (Oxford: Clarendon Press, 1993), 52–54.

50. R. B., *The Kingdom of Darkness: Or the History of Daemons, Specters, Witches, Apparitions, Possessions, Disturbances, and Other Wonderful and Supernatural Delusions, Mischievous Feats, and Malicious Impostures of the Devil* (London: Printed for Nath[aniel] Crouch, 1688).

51. John Cutts believes Robert Johnson composed this witches' dance, although he does not believe it was performed in *The Masque of Queens*; see "Robert Johnson and the Court Masque," *Music and Letters* 41 (1960): 115–16. Both Andrew Sabol and Peter Walls connect the dance with *The Masque of Queens*, although Walls avoids attributing it to Johnson; see Walls, *Music in the English Courtly Masque*, 136; and *Four Hundred Songs and Dances from the Stuart Masque*, ed. Andrew Sabol (Providence, R.I.: Brown University Press, 1978), 568. Mary Chan also believes the second witches' dance was performed in *The Masque of Queens*; see *Music in the Theatre of Ben Jonson* (Oxford: Clarendon Press, 1980), 209 n.73.

52. In the keyboard version of this piece, GB-Och. MS Mus. 93 (fol. 15), some of the meter changes were omitted; see the discussion in Walls, *Music in the English Courtly Masque*, 136.

53. The clef in the top part has been modernized. The time signature in the lower part is given as 3/1, an obvious error.

54. Anne Lancashire has argued persuasively that Middleton's play was removed from the stage because of its unflattering parallel to the Essex-Howard divorce case; "*The Witch*: Stage Flop or Political Mistake?," in "*Accompanying the Players*": *Essays Celebrating Thomas Middleton, 1580–1980*, ed. Kenneth Friedenreich, AMS Studies in the Renaissance (New York: AMS Press, 1983), 161–81.

55. Thomas Middleton, *The Witch*, ed. Elizabeth Schafer, *The New Mermaids* (London: A. & C. Black, 1994), 22.

56. Ibid., 35.

57. All quotations are from Middleton, *The Witch*, ed. Elizabeth Schafer.

58. John P. Cutts, "Robert Johnson and the Court Masque," 115–16. For a summary of Renaissance views about the presentation of the aristocratic body, see Barbara Ravelhofer, "Unstable Movement Codes in the Stuart Masque," in *The Politics of the Stuart Court Masque*, 248–49.

59. "Hecate, Come Away," and "Black Spirits and White" were taken from Middleton's play. On this subject, see Nicholas Brooke's commentary in William Shakespeare, *The Tragedy of Macbeth*, ed. Nicholas Brooke, The Oxford Shakespeare (Oxford: Clarendon Press, 1990), 64–66, 225–33. Brooke discusses the relationship between Middleton's *The Witch* and *Macbeth* at length, and posits that Middleton revised the witches' scenes for *Macbeth* first and then reused the music for his play, *The Witch*. Brooke's evidence for this assertion is slight; nevertheless, his discussion of the Hecate problem in *Macbeth* is enlightening.

60. For the typical view of the interpolations into *Macbeth*, see Inga-Stina Ewbank, "The Middle of Middleton," in *The Arts of Performance in Elizabethan and Early Stuart Drama*, ed. Murray Biggs et al. (Edinburgh: Edinburgh University Press, 1991), 157–58.

61. Diane Purkiss makes a similar point; however, she argues that Duncane's performance before the king served to "[affirm] royal power as the privileged spectator and interpreter of a spectacle offering otherness only to be dispelled by legitimate authority." "The All-Singing, All-Dancing Plays of the Jacobean Witch-Vogue: *The Masque of Queens, Macbeth, The Witch*, in *The Witch in History: Early Modern and Twentieth-Century Representations*, ed. Diane Purkiss (London: Routledge, 1996), 200.

62. The playwrights take whole passages from Henry Goodcole's pamphlet, which describes Sawyer's trial, conviction, and execution; see Arthur F. Kinney's introduction to Thomas Dekker, John Ford, and William Rowley, *The Witch of Edmonton* (London: A. & C. Black, 1998), xiii.

63. John Forrest, *The History of Morris Dancing, 1458–1750*, ed. J. A. B. Somerset, vol. 5 of *Studies in Early English Drama* (Toronto: University of Toronto Press, 1999), 168–69. See also Bruce R. Smith's description of the aurally disruptive morris in *The Acoustic World of Early Modern England*, 139–49.

64. In 1618 James issued a proclamation in defense of rural pastimes, "The King's Majesties Declaration to his Subjects concerning Lawfull Sports to be Used," now known as the *Book of Sports*. His son Charles republished it in an attempt to rally his subjects against Puritan reforms; see Forrest, *The History of Morris Dancing*, 140, 202, and Anthony B. Dawson, "Witchcraft/Bigamy: Cultural Conflict in *the Witch of Edmonton*," *Renaissance Drama* 20 (1989): 79.

65. On the unstable alliance between the Stuarts and the rural poor, see David Underdown, *Revel, Riot, and Rebellion: Popular Politics and Culture in England, 1603–1660* (Oxford: Clarendon Press, 1985), 64–72.

66. Forrest, *The History of Morris Dancing*, 3–4.

67. Phillip Stubbes, *The Anatomie of Abuses* (London: Printed . . . by Richard Jones, 1583), M2$^{\mathrm{r-v}}$.

68. Harsnett, *A Declaration of Egregious Popish Impostures*, 49.

69. Although I do not find Dawson's claim that the morris is a symbol of "social cohesion" convincing, I do agree with his reading of its ambivalent presentation within the play; see Dawson, "Witchcraft/Bigamy," 79, 91–93.

70. On the history of the jig, see Charles Read Baskervill, *The Elizabethan Jig and Related Song Drama* (Chicago: University of Chicago Press, 1929).

71. See "Millisons Jegge," "Kemps Jegg," "The Punk's Delight" (also known as "The Jig of 'Garlick' ").

72. *Hic Mulier: or, The Man-Woman: Being a Medicine to Cure the Coltish Disease of the Staggers in the Masculine-Feminine, of our Times* (London, Printed for J. T. [John Trundle], 1620), A4^{r-v}.

73. Laird H. Barber, ed., *An Edition of the Late Lancashire Witches by Thomas Heywood and Richard Brome*, Renaissance Drama: A Collection of Critical Editions (New York: Garland, 1979), 153. This is reminiscent of the witches in Nahum Tate and Henry Purcell's *Dido and Aeneas* (ca. 1687), who want to spoil the courtiers' hunting sport.

74. On the music for Davenant's *Macbeth* see my introduction to *Music for Macbeth*; Roger Fiske, "The *Macbeth* Music," *Music and Letters* 45 (April 1964): 114–25, Robert E. Moore, "The Music to *Macbeth*," *Musical Quarterly* 47 (January 1961): 22–40.

75. The text is not printed with the dance attributed to Locke; however, Robert Moore demonstrates that the words of "Let's Have a Dance" fit with this tune; see Moore, "The Music to *Macbeth*," 26–27.

76. On the jigging actresses, see Howe, *The First English Actresses*, 73.

77. Thomas Mace, *Musick's Monument (1676)*, vol. 17 of Monuments of Music and Music Literature in Facsimile (New York: Broude Brothers, 1966), 129.

78. This excerpt is transposed down an octave from the original source.

79. Citations from Davenant's *Macbeth* are taken from *Five Restoration Adaptations of Shakespeare*, ed. Christopher Spencer (Urbana: University of Illinois Press, 1965).

80. Keith Thomas, *Religion and the Decline of Magic* (London: Weidenfeld and Nicolson, 1971).

81. Scot, *Discoverie of Witchcraft*, 52–53.

82. Webster, *The Displaying of Supposed Witchcraft*, 66.

83. Bostridge traces these changes in *Witchcraft and its Transformations*.

84. Joseph Glanvill, *Saducismus Triumphatus: Or Full and Plain Evidence Concerning Witches and Apparitions* (London: Printed for J. Collins and S. Lownds, 1681), F3^{v}.

85. J. C. D. Clark, *English Society, 1688–1832* (Cambridge: Cambridge University Press, 1985), 169. On Joseph Glanvill and the Restoration debate about witchcraft, see Jackson I. Cope, *Joseph Glanvill: Anglican Apologist* (St. Louis: Washington University Studies, 1956); Jobe, "The Devil in Restoration Science," 343–56.

86. Clefs have been modernized.

87. Clefs have been modernized.

88. Some plays do have an anti-Catholic resonance. The witches in *Macbeth*, for example, may have represented the Jesuits behind the Gunpowder Plot; see Wills, *Witches and Jesuits: Shakespeare's Macbeth*, 8.

89. Paul Seaward, *The Restoration, 1660–1688* (New York: St. Martin's Press, 1991), 61–69.

90. Charles II was married to a Catholic queen, kept Catholic mistresses, and supposedly converted to Catholicism on his deathbed. For late seventeenth-century critiques of Charles's Catholic sympathies see Rachel Weil, "Sometimes a Scepter Is Only a Scepter: Pornography and Politics in Restoration England," in *The Invention of Pornography: Obscenity and the Origins of Modernity, 1500–1800*, ed. Lynn Hunt (New York: Zone Books, 1996), 125–56.

91. Seaward, *The Restoration*, 109. For a sample of anti-Catholic literature, see Titus Oates, *The Witch of Endor; or the Witchcrafts of the Roman Jesebel* (London: Printed for Thomas Parkhurst and Thomas Cockeril, 1679).

92. The conflict continued throughout most of the eighteenth century; see Patricia Crawford, *Women and Religion in England, 1500–1720* (London: Rout-

ledge, 1993), 186–87; and G. V. Bennet, *The Tory Crisis in Church and State, 1688–1730* (Oxford: Clarendon Press, 1975), 5–21, 44–45, 63.

93. Samuel Johnson, "The Church of England as by Law Established," in *A Second Five Years Struggle against Popery and Tyranny* (London: Printed for the author . . . sold by Richard Baldwin, 1689), 45.

94. Oates, *The Witch of Endor,* unpaginated dedication to the Earl of Shaftesbury.

95. Shadwell, *The Lancashire Witches,* 101.

96. Unfortunately, none of the witches' music survives; for the song text, see Shadwell, *The Lancashire Witches,* 115.

97. Ibid., 101.

98. Ibid., 116. I am grateful to Steven Plank for this observation.

99. Clefs have been modernized.

100. Clefs have been modernized.

101. Jack Westrup, "A Flawed Masterpiece," in *Dido and Aeneas: An Opera,* ed. Curtis Price (New York: W. W. Norton, 1986), 197.

102. Wilfrid Mellers, "The Tragic Heroine and the Un-Hero," in *Dido and Aeneas: An Opera,* 208–209.

103. Steven E. Plank, " 'And Now about the Cauldron Sing': Music and the Supernatural on the Restoration Stage," *Early Music* 18 (1990): 396.

104. Weil, "Sometimes a Scepter Is Only a Scepter," 136–37.

105. On the witches as symbols of disorder on the Restoration stage see Bruce Wood and Andrew Pinnock, " 'Unscarr'd by Turning Times'? The Dating of Purcell's *Dido and Aeneas,*" *Early Music* 20 (1992): 373–90; Curtis Price, "*Dido and Aeneas* in Context," in *Dido and Aeneas: An Opera,* 3–41; Mellers, "The Tragic Heroine and the Un-Hero," 204–213; John Buttrey, "A Cautionary Tale," in *Dido and Aeneas: An Opera,* 228–35; Joanne Altieri, *The Theatre of Praise: The Panegyric Tradition in Seventeenth-Century English Drama* (Newark: University of Delaware Press, 1986), 31–32.

106. Virgil, *The Aeneid,* trans. Edward McCrorie (Ann Arbor: University of Michigan Press, 1995), 91.

107. Richard Fanshawe, *Il Pastor Fido: The Faithfull Shepheard with an Addition of Divers Other Poems,* (London: Printed for Humphrey Moseley, 1648), 291.

108. Ibid., 292.

109. Ibid., 292.

110. Andrew Pinnock, "Book IV in Plain Brown Wrappers: Translations and Travesties of Dido," in *A Woman Scorn'd: Responses to the Dido Myth,* ed. Michael Burden (London: Faber and Faber, 1998), 249–71.

111. John Dryden, *Virgil's Aeneid (1697),* ed. Frederick M. Keener (London: Penguin Books, 1997), 108.

112. Buttrey believed that *Dido* was performed in 1689 and was an allegory of William's mistreatment of the popular Queen Mary; see "A Cautionary Tale," 232. Price originally followed Buttrey's suggestion, but nuanced his reading with more historical evidence and posited that the witches represented the Roman Catholic threat to the kingdom; see "*Dido and Aeneas* in Context," 3–4. Price recently renounced his previous interpretation in "*Dido and Aeneas:* Questions of Style and Evidence," *Early Music* 22 (1994): 122, to refute Andrew Pinnock and Bruce Wood's interpretation in " 'Unscarr'd by Turning Times,' " 373–90. Pinnock and Wood, like Andrew Walkling, have suggested that the opera was performed earlier than 1689; for Walkling's reading connecting the opera with pro-Catholic policies of James II, see "Politics and the Restoration Masque: The Case of *Dido and Aeneas,*" in *Culture and Society in the Stuart Restoration: Literature, Drama, History,* ed. Gerald MacLean (Cambridge: Cambridge University Press,

1995), 52–69; and "Political Allegory in Purcell's *Dido and Aeneas,*" *Music and Letters* 76 (November 1995): 540–71.

113. Thomas D'Urfey, "Epilogue to the Opera of DIDO and AENEAS, performed at Mr. *Preist's* Boarding School at *Chelsey:* Spoken by the Lady *Dorothy Burk,*" in *New Poems, consisting of Satyrs, Elegies, and Odes* (London: J. Bullord and A. Roper, 1690), 83.

114. Wood and Pinnock, " 'Unscarr'd by Turning Times,' " 374–75.

115. Ibid., 374.

116. Following Thurston Dart and Margaret Laurie's edition, I am using the act divisions from the 1689 libretto, not the Tenbury manuscript. All the measure number references are taken from *Dido and Aeneas,* ed. Margaret Laurie and Thurston Dart, as reprinted in the Norton Critical Score, *Dido and Aeneas: An Opera.*

117. In "Hecate, Come Away," the situation is reversed, as Hecate's coven sings to summon their leader.

118. For Roger Savage's reading of the opera, see "Producing Dido and Aeneas," in *Dido and Aeneas: An Opera,* 255–77.

119. For examples of such critiques, see Jonas Barish's *The Antitheatrical Prejudice* (Berkeley: University of California Press, 1981).

3. "REMEMBER ME, BUT AH, FORGET MY FATE"

1. I am not completely disagreeing with Heller and Schmalfeldt; rather, I suggest an alternative frame through which we can interpret Dido's character. For their fascinating arguments, see Wendy Heller, " 'A Present for the Ladies': Ovid, Montaigne, and the Redemption of Purcell's Dido," *Music and Letters* 84, no. 2 (2003): 189–208; and Janet Schmalfeldt, "In Search of Dido," *The Journal of Musicology* 18, no. 4 (Fall 2001): 584–615.

2. "Erotic melancholy," "lovesickness," and "erotomania" were common terms for this ailment during the early modern period. See, for example, James [Jacques] Ferrand, *Erotomania: Or a Treatise Discoursing of the Essence, Causes, Symptomes, Prognosticks, and Cure of Love or Erotique Melancholy,* trans. E. Chilmead (Oxford: L. Lichfield, 1640). All citations from Ferrand (originally published in Paris in 1623) are from the 1640 English translation from the French by Edmund Chilmead. Many treatises on lovesickness, melancholy, and madness circulated at the time, and it is a testament to Ferrand's popularity that his work was chosen for translation. On Ferrand's influence on English thought, see Donald A. Beecher and Massimo Ciavolella, "Introduction," in *Jacques Ferrand, a Treatise on Lovesickness,* ed. Donald A. Beecher and Massimo Ciavolella (Syracuse, N.Y.: Syracuse University Press, 1990), 15.

3. On female lasciviousness and lovesickness, see Harvey, *Morbus Anglicus,* 20–25.

4. Richard Brathwaite, *The English Gentleman; and the English Gentlewoman: Both in One Volume Couched* (London: Printed by John Dawson, 1641), 320.

5. Richard Allestree, *The Ladies Calling* (Oxford: n.p., 1673), 6–7.

6. Susan McClary has identified the tendency to give scenes of madness a rational, masculine frame in order to set the feminine excess apart from the male spectator; see "Excess and Frame: The Musical Representation of Madwomen" in *Feminine Endings: Music, Gender, and Sexuality* (Minneapolis: University of Minnesota Press, 1991), 80–111.

7. Laurent Joubert, *The Second Part of the Popular Errors (1587)*, trans. Gregory David de Rocher (Tuscaloosa: University of Alabama Press, 1995), 51.

8. Jacques Ferrand, *Erotomania*, 214–15.

9. Michael MacDonald, *Mystical Bedlam: Madness, Anxiety, and Healing in Seventeenth-Century England* (Cambridge: Cambridge University Press, 1981), 73.

10. On women's exclusion from the more positive melancholic tradition, see Laurinda Dixon, *Perilous Chastity: Women and Illness in Pre-Enlightenment Art and Medicine* (Ithaca, N.Y.: Cornell University Press, 1995); and Juliana Schiesari, *The Gendering of Melancholia: Feminism, Psychoanalysis, and the Symbolics of Loss in Renaissance Literature* (Ithaca, N.Y.: Cornell University Press, 1992).

11. For a dissertation on this subject, see Jorden, *A Briefe Discourse of a Disease Called the Suffocation of the Mother.*

12. The published sermons of the seventeenth-century Dissenter Richard Baxter state that "sinful Pleasure" and the "Baits of Lust" caused melancholy; "The Cure of Melancholy and Overmuch Sorrow by Faith and Physick," in *A Continuation of Morning-Exercise Questions and Cases of Conscience, Practically Resolved by Sundry Ministers* (London: Printed by J. A. for John Dunton, 1683), 282. See also Richard Baxter, *The Signs and Causes of Melancholy*, ed. Samuel Clifford (Glasgow: John Robertson & Mrs. McLean, 1749), published posthumously; and Harvey, *Morbus Anglicus*, 44.

13. Ferrand, *Erotomania*, 61.

14. For this reason, parents were advised not to oppose marriages; see Fletcher, *Gender, Sex and Subordination in England*, 52.

15. Burton, *Anatomy of Melancholy*, book 1, 234–35. William Ramesey also discussed this in his conduct book, *The Gentleman's Companion: Or, a Character of True Nobility and Gentility* (London: n.p., 1672), 175–77.

16. Burton, *The Anatomy of Melancholy*, book 3, 187.

17. Ellen Rosand, "The Descending Tetrachord: An Emblem of Lament," *Musical Quarterly* 65 (July 1979): 346–59.

18. Ibid., 349.

19. Ibid., 350.

20. Suzanne Cusick, " 'There Was Not One Lady Who Failed to Shed a Tear': Arianna's Lament and the Construction of Modern Womanhood," *Early Music* 22 (Februrary 1994): 22.

21. Wendy Heller, *Emblems of Eloquence: Opera and Women's Voices in Seventeenth-Century Venice* (Berkeley: University of California Press, 2003), 84.

22. Cusick, " 'There Was Not One Lady Who Failed to Shed a Tear,' " 25.

23. All quotations are from *Cynthia's Revels* in *Ben Jonson*, ed. C. H. Herford and Percy Simpson, vol. 4 (Oxford: Clarendon Press, 1932).

24. For a discussion of Youll's setting, see Chan, *Music in the Theatre of Ben Jonson*, 54.

25. Mario Digangi, " 'Male Deformities': Narcissus and the Reformation of Courtly Manners in *Cynthia's Revels*," in *Ovid and the Renaissance Body*, ed. Goran V. Stanivukovic (Toronto: University of Toronto Press, 2001), 98–99.

26. Linda Austern, " 'No Women Are Indeed': The Boy Actor as Vocal Seductress in Late Sixteenth- and Early Seventeenth-Century English Drama," in *Embodied Voices: Representing Female Vocality in Western Culture*, ed. Leslie C. Dunn and Nancy A. Jones (Cambridge: Cambridge University Press, 1994), 83–102; Orgel, *Impersonations.*

27. Levine considers this problem in her brilliant study, *Men in Women's Clothing: Anti-Theatricality and Effeminization, 1579–1642* (Cambridge: Cambridge University Press, 1994).

28. "Ingle," *Oxford English Dictionary Online* (accessed 18 February 2005), http://www.oed.com.

29. "Crack," *Oxford English Dictionary Online* (accessed 28 February 2004), http://www.oed.com.

30. On *Cynthia's Revels* as social critique, see Digangi, " 'Male Deformities,' " 94–110.

31. F. W. Sternfeld, *Music in Shakespearean Tragedy* (London: Routledge and Kegan Paul, 1963), 32. On the various manuscript sources for Desdemona's "Willow Song," see Peter J. Seng, "The Earliest Known Music for Desdemona's 'Willow Song,' " *Shakespeare Quarterly* 9, no. 1 (Winter 1958): 419–20. As Seng notes, this ballad certainly did not originate with Shakespeare. Earlier versions in lute tablature of the music occur in Thomas Dallis's manuscript Lute Book (1583), Trinity College, Dublin. Seng claims the earliest setting of the "Willow Song," also in lute tablature, is in Folger MS. V.a.I.59 (olim 448.16, fol. 19) (ca. 1572). John Ward dates fragments found in Drexel 4183 (discovered by Thurston Dart) and fragments in the Case Western Reserve library to the 1530s or '40s; see John M. Ward, "Joan Qd John and Other Fragments at Western Reserve University," in *Aspects of Medieval and Renaissance Music: A Birthday Offering to Gustave Reese*, ed. Jan LaRue (New York: W. W. Norton, 1966), 852. A more recent discussion of the sources for the "Willow Song" can be found in Ross W. Duffin's *Shakespeare's Songbook* (New York: W. W. Norton, 2004), 469–70.

32. Peter Seng, *The Vocal Songs in the Plays of Shakespeare: A Critical History* (Cambridge: Harvard University Press, 1967), 195. Duffin notes that two unregistered broadsides from the early seventeenth century also have texts similar to Shakespeare's; *Shakespeare's Songbook*, 469.

33. For a comparison of the text in GB-Lbl. Add. MS 15117 with the text sung by Desdemona, see Ernest Brennecke, " 'Nay, That's Not Next!' The Significance of Desdemona's 'Willow Song,' " *Shakespeare Quarterly* 4, no. 1 (January 1953): 35–38.

34. In measure 8 of the manuscript notes 1–2 are e'. I have corrected this obvious error.

35. For numerous examples of this iconographic trope, see Dixon, *Perilous Chastity*.

36. John M. Major, "Desdemona and Dido," *Shakespeare Quarterly* 10, no. 1 (Winter 1959): 123–25.

37. Linda Austern, "Thomas Ravenscroft: Musical Chronicler of an Elizabethan Theater Company," *Journal of the American Musicological Society* 38 (1985): 258–63; Rochelle Smith, "Admirable Musicians: Women's Songs in *Othello* and *The Maid's Tragedy*," *Comparative Drama* 28, no. 3 (Fall 1994): 311–23.

38. Rochelle Smith, "Admirable Musicians," 320.

39. Henry Jackson's reaction from 1610 suggests the potency of the boy actor's portrayal of Desdemona: "Desdemona, killed in front of us by her husband, although she acted her part excellently throughout, in her death moved us especially when, as she lay in her bed, with her face alone she implored the pity of the audience"; quoted in Anthony B. Dawson, "Performance and Participation: Desdemona, Foucault, and the Actor's Body," in *Shakespeare, Theory, and Performance*, ed. James C. Bulman (London: Routledge, 1996), 35.

40. Quotations are taken from Francis Beaumont and John Fletcher, *The Maid's Tragedy*, ed. T. W. Craik, The Revels Plays (Manchester: Manchester University Press, 1988).

41. Rochelle Smith makes a similar point in "Admirable Musicians," 318–20.

42. On Aspatia's masochism and self-involvement, see Cristina León Alfar,

"Staging the Feminine Performance of Desire: Masochism in *The Maid's Tragedy,*" *Papers on Language and Literature* 31, no. 3 (Summer 1995): 313–33; William Shullenberger, " 'This for the Most Wrong'd of Women': A Reappraisal of *The Maid's Tragedy,*" *Renaissance Drama* 13 (1982): 131–56.

43. John H. Long discusses this tradition in *Shakespeare's Use of Music: The Final Comedies* (New York: Da Capo Press, 1977), 20–21.

44. Burton, *The Anatomy of Melancholy,* book 2, 118.

45. Wilson, born in 1595, would have only been nine years old at the time of the first production. See Ian Spink, "John Wilson," *Grove Music Online,* ed. Laura Macy (accessed 9 December 2003), http://www.grovemusic.com.

46. Seng, *The Vocal Songs in the Plays of Shakespeare,* 182.

47. Curtis Price, *Henry Purcell and the London Stage* (Cambridge: Cambridge University Press, 1984), 22.

48. Quotations taken from *The Renegado* in *The Plays and Poems of Philip Massinger,* ed. Philip Edwards and Colin Gibson, vol. 2 (Oxford: Clarendon Press, 1976).

49. For an example of the empowered musical female argument, see Leslie C. Dunn, "Ophelia's Songs in *Hamlet:* Music, Madness, and the Feminine," in *Embodied Voices: Representing Female Vocality in Western Culture,* ed. Leslie C. Dunn and Nancy A. Jones (Cambridge: Cambridge University Press, 1994), 63–64.

50. Elaine Showalter notes that contemporaries would have recognized that Ophelia suffered from erotomania, resulting from Hamlet's rejection; see "Representing Ophelia: Women, Madness, and the Responsibilities of Feminist Criticism," in *Shakespeare and the Question of Theory,* ed. Patricia Parker and Geoffrey Hartman (New York: Methuen, 1985), 81.

51. Jacquelyn Fox-Good makes a similar claim in "Ophelia's Mad Songs: Music, Gender, Power," in *Subjects on the World's Stage: Essays on British Literature of the Middle Ages and Renaissance,* ed. David G. Allen and Robert A. White (Newark: University of Delaware Press, 1995), 217–38. Fox-Good uses French feminist theory to recover Ophelia's voice and does a close reading of the surviving music. The problem with Fox-Good's approach is that it reifies the musical text; she acknowledges that the musical sources for Ophelia's songs are fluid, but eventually her entire thesis rests on a close reading of a musical score. Leslie Dunn also makes a similar argument (although she does not attempt a close musical analysis of Ophelia's songs) in "Ophelia's Songs in *Hamlet,*" 50–64.

52. Duffin, *Shakespeare's Songbook,* 18.

53. Baldassare Castiglione, *The Book of the Courtier,* trans. Sir Thomas Hoby (London: J. M. Dent and Sons, 1974), 194. Castiglione's *Courtier* was first published in 1528 and was translated into English by Hoby in 1561.

54. Sternfeld comments on the transgression of female public musical performance; see *Music in Shakespearean Tragedy,* 54–57.

55. The music for "Walsingham" exists in numerous sixteenth- and seventeenth-century sources, but I accept F. W. Sternfeld's suggestion that the version for orpharion found in William Barley's *A New Book of Tablature* (1596) is the most appropriate for solo song performance (Shakespeare's text fits quite neatly if one detaches the treble from the lower voices). Other versions, such as those by Byrd and Bull, are less conducive to adaptation for solo performance. See Sternfeld, "Ophelia's Version of the Walsingham Song," *Music and Letters* 45 (1964): 108–113. Duffin reproduces a version of Byrd's "Walsingham" from *My Lady Nevells Booke* (1591) in *Shakespeare's Songbook,* 423.

56. Although the earliest source for this song dates from eighteenth-century Drury Lane productions of *Hamlet,* the tune actually is a version of a melody current at Shakespeare's time, "The Soldier's Life" or "The Soldier's Dance." It

is therefore possible that Ophelia's plaint would have been sung to a version of this tune in the early seventeenth century. See Duffin, *Shakespeare's Songbook*, 408. Duffin reproduces a version of the melody based on a keyboard setting attributed to William Byrd in Paris Conservatoire MS Rés. 1186 (ca. 1630–40). The tune was also reprinted in several editions of John Playford's *English Dancing Master*. On the version from Drury Lane see Sternfeld, *Music in Shakespearean Tragedy*, 63.

57. Seng, *The Vocal Songs in the Plays of Shakespeare*, 150. This snippet may have been sung to the "Bonny Sweet Robin" tune, discussed below; see Duffin, *Shakespeare's Songbook*, 72–73. Duffin believes that the "hey nonny" refrain, found in the Folio of 1623, is a later interpolation or an aside.

58. Sternfeld, *Music in Shakespearean Tragedy*, 68; see also Duffin, *Shakespeare's Songbook*, 72–73.

59. Sternfeld, *Music in Shakespearean Tragedy*, 69.

60. Ibid., 58.

61. This song does not have an extant seventeenth-century version. A traditional version exists in the eighteenth-century Drury Lane copy; see Sternfeld, *Music in Shakespearean Tragedy*, 67.

62. On women as watery and leaky vessels, see Paster, *The Body Embarrassed*, ch. 1.

63. Elaine Showalter, "Representing Ophelia," 81.

64. For an excellent discussion of how the Jailer's Daughter represents contemporary ideas about female lovesickness, see Neely, *Distracted Subjects*, 83–91.

65. S[arah] F[yge], *The Female Advocate: or, an Answer to a late Satyr against the Pride, Lust and Inconstancy of Woman* (London: H. C. for John Taylor, 1686), unpaginated preface.

66. Michel Foucault, in his groundbreaking study, *Madness and Civilization*, noted what he called "the Great Confinement," claiming that attitudes toward madness shifted in the mid seventeenth century. Madness, which in the past could be seen in every village, every town, and on the European stage, was subjected to an increasingly rigorous confinement, as exemplified by the rise of the "mad house" in both England and France; Michel Foucault, *Madness and Civilization: A History of Insanity in the Age of Reason*, trans. Richard Howard (New York: Vintage Books, 1988). See particularly ch. 2, "The Great Confinement."

67. Howe, *The First English Actresses*, 21.

68. William Van Lennep, *The London Stage 1660–1800, Part 1: 1660–1700* (Carbondale: Southern Illinois University Press, 1960), 83, 124. The first cast of *The Rivals* (1664) listed Mrs. Gosnell in the role of Celania.

69. John Downes, *Roscius Anglicanus*, ed. Judith Milhous and Robert D. Hume (London: Society for Theatre Research, 1987), 55. Milhous and Hume note that Charles II definitely saw a performance of the play on 19 November 1667.

70. Unfortunately, very few of these songs are extant. The only music from the show that remains is "Under the Willow Shades They Were," a song for another character, Theocles (*New Ayres and Dialogues*, 1678), and "My Lodging it is on the Cold Ground," a popular tune that exists in many printed collections.

71. Jeremy Collier, the infamous anti-theatricalist, both recognized and rejected the onstage transgression of idealized female behavior, taking particular exception to mad scenes, which, he believed, allowed women's "Impudence" to be "screened from Censure"; see *A Short View of the Immorality and Profaneness of the English Stage, Together with the Sense of Antiquity Upon This Argument* (London: Printed for S. Keble . . . R. Sare . . . and H. Hindmarsh, 1698), 7–11.

72. Anne Bracegirdle was one of the most popular singers and actresses of

her generation. She studied voice with John Eccles and was particularly known for her performances of mad songs as well as her breeches roles. During the peak of her career (ca. 1690–1707), much ink was spilled speculating about her chastity or lack thereof; see Philip H. Highfill Jr., Kalman A. Burnim, Edward A. Langhans, s.v. "Bracegirdle, Anne," in *A Biographical Dictionary of Actors, Actresses, Musicians, Dancers, Managers, and Other Stage Personnel in London, 1660–1800*, vol. 2 (Carbondale: Southern Illinois University Press, 1973), 269–81.

73. Howe, *The First English Actresses*, 22.

74. William Mountfort was murdered on 10 December 1692 by a Captain Hill, who believed the actor was having an affair with Bracegirdle; see Howe, *The First English Actresses*, 83.

75. On Bracegirdle as a sexual object, see Howe, *The First English Actresses*, 35–36, and Cynthia Lowenthal, "Sticks and Rags, Bodies and Brocade: Essentializing Discourses and the Late Restoration Playhouse," in *Broken Boundaries: Women and Feminism in Restoration Drama*, ed. Katherine M. Quinsey, 219–33 (Lexington: University Press of Kentucky, 1996), 220.

76. Thomas D'Urfey, "Dramatis Personae," *The Comical History of Don Quixote, Part I* (London: Printed for Samuel Briscoe, 1694).

77. Price makes the connection between the death of Mountfort and the death of Chrysostome in *Don Quixote, Part I*; see *Henry Purcell and the London Stage*, 210.

78. Ibid.

79. D'Urfey, *Don Quixote, Part I*, 21.

80. Thomas D'Urfey, "*The Representers Names, and Characters*," *The Comical History of Don Quixote, Part II* (London: Printed for Samuel Briscoe, 1694).

81. D'Urfey, "The Preface," *Don Quixote, Part II*.

82. D'Urfey, "The Preface," *Don Quixote, Part II*.

83. Ibid., 60.

84. Ibid.

85. Ibid.

86. See Curtis Price's discussion of Finger's and Purcell's musical responses to Bracegirdle in *Henry Purcell and the London Stage*, 86–89.

87. In *Deliciae Musicae* Bracegirdle's name is misspelled "Bracegidle."

88. Price, *Henry Purcell and the London Stage*, 88.

89. On *Dido and Aeneas* as a morality play, see Ellen Harris, *Henry Purcell's Dido and Aeneas* (Oxford: Clarendon Press, 1987).

90. Virgil, *The Aeneid*, trans. McCrorie, 79–97.

91. Heller makes the argument that elements of other, non-Virgilian versions of Dido shape Tate's sympathetic portrayal. The Dido found in Ovid had, according to Heller, a particular influence on the libretto; " 'A Present for the Ladies,' " particularly from p. 198 onward. See also Schmalfeldt, "In Search of Dido," 613.

92. The ballad was immensely popular and was reprinted numerous times throughout the seventeenth century; see Duffin, *Shakespeare's Songbook*, 321–25.

93. This translation, first published in 1596, went through several editions. I consulted Thomas Phaer and Thomas Twyne, *The Thirteene Bookes of Aeneidos* (London: Printed by Bernard Alsop, by the Assignement of Clement Knight, 1620), F2ᵛ.

94. For a discussion of the bawdy parodies of Dido's lustful nature, see Pinnock, "Book IV in Plain Brown Wrappers," 249–71.

95. Ferrand, *Erotomania*, 107–108.

96. Burton, *Anatomy of Melancholy*, book 3, 134.

97. On the types of music thought to cure melancholy, see Linda Phyllis

Austern, " 'No Pill's Gonna Cure My Ill': Gender, Erotic Melancholy and Traditions of Musical Healing in the Modern West," in *Musical Healing in Cultural Contexts*, ed. Penelope Gouk (Aldershot, U.K.: Ashgate/Scolar Press, 2000), 115.

98. Burton, *Anatomy of Melancholy*, book 3, 228.

99. Michael Burden presents an alternative reading. He disagrees that Tate expected his audience to fill in the blanks from Virgil. Rather, "she [Dido] is presented by Tate as a virginal queen, thus allowing a more momentous interpretation of the moment she yields to Aeneas." Whatever Tate's intentions were in omitting mention of Dido's widowhood (and this, we can never know), it seems plausible that a seventeenth-century educated audience would have compared Purcell and Tate's *Dido* with her classical counterpart. For Burden's argument, see " 'Great Minds against Themselves Conspire': Purcell's Dido as a Conspiracy Theorist," in *A Woman Scorn'd: Responses to the Dido Myth*, 232.

100. See Price, "*Dido and Aeneas* in Context," 22, and Burden, " 'Great Minds against Themselves Conspire,' " 234.

101. *The Diall of Destiny* (London: Imprinted by Thomas Marshe, 1581), fols. 62–63. Quoted in Robin Headlam Wells, *Elizabethan Mythologies: Studies in Poetry, Drama, and Music* (Cambridge: Cambridge University Press, 1994), 196.

102. Burton, *Anatomy of Melancholy*, book 3, 187.

103. Heller, " 'A Present for the Ladies,' " 207.

104. Susan McClary, "Excess and Frame," 80–111, and Ellen Rosand, "Operatic Madness: A Challenge to Convention," in *Music and Text: Critical Inquiries* (Cambridge: Cambridge University Press, 1992), 241–87.

4. "O LET US HOWLE SOME HEAVY NOTE"

1. On appropriate behavior for men, see Jacqueline Pearson, *The Prostituted Muse: Images of Women and Women Dramatists, 1642–1737* (New York: Harvester-Wheatsheaf, 1988), 69; and Anthony Fletcher, "Effeminacy and Manhood," and "The Construction of Masculinity," in *Gender, Sex, and Subordination in England*, 83–98, 322–46.

2. T[imothy] Bright, *A Treatise of Melancholie: Containing the Causes Thereof, & Reasons of the Strange Effects It Worketh in Our Minds and Bodies* (London: Imprinted . . . by Thomas Vautrolier, 1586), 1–2.

3. For the symptoms associated with natural melancholy, see Bright, *A Treatise of Melancholie*, 2; and Burton, *Anatomy of Melancholy*, book 1, 398–99. The quotation is from Burton.

4. Burton, *Anatomy of Melancholy*, book 1, 383.

5. Bright, *A Treatise of Melancholie*, 2.

6. For an excellent summary of the causes and symptoms of melancholy, see Lawrence Babb, *The Elizabethan Malady: A Study of Melancholia in English Literature from 1580 to 1642* (East Lansing: Michigan State College Press, 1951).

7. Ferrand, *Erotomania*, 17.

8. Roy Porter, *Mind-Forg'd Manacles* (London: Athlone Press, 1987), 22. Some considered all musicians to be mad: "in comes music at one ear, out goes wit at another," Burton, *The Anatomy of Melancholy*, book 1, 116.

9. Excerpts from Aristotle's *Problemata* are reprinted by Raymond Klibansky, Erwin Panofsky, and Fritz Saxl in *Saturn and Melancholy: Studies in the History of Natural Philosophy, Religion, and Art* (New York: Basic Books, 1964), 18–29.

10. Andreas Laurentius, *A Discourse of the Preservation of the Sight; of Melancholike Diseases; of Rheumes, and of Old Age* (London: Imprinted by Felix Kingston for Ralph Jacson, 1599), 86.

11. Burton, *The Anatomy of Melancholy*, book 1, 383–84.

12. Laurentius, *A Discourse of the Preservation of the Sight*, 86.

13. Porter, *Mind-Forg'd Manacles*, 22. See also MacDonald, *Mystical Bedlam*.

14. On the tradition of Elizabethan melancholy and its relationship to Dowland, see Wells, 189–207; Anthony Rooley, "New Light on John Dowland's Songs of Darkness," *Early Music* 11 (1983): 153–65; and Peter Holman, *Dowland: Lachrimae (1604)*, Cambridge Music Handbooks (Cambridge: Cambridge University Press, 1999), 50–52.

15. See particularly Austern's " 'Alluring the Auditorie to Effeminacie,' " 343–54.

16. See Ann Rosalind Jones and Peter Stallybrass, "Fetishizing Gender: Constructing the Hermaphrodite in Renaissance Europe," in *Body Guards: The Cultural Politics of Gender Ambiguity*, ed. Julia Epstein and Kristina Straub (New York: Routledge, 1991), 97.

17. Stubbes, *The Anatomie of Abuses*, sig. O5^r.

18. Thomas Morley, *A Plaine and Easie Introduction to Practicall Musicke* (London: Imprinted . . . by Peter Short, 1597), 177. Morley is paraphrasing Zarlino's *Institutioni harmoniche*, IV, ch. 32; see *Music in the Western World: A History in Documents*, selected and annotated by Piero Weiss and Richard Taruskin (New York: Schirmer Books, 1984), 144.

19. Charles Butler, *The Principles of Musik, in Singing and Setting: With the Two-Fold Use Therof, [Ecclesiasticall and Civil]* (London: Printed by John Haviland, 1636), 96.

20. See John Playford's discussion of the affective properties of the modes, *An Introduction to the Skill of Musick (1674)*, facsimile of the 7th ed. (Ridgewood, N.J.: Gregg Press, 1966), 61; Henry Purcell, ed., *John Playford, An Introduction to the Skill of Musick (1694)*, facsimile 12th ed. (New York: Da Capo Press, 1972), 41; William Holder, *Treatise of the Natural Grounds and Principals of Harmony (1694)*, facsimile ed. (New York: Broude Brothers, 1967), 197–99; and Mace, *Musick's Monument*, 2–3.

21. Prynne is quoting the Church Father Clement of Alexandria; see *Histriomastix*, 275.

22. Collier, *A Short View of the Immorality and Profaneness of the English Stage*, 279–80.

23. Jonathan Gil Harris, *Foreign Bodies and the Body Politic*, 2.

24. See Jonathan Gil Harris, *Foreign Bodies and the Body Politic*, and Duncan Salkeld, *Madness and Drama in the Age of Shakespeare* (Manchester: Manchester University Press, 1993), 60.

25. As Lawrence Babb suggests, the malcontent was a frequent presence in seventeenth-century culture, where "he represents a popular conception of melancholy in which the two melancholic traditions [the positive and the negative] are fused." Babb, *The Elizabethan Malady*, 76.

26. All citations are from John Marston, *The Malcontent and Other Plays*, ed. Keith Sturgess, The World's Classics (Oxford: Oxford University Press, 1997).

27. On the relationship of these analogies to *The Malcontent*, see Christian Kiefer, "Music and Marston's *The Malcontent*," *Studies in Philology* 51 (1954): 164.

28. For a detailed examination of the early modern concept of disease and the body politic, see Jonathan Gil Harris, *Foreign Bodies and the Body Politic*, 19–75.

29. Agrippa, *Three Books of Occult Philosophy*, 257.

30. Elise Bickford Jorgens notes the early modern use of onstage music to nurture rather than cure melancholy and places this tendency within the anti-theatricalists' polemic about the abuse of music; see "The Singer's Voice in Eliz-

abethan Drama," in *Renaissance Rereadings: Intertext and Context*, ed. Anne J. Cruz, Maryanne Cline Horowitz, and Wendy A. Furman (Urbana: University of Illinois Press, 1988), 38–40.

31. Babb, *The Elizabethan Malady*, 17–19.

32. Philip Barrough, *The Method of Physick, Containing the Causes, Signes, and Cures of Inward Diseases in Mans Body, from the Head to the Foote*, 7th ed. (London: Printed by George Miller, 1634), 45.

33. On the proper types of music and performance for noblemen in seventeenth-century England, see Penelope Gouk, *Music, Science and Natural Magic in Seventeenth-Century England* (New Haven, Conn.: Yale University Press, 1999), 34. As Gouk notes, the most fundamental convention was that music making be a private activity. For these noblemen to sing in public, then, was another signifier of their mental disorder.

34. Castiglione, *The Book of the Courtier*, 100.

35. The broadside ballad quoted by Falstaff and Malevole was sung to the tune "Flying Fame," also known as "Chevy Chace." The text of the ballad details the heroic exploits of Arthur, but also makes prominent mention of the man who cuckolded him, "Sir Lancelot du Lake." For more on this ballad, see Seng, *The Vocal Songs in the Plays of Shakespeare*, 44–46; and Duffin, *Shakespeare's Songbook*, 435–37.

36. "Pox" was omitted in all printed editions. Either it was censored or Marston himself cut it; see Marston, *The Malcontent*, 399.

37. All citations are from John Webster, *The Duchess of Malfi*, ed. Brian Gibbons, 4th ed., New Mermaids (London: A. & C. Black, 2001).

38. Lynn Enterline also notices the Duchess's resistance. However, Enterline believes the Duchess succumbs to the contagion before the mad masque even begins, when she is confronted with the wax figures of her husband and children, which she believes to be real; see Lynn Enterline, *The Tears of Narcissus: Melancholia and Masculinity in Early Modern Writing* (Stanford, Calif.: Stanford University Press, 1995), 269–70.

39. On the dating of this manuscript, see John Cutts, "Songs unto the Violl and Lute: Drexel MS 4175," *Musica Disciplina* 16 (1962): 73.

40. For a more complete description of the manuscript, see Elise Bickford Jorgens's introduction to *English Song 1600–1675, Facsimiles of Twenty-six Manuscripts and an Edition of the Texts*, part 1 (New York: Garland, 1986). Jorgens speculates that the volume may have been for student use.

41. On the revival of *The Duchess of Malfi*, see Brian Gibbons's introduction to the New Mermaids edition of the play, lx.

42. John Cutts dates the manuscript before 1649; see "Drexel Manuscript 4041," *Musica Disciplina* 18 (1964): 154.

43. Inga-Stina Ekeblad, "The 'Impure Art' of John Webster," *Review of English Studies* 9, no. 35 (1958): 253–67.

44. Frederick Kiefer, "The Dance of the Madmen in *the Duchess of Malfi*," *Journal of Medieval and Renaissance Studies* 17 (1987): 211–33.

45. Burton, *Anatomy of Melancholy*, book 1, 141. Peter B. Murray sees the mad song and dance as extensions of the Duke's derangement: they are "symbolic of his own mad world," *A Study of John Webster* (The Hague: Mouton, 1969), 131. Catherine Belsey believes that "they function dramatically as transformations not of the Duchess but of Ferdinand," "Emblem and Antithesis in *The Duchess of Malfi*," *Renaissance Drama* 11 (1980): 131.

46. Michel Bitot observes the similarity between the plays in "Inversion et folie dans la comedie de Richard Brome, 'The Antipodes' (1638)," in *L'Image du monde renverse et ses representations littéraires et paralittéraires de la fin du XVIe siècle*

a milieu du XVIIe: colloque international, Tours, 17–19 Novembre 1977: etudes, ed. Jean Lafond and Austin Redondo (Paris: J. Vrin, 1979), 171–78.

47. All citations are from Richard Brome, *The Antipodes*, ed. Ann Haaker, Regents Renaissance Drama Series (Lincoln: University of Nebraska Press, 1966).

48. Each member of the family has a specific type of the disease, information that Brome drew directly from Robert Burton's *Anatomy of Melancholy*, which, although it was first published in 1621, continued to be widely read, enjoying several reprintings, including a significant revision in 1638. Beyond Mandeville, Peregrine's delusions are drawn from *Gargantua and Pantagruel*. On the sources for Brome's play, see Ann Haaker's introduction to Richard Brome, *The Antipodes*, xii–xiv.

49. Babb, *The Elizabethan Malady*, 140.

50. On the celebration of marriage at the Caroline court, see Erica Veevers, *Images of Love and Religion: Queen Henrietta Maria and Court Entertainments* (Cambridge: Cambridge University Press, 1989), 36.

51. It is instructive to compare this masque of Discord to William Davenant's in *Salmacida Spolia* (1640), the last masque presented before the outbreak of Civil War. Discord also resists containment in Davenant's masque, as it features two antimasques, one featuring furies and the other stock grotesque characters, including "four mad lovers."

52. Ferrand, *Erotomania*, 215.

53. Laurentius, *A Discourse of the Preservation of the Sight*, 118.

54. Ferrand, *Erotomania*, 112.

55. Ibid., 107.

56. Austern, " 'No Women Are Indeed,' " 90–91.

57. See Austern, " 'No Women Are Indeed,' " 86–87. See also Stephen Greenblatt's discussion of effeminacy and boys in *Shakespearean Negotiations*, 78.

58. Ferrand, *Erotomania*, 46.

59. *The Rivall Friends*, (London: Printed by Aug. Matthewes for Humphrey Robinson, 1632), act 1, scene 3, C1^r. This play was performed for the king and queen during their trip to Cambridge in 1631.

60. Ibid., C1^r.

61. Ibid., C1^v.

62. This play was performed for the king and queen at Whitehall.

63. J[oseph] R[utter], *The Shepheards Holy-day* (London: Printed for N. and I. Okes, for John Benson, 1635), B3^r.

64. Ibid., B3^v.

65. Quotations are from Nathaniel Lee, *Mithridates: King of Pontus*, in *The Works of Nathaniel Lee*, ed. Thomas B. Stroup and Arthur L. Cooke, vol. 1 (New Brunswick, N.J.: Scarecrow Press, 1954).

66. The lyrics for this song are not Lee's; the playtext lists "Sir Car. Scroop" as the author; see *Mithridates*, 344.

67. Price, *Henry Purcell and the London Stage*, 22.

68. This satire, *Female Excellence: Or Woman Display'd, in Several Satyrick Poems* (London: Printed for Norman Nelson, 1679), is commonly attributed to Robert Gould, although this attribution has recently been questioned. Another misogynist tract that Gould is widely believed to have penned is *Love Given O're; or, a Satyr Against the Pride, Lust, and Inconstancy &c. of Woman* (London: Printed for Andrew Green, 1682).

69. [Robert] Gould, *The Rival Sisters: or, The Violence of Love* (London: Printed for Richard Bently . . . , Francis Saunders . . . , and James Knapton, 1696), 14.

70. Joseph Kerman, "A Glimmer from the Dark Ages," in *Dido and Aeneas:*

An Opera, ed. Curtis Price (New York: W. W. Norton, 1986), 224. This material is reprinted from *Opera as Drama*.

71. Price, "*Dido and Aeneas* in Context," 4. Recently, Michael Burden has sought to recuperate the image of the maligned Aeneas, arguing that the Trojan prince wasn't such a bad chap after all. He got Dido to admit her love, spent a passionate night with her, and offered to defy destiny; see "Great Minds Against Themselves Conspire," especially 234–35.

72. Burton, *Anatomy of Melancholy*, book 1, 235.

73. For literary antecedents to Tate's libretto, see Price, "*Dido and Aeneas* in Context"; Wood and Pinnock, " 'Unscarr'd by Turning Times'?" 373–90; and Pinnock, "Book IV in Plain Brown Wrappers," 249–71.

74. For a summary of political and moralistic readings of this myth in the seventeenth century see my article " 'O Ravishing Delight': The Politics of Pleasure in *The Judgment of Paris*," *Cambridge Opera Journal* 15 (2003): 1–17.

75. This quotation from Virgil's *Aeneid* is from Robert Fitzgerald's translation (New York: Vintage Classics, 1990), 103.

76. Richard Fanshawe, *Il Pastor Fido: The Faithfull Shepheard with an Addition of Divers Other Poems* (London: Printed for Humphrey Moseley, 1648), 281.

77. Sir Robert Howard, "The Fourth Book of Virgill, Of the Loves of Dido and Aeneas," in *Poems* (London: Printed for Henry Herringman, 1660), 150.

78. Ibid., 152.

79. Burton, *Anatomy of Melancholy*, book 3, 268.

80. In keeping with the presentation of the other musical examples in the book, slur lines have been replaced with protraction lines.

81. On the authorship of the play see George Walton Williams's textual introduction to *The Nice Valour, or The Passionate Mad-Man*, in *The Dramatic Works in the Beaumont and Fletcher Canon*, ed. Fredson Bowers, vol. 7 (Cambridge: Cambridge University Press, 1989), 427–29. The quotations are taken from this edition.

82. Babb, *The Elizabethan Malady*, 92.

83. On the dating of the manuscript, see Ian Spink, *English Song: Dowland to Purcell* (New York: Taplinger, 1986), 272.

84. *La musique de scène de la troupe de Shakespeare: The King's Men sous la règne de Jacques Ier*, ed. John P. Cutts, 2nd ed. (Paris: Éditions du Centre National de la Recherche Scientifique, 1971), 188. For a biographical sketch of Hilton's career, see Peter LeHuray and Ian Spink, "John Hilton," *Grove Music Online*, ed. Laura Macy (accessed 5 December 2004), http://www.grovemusic.com.

85. The Christ Church music catalogue fully describes the manuscript's contents; see *Christ Church Library: Music Catalogue* (accessed 18 April 2005), http://www2.chch.ox.ac.uk/library/music/page.html?set=Mus.+350.

86. On bleeding as a cure for lovesickness, see Babb, *The Elizabethan Malady*, 138.

87. Thomas D'Urfey, *A Fool's Preferment, or the Three Dukes of Dunstable* (London: Printed for Jos. Knight, and Fra. Saunders, 1688), L3ᵛ.

88. Ibid., 1.

89. Babb, *The Elizabethan Malady*, 46.

90. Laurentius, *A Discourse of the Preservation of the Sight*, 98.

91. Curtis Price has speculated that the song was beyond Mountfort's abilities and therefore would have been sung between the acts by an anonymous professional. See *Henry Purcell and the London Stage*, 158. For Baldwin and Wilson's hypothesis, see Olive Baldwin and Thelma Wilson, "Purcell's Stage Singers," in *Performing the Music of Henry Purcell*, ed. Michael Burden (Oxford: Clarendon Press, 1996), 108.

92. Citing as evidence the fact that John Walsh, thirty years hence, included "I'le Sail Upon the Dog-Star" in a collection of sea songs, Baldwin and Wilson claim that the music isn't inherently mad—the actor must project the necessary irrationality through stage actions ("Purcell's Stage Singers," 108). Although Walsh may have favored the nautical imagery over the other, obviously delusional, implications of the text, there is no indication that audiences in the 1680s would have heard things this way. Indeed, "I'le Sail Upon the Dog-Star" incorporates typical conventions of musical madness and contains textual allusions to another male mad song, "Tom a Bedlam," printed in *Choice Ayres, Songs, and Dialogues to Sing to the Theorbo-Lute, or Bass-Viol being Most of the Newest Ayres and Songs, Sung at Court, and at the Publick Theatres* (London: Printed by William Godbid . . . and Sold by John Playford, 1676). In the second verse of "Tom a Bedlam" the hallucinating madman thinks he hears the "dog star bark" and also mentions Vulcan's horns (he was cuckolded by Venus) and the man in the moon. In "I'le Sail Upon the Dog-Star" Lyonel uses the dog star to guide him. He then chases the moon, who has been "horning."

93. On the shift in the idea of the body politic, see Richard Braverman, *Plots and Counterplots: Sexual Politics and the Body Politic in English Literature, 1660–1730* (Cambridge: Cambridge University Press, 1993); Paul Hammond, "The King's Two Bodies: Representations of Charles II," in *Culture, Politics and Society in Britian, 1660–1800*, ed. Jeremy Black and Jeremy Gregory (Manchester: Manchester University Press, 1991), 13–48; and John Rogers, *The Matter of Revolution: Science, Poetry, and Politics in the Age of Milton* (Ithaca, N.Y.: Cornell University Press, 1996).

94. On eighteenth-century adaptations of the play, see Brian Gibbons's introduction to the New Mermaids edition of *The Duchess of Malfi*, xl–xli.

95. Kathryn Lowerre examined the connection between the Johnson and Eccles settings in her conference paper "Gothic Elements in English Theater Music" for the American Musicological Society, Columbus, Ohio, 2003. Lowerre also discusses Eccles's setting in "Music in the Productions at London's Lincoln's Inn Fields Theater, 1695–1705" (Ph.D. diss., Duke University, 1997), 616–17.

5. DISORDER IN THE EIGHTEENTH CENTURY

1. Joseph Addison, *Spectator,* no. 45 (Saturday, 21 April 1711).

2. Arthur Bedford, *A Serious Remonstrance on Behalf of the Christian Religion* (London: Printed by John Darby for Henry Hammond, 1719), 24.

3. Bedford, *A Serious Remonstrance*, 26. For more background on Bedford, see Jonathan Barry, "Hell upon Earth or the Language of the Playhouse," in *Languages of Witchcraft: Narrative, Ideology, and Meaning in Early Modern Culture*, ed. Stuart Clark (London: Macmillan Press, 2001), 139–58. As Barry notes, Bedford only read these plays and heard about audience response through hearsay; his religious beliefs precluded his attending the theater.

4. Roger Fiske, *English Theatre Music in the Eighteenth Century*, 2nd ed. (Oxford: Oxford University Press, 1986), 81. None of the music for this pantomime survives.

5. On the confusion over who composed *Macbeth*'s "Famous Music" see Eubanks Winkler, introduction, *Music for Macbeth*, viii–ix; Fiske, "The *Macbeth* Music," 114–25; and Moore, "The Music to *Macbeth*," 22–40.

6. Irena Bozena Cholij, "Music in Eighteenth-Century London Shakespeare Productions" (Ph.D. diss., King's College, University of London, 1996), 140–41.

7. Quoted in Marvin Rosenberg, *The Masks of Macbeth* (Berkeley: University of California Press, 1978), 8.

8. Ibid., 9.

9. Ibid. Some of the song texts interpolated into *Macbeth* were from Middleton's *The Witch*. See chapter 2.

10. On the anatomical discoveries that fed into these changing notions of gender, see Laqueur, *Making Sex*, 149–92.

11. Randolph Trumbach, "Sodomitical Assaults, Gender Role, and Sexual Development in Eighteenth-Century London," *Journal of Homosexuality* 16, no. 1 (1989): 408.

12. Kristina Straub, *Sexual Suspects: Eighteenth-Century Players and Sexual Ideology* (Princeton, N.J.: Princeton University Press, 1992), ch. 3. On the molly, see Rictor Norton, *Mother Clap's Molly House: The Gay Subculture in England 1700–1830* (London: GMP Publishers, 1992); and Randolph Trumbach, "Sodomy Transformed: Aristocratic Libertinage, Public Reputation and the Gender Revolution of the Eighteenth Century," in *Love Letters between a Certain Late Nobleman and the Famous Mr. Wilson*, ed. M. S. Kimmel (New York: Harrington Park Press, 1990), 105–124. Ellen Harris, in the opening chapter to her excellent study, *Handel as Orpheus: Voice and Desire in the Chamber Cantatas* (Cambridge, Mass.: Harvard University Press, 2001), also summarizes standard sources on gender and sexuality (although Straub appears to have been unknown to her). Harris, following Michel Foucault's *The History of Sexuality: An Introduction*, vol. 1, trans. Robert Hurley (New York: Vintage Books, 1990), 43, asserts that a homosexual identity did not become established until the nineteenth century, an assertion that has been critiqued by some gay and lesbian historians; see, for example, Valerie Traub's *The Renaissance of Lesbianism in Early Modern England* (Cambridge: Cambridge University Press, 2002). Trumbach himself questions this notion, suggesting that, in fact, the homosexual as a discrete category began to emerge in the early eighteenth century. While acknowledging, as does Harris, that some men who engaged in homosexual behaviors were married and had children, Trumbach is quick to point out that regardless of marital status, in the "public estimate, all sodomites were effeminate and exclusively interested in men." See Trumbach, "Sodomitical Assaults," 408. In such discussions, it is important to make a distinction between historical actualities (some sodomites were married) and historical perceptions (all sodomites were exclusively interested in men).

13. Straub makes this argument in *Sexual Suspects*, 28–29.

14. Max Byrd, *Visits to Bedlam: Madness and Literature in the Eighteenth Century* (Columbia: University of South Carolina Press, 1974), 14.

15. Foucault, *Madness and Civilization*, 38–64.

16. Byrd, *Visits to Bedlam*, 44. Roy Porter also questions the applicability of Foucault's model of confinement for England; see *Mind-Forg'd Manacles*, 6–9.

17. Byrd, *Visits to Bedlam*, 54.

18. Straub, *Sexual Suspects*, 90.

19. Elaine Showalter documents the changing performance and reception of Ophelia in "Representing Ophelia," 77–94.

20. Collier, *A Short View of the Immorality and Profaneness of the English Stage*, 10–11.

21. Ibid., 10.

22. Ibid., 10.

23. Ibid., 11.

24. Thomas D'Urfey, "Preface," *The Campaigners: or, the Pleasant Adventures at Brussels* (London: Printed for A. Baldwin, 1698), 9.

25. James Drake, *The Antient and Modern Stages Survey'd. Or, Mr Collier's*

View of the Immorality and Profaness of the English Stage set in a True Light (London: Printed for Abel Roper, 1699), 295.

26. Ibid., 296.

27. Ibid., 297.

28. Quoted in Showalter, "Representing Ophelia," 82.

29. Ibid., 82.

30. Showalter seems to suggest that highlighting the musical component would have been another way to render Ophelia more benign, ibid., 83; I believe it's a bit more complicated.

31. See chapter 3, in particular n. 56.

32. Fiske, *English Theatre Music in the Eighteenth Century*, 31; Curtis Price, *Music in the Restoration Theatre: With a Catalogue of Instrumental Music in the Plays 1665–1713* (Ann Arbor, Mich.: UMI Research Press, 1979), 112.

33. On *Arsinoe, The Loves of Ergasto*, Bononcini's immensely successful *Camilla*, and the reform of the play and the removal of the musical elements, see Price, *Music in the Restoration Theatre*, 110–16; for a detailed analysis of the gradual rise of Italian opera, see "The English Background: Italian Opera in London 1705–1710," chapter 9 in Winton Dean and John Merrill Knapp, *Handel's Operas, 1704–1726* (Oxford: Clarendon Press, 1987), 140–50.

34. In a recent article Roger Freitas claims that castrati, by virtue of their boyish effeminacy, were perfectly cast as the amorous lovers in Italian opera. He understands the castrato's body through the lens of the one-sex body as described by Laqueur and equates them with boys, who had frequently (as we have seen in the current study) been the objects of desire for adult men in the early modern period. Freitas's analysis works quite well for the seventeenth century, but is less applicable to eighteenth-century London, where quite clearly, as the previous discussion demonstrates, the one-sex model was no longer the only way people understood biological sex. For Freitas's argument see "The Eroticism of Emasculation."

35. Joseph Addison had a personal vendetta against Italian opera. His English opera, *Rosamond*, with music by Thomas Clayton, had failed a few years before; see Charles Burney, *A General History of Music from the Earliest Ages to the Present Period (1789)*, vol. 2, ed. Frank Mercer (New York: Dover, 1957), 657–59.

36. See *Spectator*, no. 13 (Tuesday, 15 March 1711).

37. John Dennis, *An Essay on the Opera's After the Italian Manner. Which are About to be Establish'd on the English Stage: With some Reflections on the Damage which They may Bring to the Publick* (London: Printed for John Nutt, 1706), unpaginated preface.

38. Quoted in Todd Gilman, "The Italian (Castrato) in London," in *The Work of Opera: Genre, Nationhood and Sexual Difference*, ed. Richard Dellamora and Daniel Fischlin (New York: Columbia University Press, 1997), 54.

39. On the danger castrati and Italian opera posed for the male spectators, see Thomas McGeary, " 'Warbling Eunuchs': Opera, Gender, and Sexuality on the London Stage, 1705–1742," *Restoration and 18th-Century Theatre Research* 7 (1992): 1–22; and Gilman, "The Italian (Castrato) in London," 49–70.

40. John Dennis, *An Essay on the Opera's After the Italian Manner*, unpaginated preface.

41. For a full discussion of Italian opera, see Dennis, *An Essay upon Publick Spirit, Being a Satyr in Prose upon the Manners and Luxury of the Times* (London: Printed for Bernard Lintott, 1711), 18–25.

42. On the construction of British identity in the eighteenth century, see Linda Colley, *Britons: Forging the Nation, 1707–1837* (New Haven, Conn.: Yale University Press, 1992).

43. Ellen Harris also notes this political component in *Handel as Orpheus*, ch. 1.

44. Richard Steele, *The Tender Husband; or the Accomplish'd Fools. A Comedy* (London: Printed for Jacob Tonson, 1705).

45. On the Royal Academy and its aesthetic and moral goals, see Elizabeth Gibson, "The Royal Academy of Music (1719–28) and its Directors," in *Handel Tercentenary Collection*, ed. Stanley Sadie and Anthony Hicks (London: Macmillan Press, 1987), 149–51.

Bibliography

MUSIC

Manuscript Sources

GB-Cfm. Mu MS 87
GB-Lbl. Add. MS 10444
GB-Lbl. Add. MS 12219
GB-Lbl. Add. MS 15117
GB-Lbl. Add. MS 29481
GB-Lbl. Egerton MS 2013
GB-Ob. MS Mus. Sch. F.575
GB-Ob. MS Mus. Sch. B.1
GB-Och. MS Mus. 350
US-NYp. Drexel MS 4041
US-NYp. Drexel MS 4175

Seventeenth- and Eighteenth-Century Songbooks

Apollo's Banquet. London: John Playford, 1669.
Choice Ayres, Songs, and Dialogues to Sing to the Theorbo-Lute, or Bass-Viol being Most of the Newest Ayres and Songs, Sung at Court, and at the Publick Theatres. London: Printed by William Godbid . . . and Sold by John Playford, 1676.
Choice Ayres and Songs . . . The Third Book. London: Printed by William Godbid . . . and Sold by John Playford, 1681.
Deliciae Musicae . . . The First Book. London: Printed by J. Heptinstall, for Henry Playford, 1695.
Eccles, John. *A Collection of Songs for One, Two, and Three Voices, Together with Such Symphonies for Violins or Flues as were by the Author Design'd.* London: J. Walsh, [1704].
Purcell, Henry. *Orpheus Britannicus, A collection of All the Choicest Songs for One, Two, and Three Voices Compos'd by Mr. Henry Purcell.* London: Printed by J. Heptinstall for Henry Playford, 1698.
———. *New Songs Sung in The Fool's Preferment, or the Three Dukes of Dunstable.* London: Printed by E. Jones, for Jos. Knight and Fran. Saunders, 1688.
The Songs to the New Play of Don Quixote . . . Part the First. London: Printed by J. Heptinstall for Samuel Briscoe, 1694.
The Songs to the New Play of Don Quixote . . . Part the Second. London: Printed by J. Heptinstall for Samuel Briscoe, 1694.
Thesaurus Musicus: Being, a Collection of the Newest Songs Performed at His Majesties Theatres; and at the Consorts in Viller-Street in York-Buildings, and in Charles-Street Covent-Garden . . . The Fourth Book. London: Printed by J. Heptinstall for John Hudgebutt, 1695.
Wilson, John. *Cheerfull Ayres.* Oxford: Printed by W. Hall for Ric. Davis, 1659.
Youll, Henry. *Canzonets to Three Voyces Newly Composed by Henry Youll Practicioner in the Art of Musicke.* London: Printed by Thomas Este, the assigne of William Barley, 1608.

Modern Editions

Duffin, Ross W. *Shakespeare's Songbook*. New York: W. W. Norton, 2004.

English Song 1600–1675, Facsimiles of Twenty-six Manuscripts and an Edition of the Texts. Ed. Elise Bickford Jorgens. New York: Garland, 1986.

Four Hundred Songs and Dances from the Stuart Masque. Ed. Andrew Sabol. Providence, R.I.: Brown University Press, 1978.

Music for Macbeth. Ed. Amanda Eubanks Winkler. Vol. 133 of Recent Researches of the Baroque Era. Middleton, Wisc.: A-R Editions, 2004.

La musique de scène de la troupe de Shakespeare: The King's Men sous la règne de Jacques Ier. Ed. John P. Cutts. 2d rev. ed. Paris: Éditions du Centre National de la Recherche Scientifique, 1971.

Purcell, Henry. *Dido and Aeneas*. Ed. Margaret Laurie and Thurston Dart. Reprinted in *Dido and Aeneas: An Opera*, ed. Curtis Price. New York: W. W. Norton, 1986.

TEXTS

Early Modern Editions

Agrippa, Henry [Heinrich] Cornelius. *Three Books of Occult Philosophy*. Trans. J. F. London: R. W. for Gregory Moule, 1651.

Allestree, Richard. *The Ladies Calling*. Oxford: n.p., 1673.

Barrough, Philip. *The Method of Physick, Containing the Causes, Signes, and Cures of Inward Diseases in Mans Body, from the Head to the Foote*. 7th ed. London, Printed by George Miller, 1634.

Baxter, Richard. "The Cure of Melancholy and Overmuch Sorrow by Faith and Physick." In *A Continuation of Morning-Exercise Questions and Cases of Conscience, Practically Resolved by Sundry Ministers*, 163–303. London: Printed by J. A. for John Dunton, 1683.

———. *The Signs and Causes of Melancholy*. Ed. Samuel Clifford. Glasgow: John Robertson and Mrs. McLean, 1749.

Bedford, Arthur. *A Serious Remonstrance on Behalf of the Christian Religion*. London: Printed by John Darby for Henry Hammond, 1719.

Brathwaite, Richard. *The English Gentleman; and the English Gentlewoman: Both in One Volume Couched*. London: Printed by John Dawson, 1641.

Bright, T[imothy]. *A Treatise of Melancholie: Containing the Causes Thereof, & Reasons of the Strange Effects it Worketh in our Minds and Bodies*. London: Imprinted . . . by Thomas Vautrolier, 1586.

Butler, Charles. *The Principles of Musik, in Singing and Setting: With the Two-Fold Use Therof, [Ecclesiasticall and Civil]*. London: Printed by John Haviland, 1636.

Charlton, Walter. *A Natural History of the Passions*. 2nd enlarged ed. London: Printed for R. Wellington, 1701.

Collier, Jeremy. *A Short View of the Immorality and Profaneness of the English Stage, Together with the Sense of Antiquity Upon This Argument*. London: Printed for S. Keble . . . R. Sare . . . and H. Hindmarsh, 1698.

Dennis, John. *An Essay on the Opera's After the Italian Manner. Which are About to Be Establish'd on the English Stage: With some Reflections on the Damage Which They May Bring to the Publick*. London: Printed for John Nutt, 1706.

———. *An Essay Upon Publick Spirit, Being a Satyr in Prose upon the Manners and Luxury of the Times*. London: Printed for Bernard Lintott, 1711.

Drake, James. *The Antient and Modern Stages Survey'd. Or, Mr Collier's View of the*

Immorality and Profaness of the English Stage set in a True Light. London: Printed for Abel Roper, 1699.

D'Urfey, Thomas. *The Campaigners: or, the Pleasant Adventures at Brussels.* London: Printed for A. Baldwin, 1698.

———. *The Comical History of Don Quixote, Part I.* London: Printed for Samuel Briscoe, 1694.

———. *The Comical History of Don Quixote, Part II.* London: Printed for Samuel Briscoe, 1694.

———. *A Fool's Preferment, or the Three Dukes of Dunstable.* London: Printed for Jos. Knight, and Fra. Saunders, 1688.

———. *New Poems, Consisting of Satyrs, Elegies, and Odes.* London: J. Bullord and A. Roper, 1689.

Fanshawe, Richard. *Il Pastor Fido: The Faithfull Shepheard with an Addition of Divers Other Poems.* London: Printed for Humphrey Moseley, 1648.

Ferrand, James [Jacques]. *Erotomania: Or a Treatise Discoursing of the Essence, Causes, Symptomes, Prognosticks, and Cure of Love or Erotique Melancholy.* Trans. E. Chilmead. Oxford: L. Lichfield, 1640.

The Full Tryals, Examination, and Condemnation of Four Notorious Witches. London: n.p., 1670.

F[yge], S[arah]. *The Female Advocate: or, an Answer to a late Satyr against the Pride, Lust and Inconstancy of Woman.* London: H. C. for John Taylor, 1686.

Glanvill, Joseph. *Saducismus Triumphatus: Or Full and Plain Evidence Concerning Witches and Apparitions.* London: Printed for J. Collins and S. Lownds, 1681.

[Gould, Robert]. *Female Excellence: Or Woman Display'd, in Several Satyrick Poems.* London: Printed for Norman Nelson, 1679.

[Gould, Robert]. *Love Given O're; or, a Satyr against the Pride, Lust, and Inconstancy & c. of Woman.* London: Andrew Green, 1682.

Gould, [Robert]. *The Rival Sisters: or, The Violence of Love.* London: Printed for Richard Bently . . . , Francis Saunders . . . , and James Knapton, 1696.

Harsnett, Samuel. *A Declaration of Egregious Popish Impostures.* London: Printed by James Roberts, 1603.

Harvey, Gideon. *Morbus Anglicus: Or the Anatomy of Consumptions.* London: Printed for William Thackeray, 1672.

Hausted, Peter. *The Rivall Friends.* London: Printed by Aug. Matthewes for Humphrey Robinson, 1632.

Hic Mulier: or, The Man-Woman: Being a Medicine to Cure the Coltish Disease of the Staggers in the Masculine-Feminine, of our Times. London: Printed for J. T. [John Trundle], 1620.

Holland, Henry. *A Treatise against Witchcraft.* Cambridge: Printed by John Legatt, 1590.

Howard, Sir Robert. "The Fourth Book of Virgill, Of the Loves of Dido and Aeneas." In *Poems.* London: Printed for Henry Herringman, 1660.

Johnson, Samuel. "The Church of England as by Law Established." In *A Second Five Years Struggle against Popery and Tyranny,* 27–46. London: Printed for the author . . . sold by Richard Baldwin, 1689.

Jorden, Edward. *A Briefe Discourse of a Disease Called the Suffocation of the Mother.* London: Printed by John Windet, 1603.

Laurentius, Andreas. *A Discourse of the Preservation of the Sight; of Melancholike Diseases; of Rheumes, and of Old Age.* London: Imprinted by Felix Kingston for Ralph Jacson, 1599.

Maplet, John. *The Diall of Destiny.* London: Imprinted by Thomas Marshe, 1581.

Marcelline, George. *The Triumphs of King James the First.* London: Printed . . . for John Budge, 1610.

Morley, Thomas. *A Plaine and Easie Introduction to Practicall Musicke*. London: Imprinted . . . by Peter Short, 1597.

Oates, Titus. *The Witch of Endor; or the Witchcrafts of the Roman Jesebel*. London: Printed for Thomas Parkhurst and Thomas Cockeril, 1679.

Overbury, Sir Thomas. *The Wife, with Additions of New Characters: And many other Witty Conceits never before Printed*. 17th Impression. London: Peter Lillicrap for Philip Chetwin, 1664.

Phaer, Thomas, and Thomas Twyne. *The Thirteene Bookes of Aeneidos*. London: Printed by Bernard Alsop, by the Assignement of Clement Knight, 1620.

Prynne, William. *Histriomastix*. London: E. A. and W. I. for Michael Sparke, 1633.

R. B. *The Kingdom of Darkness: Or the History of Daemons, Specters, Witches, Apparitions, Possessions, Disturbances, and Other Wonderful and Supernatural Delusions, Mischievous Feats, and Malicious Impostures of the Devil*. London: Printed for Nath[aniel] Crouch, 1688.

Ramesey, William. *The Gentleman's Companion: Or, a Character of True Nobility and Gentility*. London: n.p., 1672.

Robinson, Thomas. *The Schoole of Musicke*. London: Printed by Tho. Este for Simon Waterson, 1603.

Rowley, Samuel. *When You See Me, You Know Me*. London: Imprinted for Nathaniell Butter, 1605.

R[utter], J[oseph]. *The Shepheards Holy-day*. London: Printed for N. and I. Okes, for John Benson, 1635.

Scot, Reginald. *The Discoverie of Witchcraft*. London: Imprinted by William Brome, 1584.

Spectator. Tuesday, 15 March 1711.

Spectator. Saturday, 21 April 1711.

Steele, Richard. *The Tender Husband; or the Accomplish'd Fools. A Comedy*. London: Printed for Jacob Tonson, 1705.

Stubbes, Phillip. *The Anatomie of Abuses*. London: Printed . . . by Richard Jones, 1583.

Webster, John. *The Displaying of Supposed Witchcraft*. London: Printed by J. M., 1677.

The Wonderful Discouerie of the Witchcrafts of Margaret and Phillip Flower . . . Together with the Seuerall Examinations and Confessions of Anne Baker, Ioan Wilimot, and Ellen Greene. London: By G. Eld for I. Barnes, 1619.

Modern Editions

Beaumont, Francis, and John Fletcher. *The Maid's Tragedy*. Ed. T. W. Craik. The Revels Plays. Manchester: Manchester University Press, 1988.

Brome, Richard. *The Antipodes*. Ed. Ann Haaker. Regents Renaissance Drama Series. Lincoln: University of Nebraska Press, 1966.

Burney, Charles. *A General History of Music from the Earliest Ages to the Present Period (1789)*. Vol. 2. Ed. Frank Mercer. New York: Dover, 1957.

Burton, Robert. *The Anatomy of Melancholy*. Ed. Holbrook Jackson. New York: New York Review Books, 2001.

Castiglione, Baldassare. *The Book of the Courtier*. Trans. Sir Thomas Hoby. London: J. M. Dent and Sons, 1974.

Davanant, William. *Macbeth*. In *Five Restoration Adaptations of Shakespeare*, ed. Christopher Spencer. Urbana: University of Illinois Press, 1965.

Dekker, Thomas, John Ford, and William Rowley. *The Witch of Edmonton*. Ed. Arthur F. Kinney. London: A. & C. Black, 1998.

Downes, John. *Roscius Anglicanus.* Ed. Judith Milhous and Robert D. Hume. London: Society for Theatre Research, 1987.

Dryden, John. *Virgil's Aeneid (1697).* Ed. Frederick M. Keener. London: Penguin Books, 1997.

Fletcher, John. *The Nice Valour, or The Passionate Mad-Man.* In *The Dramatic Works in the Beaumont and Fletcher Canon.* Ed. Fredson Bowers. Vol. 7. Cambridge: Cambridge University Press, 1989.

Heywood, Thomas, and Richard Brome. *An Edition of the Late Lancashire Witches.* Ed. Laird H. Barber. Renaissance Drama: A Collection of Critical Editions. New York: Garland Publishing, 1979.

Hobbes, Thomas. *Leviathan (1651).* Ed. Richard Tuck. Cambridge Texts in the History of Political Thought. Cambridge: Cambridge University Press, 1991.

Holder, William. *Treatise of the Natural Grounds and Principals of Harmony (1694).* Facsimile ed. New York: Broude Brothers, 1967.

James I. *Daemonlogie* (1597). In *The Bodley Head Quartos,* vol. 9, ed. G. B. Harrison. London: John Lane, The Bodley Head, 1924.

Jonson, Ben. "Cynthia's Revels." In *Ben Jonson,* ed. C. H. Herford and Percy Simpson. Vol. 4. Oxford: Clarendon Press, 1932.

———. *Ben Jonson: The Complete Masques.* Ed. Stephen Orgel. The Yale Ben Jonson. New Haven, Conn.: Yale University Press, 1969.

Joubert, Laurent. *The Second Part of the Popular Errors (1587).* Trans. Gregory David de Rocher. Tuscaloosa: University of Alabama Press, 1995.

Lee, Nathaniel. *Mithridates: King of Pontus.* In *The Works of Nathaniel Lee,* ed. Thomas B. Stroup and Arthur L. Cooke. Vol. 1. New Brunswick, N.J.: Scarecrow Press, 1954.

Mace, Thomas. *Musick's Monument (1676).* Vol. 17 of Monuments of Music and Music Literature in Facsimile. New York: Broude Brothers, 1966.

Marston, John. *The Malcontent and Other Plays.* Ed. Keith Sturgess. The World's Classics. Oxford: Oxford University Press, 1997.

Massinger, Philip. *The Renegado.* In *The Plays and Poems of Philip Massinger,* ed. Philip Edwards and Colin Gibson. Vol. 2. Oxford: Clarendon Press, 1976.

Middleton, Thomas. *The Witch.* Ed. Elizabeth Schafer, *The New Mermaids.* London: A. & C. Black, 1994.

Newes from Scotland (1591). In *The Bodley Head Quartos,* vol. 9, ed. G. B. Harrison. London: John Lane, The Bodley Head, 1924.

Playford, John. *An Introduction to the Skill of Musick (1674).* Facsimile of the 7th ed. Ridgewood, N.J.: Gregg Press, 1966.

Purcell, Henry, ed. *John Playford, An Introduction to the Skill of Musick (1694).* Facsimile 12th ed.. New York: Da Capo Press, 1972.

Shadwell, Thomas. *The Lancashire Witches.* Vol. 4 of *The Complete Works of Thomas Shadwell.* Ed. Montague Summers. London: Benjamin Blom, 1968 reprint.

Shakespeare, William. *The Riverside Shakespeare.* Ed. G. Blakemore Evans. Boston: Houghton Mifflin, 1974.

———. *The Tragedy of Macbeth.* Ed. Nicholas Brooke. The Oxford Shakespeare. Oxford: Clarendon Press, 1990.

Virgil. *Aeneid.* Trans. Robert Fitzgerald. New York: Vintage Classics, 1990.

———. *The Aeneid.* Trans. Edward McCrorie. Ann Arbor: University of Michigan Press, 1995.

Webster, John. *The Duchess of Malfi.* Ed. Brian Gibbons. 4th ed. New Mermaids. London: A. & C. Black, 2001.

Weyer, Johann. *Witches, Devils, and Doctors in the Renaissance: Johann Weyer, De praestigiis daemonum.* Trans. John Shea. Vol. 73 of Medieval and Renaissance

Texts and Studies, ed. George Mora. Binghamton, N.Y.: Center for Medieval and Early Renaissance Studies, 1991.

Secondary Sources

Alfar, Cristina León. "Staging the Feminine Performance of Desire: Masochism in *The Maid's Tragedy*." *Papers on Language and Literature* 31, no. 3 (Summer 1995): 313–33.

Altieri, Joanne. *The Theatre of Praise: The Panegyric Tradition in Seventeenth-Century English Drama*. Newark: University of Delaware Press, 1986.

Austern, Linda. " 'Alluring the Auditorie to Effeminacy': Music and the Idea of the Feminine in Early Modern England'." *Music and Letters* 74 (1993): 347–68.

———. " 'Art to Enchant': Musical Magic and Its Practitioners in English Renaissance Drama." *Journal of the Royal Musical Association* 115 (1990): 191–206.

———. " 'For, Love's a Good Musician': Performance, Audition, and Erotic Disorders in Early Modern Europe." *Musical Quarterly* 82 (Fall/Winter 1998): 614–53.

———. " 'No Pill's Gonna Cure My Ill': Gender, Erotic Melancholy and Traditions of Musical Healing in the Modern West." In *Musical Healing in Cultural Contexts*, ed. Penelope Gouk, 113–36. Aldershot, U.K.: Ashgate/Scolar Press, 2000.

———. " 'No Women Are Indeed': The Boy Actor as Vocal Seductress in Late Sixteenth- and Early Seventeenth-Century English Drama." In *Embodied Voices: Representing Female Vocality in Western Culture*, ed. Leslie C. Dunn and Nancy A. Jones, 83–102. Cambridge: Cambridge University Press, 1994.

———. " 'Sing Againe Syren': The Female Musician and Sexual Enchantment in Elizabethan Life and Literature." *Renaissance Quarterly* 42 (Autumn 1989): 420–48.

———. "Thomas Ravenscroft: Musical Chronicler of an Elizabethan Theater Company." *Journal of the American Musicological Association* 38 (1985): 238–63.

Babb, Lawrence. *The Elizabethan Malady: A Study of Melancholia in English Literature from 1580 to 1642*. East Lansing: Michigan State College Press, 1951.

Bakhtin, Mikhail. *Rabelais and His World*, trans. Hélène Iswolsky. Bloomington: Indiana University Press, 1984.

Baldwin, Olive, and Thelma Wilson. "Purcell's Stage Singers." In *Performing the Music of Henry Purcell*, ed. Michael Burden, 105–129. Oxford: Clarendon Press, 1996.

Barish, Jonas. *The Antitheatrical Prejudice*. Berkeley: University of California Press, 1981.

Barroll, Leeds. "Inventing the Stuart Masque." In *The Politics of the Stuart Court Masque*, ed. David Bevington and Peter Holbrook, 121–43. Cambridge: Cambridge University Press, 1998.

Barry, Jonathan. "Hell upon Earth or the Language of the Playhouse." In *Languages of Witchcraft: Narrative, Ideology, and Meaning in Early Modern Culture*, ed. Stuart Clark, 139–58. London: Macmillan Press, 2001.

Baskervill, Charles Read. *The Elizabethan Jig and Related Song Drama*. Chicago: University of Chicago Press, 1929.

Beecher, Donald A., and Massimo Ciavolella. "Introduction." In *Jacques Ferrand*,

A Treatise on Lovesickness, ed. Donald A. Beecher and Massimo Ciavolella. Syracuse: Syracuse University Press, 1990.

Belsey, Catherine. "Emblem and Antithesis in *The Duchess of Malfi*." *Renaissance Drama* 11 (1980): 115–34.

Bennet, G. V. *The Tory Crisis in Church and State, 1688–1730*. Oxford: Clarendon Press, 1975.

Bitot, Michel. "Inversion et folie dans la comedie de Richard Brome, 'The Antipodes' (1638)." In *L'Image du monde renverse et ses representations littéraires et paralittéraires de la fin du XVIe siècle a milieu du XVIIe: colloque international, Tours, 17–19 Novembre 1977: etudes*, ed. Jean Lafond and Austin Redondo, 171–78. Paris: J. Vrin, 1979.

Bostridge, Ian. *Witchcraft and its Transformations, c. 1650–c. 1750*. Oxford: Clarendon Press, 1997.

Braverman, Richard. *Plots and Counterplots: Sexual Politics and the Body Politic in English Literature, 1660–1730*. Cambridge: Cambridge University Press, 1993.

Brennecke, Ernest. " 'Nay, That's Not Next!' The Significance of Desdemona's 'Willow Song.' " *Shakespeare Quarterly* 4, no. 1 (January 1953): 35–38.

Burden, Michael. " 'Great Minds against Themselves Conspire': Purcell's Dido as a Conspiracy Theorist." In *A Woman Scorn'd: Responses to the Dido Myth*, ed. Michael Burden, 227–47. London: Faber and Faber, 1998.

Buttrey, John. "A Cautionary Tale." In *Dido and Aeneas: An Opera*, ed. Curtis Price, 228–35. New York: W. W. Norton, 1986.

Byrd, Max. *Visits to Bedlam: Madness and Literature in the Eighteenth Century*. Columbia: University of South Carolina Press, 1974.

Chan, Mary. *Music in the Theatre of Ben Jonson*. Oxford: Clarendon Press, 1980.

Cholij, Irena Bozena. "Music in Eighteenth-Century London Shakespeare Productions." Ph.D. diss., King's College, University of London, 1996.

Clark, J. C. D. *English Society, 1688–1832*. Cambridge: Cambridge University Press, 1985.

Clark, Stuart. "Inversion, Misrule and the Meaning of Witchcraft." *Past and Present* 87 (1980): 98–127.

———. *Thinking with Demons: The Idea of Witchcraft in Early Modern Europe*. Oxford: Clarendon Press, 1997.

Colley, Linda. *Britons: Forging the Nation, 1707–1837*. New Haven, Conn.: Yale University Press, 1992.

Cope, Jackson I. *Joseph Glanvill: Anglican Apologist*. St. Louis: Washington University Studies, 1956.

Covey, Herbert C. *Images of Older People in Western Art and Society*. New York: Praeger, 1991.

Crawford, Patricia. *Women and Religion in England, 1500–1720*. London: Routledge, 1993.

Cusick, Suzanne. " 'There Was Not One Lady Who Failed to Shed a Tear': Arianna's Lament and the Construction of Modern Womanhood." *Early Music* 22 (February 1994): 21–41.

Cutts, John P. "Drexel Manuscript 4041." *Musica Disciplina* 18 (1964): 151–201.

———. "Robert Johnson and the Court Masque." *Music and Letters* 41 (1960): 111–26.

———. "Songs unto the Violl and Lute: Drexel MS 4175." *Musica Disciplina* 16 (1962): 73–92.

Davis, Natalie Zemon. "Women on Top: Symbolic Sexual Inversion and Political Disorder in Early Modern Europe." In *The Reversible World: Symbolic Inversion in Art and Society*, ed. Barbara A. Babcock, 147–90. Ithaca, N.Y.: Cornell University Press, 1978.

Dawson, Anthony B. "Performance and Participation: Desdemona, Foucault, and the Actor's Body." In *Shakespeare, Theory, and Performance*, ed. James C. Bulman, 29–45. London: Routledge, 1996.

———. "Witchcraft/Bigamy: Cultural Conflict in *The Witch of Edmonton*." *Renaissance Drama* 20 (1989): 77–98.

Dean, Winton, and John Merrill Knapp. *Handel's Operas, 1704–1726*. Oxford: Clarendon Press, 1987.

Digangi, Mario. " 'Male Deformities': Narcissus and the Reformation of Courtly Manners in *Cynthia's Revels*." In *Ovid and the Renaissance Body*, ed. Goran V. Stanivukovic, 94–110. Toronto: University of Toronto Press, 2001.

Dixon, Laurinda. *Perilous Chastity: Women and Illness in Pre-Enlightenment Art and Medicine*. Ithaca, N.Y.: Cornell University Press, 1995.

Dolan, Francis E. *Dangerous Familiars: Representations of Domestic Crime in England, 1550–1700*. Ithaca, N.Y.: Cornell University Press, 1994.

Dunn, Leslie C. "Ophelia's Songs in *Hamlet*: Music, Madness, and the Feminine." In *Embodied Voices: Representing Female Vocality in Western Culture*, ed. Leslie C. Dunn and Nancy A. Jones, 63–64. Cambridge: Cambridge University Press, 1994.

Eagleton, Terry. *Walter Benjamin: Towards a Revolutionary Criticism*. London: NLB/Verso, 1981.

Ekeblad, Inga-Stina. "The 'Impure Art' of John Webster." *Review of English Studies* 9, no. 35 (1958): 253–67.

Enterline, Lynn. *The Tears of Narcissus: Melancholia and Masculinity in Early Modern Writing*. Stanford: Stanford University Press, 1995.

Eubanks Winkler, Amanda. " 'O Ravishing Delight': The Politics of Pleasure in *The Judgment of Paris*." *Cambridge Opera Journal* 15 (2003): 1–17.

Ewbank, Inga-Stina. "The Middle of Middleton." In *The Arts of Performance in Elizabethan and Early Stuart Drama*, ed. Murray Biggs et al., 156–72. Edinburgh: Edinburgh University Press, 1991.

Finney, Gretchen Ludke. *Musical Backgrounds for English Literature: 1580–1650*. New Brunswick, N.J.: Rutgers University Press, [1962].

Fiske, Roger. *English Theatre Music in the Eighteenth Century*. 2nd ed. Oxford: Oxford University Press, 1986.

———. "The *Macbeth* Music." *Music and Letters* 45 (April 1964): 114–25.

Fletcher, Anthony. *Gender, Sex and Subordination in England, 1500–1800*. New Haven, Conn.: Yale University Press, 1995.

Forrest, John. *The History of Morris Dancing, 1458–1750*. Ed. J. A. B. Somerset. Vol. 5 of *Studies in Early English Drama*. Toronto: University of Toronto Press, 1999.

Fox-Good, Jacquelyn A. "Ophelia's Mad Songs: Music, Gender, Power." In *Subjects on the World's Stage: Essays on British Literature of the Middle Ages and Renaissance*, ed. David G. Allen and Robert A. White, 217–38. Newark: University of Delaware Press, 1995.

Foucault, Michel. *The History of Sexuality: An Introduction*. Vol. 1. Trans. Robert Hurley. New York: Vintage Books, 1990.

———. *Madness and Civilization: A History of Insanity in the Age of Reason*. Trans. Richard Howard. New York: Vintage Books, 1988.

———. *The Order of Things: An Archaeology of the Human Sciences*. New York: Vintage Books, 1994.

Freitas, Roger. "The Eroticism of Emasculation: Confronting the Baroque Body of the Castrato." *The Journal of Musicology* 20 (Spring 2003): 196–249.

Fuller, David. "The Jonsonian Masque and Its Music." *Music and Letters* 54 (1973): 440–52.

Gentili, Vanna. "Madmen and Fools Are a Staple Commodity: On Madness as a System in Elizabethan and Jacobean Plays." *Cahiers Elisabethains: Late Medieval and Renaissance Studies* 34 (October 1988): 11–24.

Gibson, Elizabeth. "The Royal Academy of Music (1719–28) and Its Directors." In *Handel Tercentenary Collection*, ed. Stanley Sadie and Anthony Hicks, 136–64. London: Macmillan Press, 1987.

Gilman, Todd. "The Italian (Castrato) in London." In *The Work of Opera: Genre, Nationhood and Sexual Difference*, ed. Richard Dellamora and Daniel Fischlin, 49–70. New York: Columbia University Press, 1997.

Gouk, Penelope. "Music, Melancholy, and Medical Spirits in Early Modern Thought." In *Music as Medicine: The History of Music Therapy since Antiquity*, ed. Peregrine Horden, 173–94. Aldershot, UK: Ashgate, 2000.

———. *Music, Science, and Natural Magic in Seventeenth-Century England*. New Haven, Conn.: Yale University Press, 1999.

Greenblatt, Stephen. *Shakespearean Negotiations: The Circulation of Social Energy in Renaissance England*. Berkeley: University of California Press, 1988.

Hammond, Paul. "Dryden's *Albion and Albanius:* The Apotheosis of Charles II." In *The Court Masque*, ed. David Lindley, 169–83. Manchester: Manchester University Press, 1984.

———. "The King's Two Bodies: Representations of Charles II." In *Culture, Politics, and Society in Britian, 1660–1800*, ed. Jeremy Black and Jeremy Gregory, 13–48. Manchester: Manchester University Press, 1991.

Harris, Anthony. *Night's Black Agents: Witchcraft and Magic in Seventeenth-Century English Drama*. Manchester: Manchester University Press, 1980.

Harris, Ellen. *Handel as Orpheus: Voice and Desire in the Chamber Cantatas*. Cambridge: Harvard University Press, 2001.

———. *Henry Purcell's* Dido and Aeneas. Oxford: Clarendon Press, 1987.

Harris, Jonathan Gil. *Foreign Bodies and the Body Politic: Discourses of Social Pathology in Early Modern England*. Cambridge: Cambridge University Press, 1998.

Heller, Wendy. " 'A Present for the Ladies': Ovid, Montaigne, and the Redemption of Purcell's Dido." *Music and Letters* 84, no. 2 (2003): 189–208.

———. *Emblems of Eloquence: Opera and Women's Voices in Seventeenth-Century Venice*. Berkeley: University of California Press, 2003.

Highfill, Philip H., Jr., Kalman A. Burnim, and Edward A. Langhans. *A Biographical Dictionary of Actors, Actresses, Musicians, Dancers, Managers, and Other Stage Personnel in London, 1660–1800*. Carbondale: Southern Illinois University Press, 1973–93.

Holbrook, Peter. "Jacobean Masques and the Jacobean Peace." In *The Politics of the Stuart Court Masque*, ed. David Bevington and Peter Holbrook, 67–87. Cambridge: Cambridge University Press, 1998.

Holman, Peter. *Dowland: Lachrimae (1604)*. Cambridge Music Handbooks. Cambridge: Cambridge University Press, 1999.

Howard, Jean E. *The Stage and Social Struggle in Early Modern England*. London: Routledge, 1994.

Howard, Skiles. *The Politics of Courtly Dancing in Early Modern England*. Massachusetts Studies in Early Modern Culture. Amherst: University of Massachusetts Press, 1998.

Howe, Elizabeth. *The First English Actresses: Women and Drama 1660–1700*. Cambridge: Cambridge University Press, 1992.

Hughes-Hughes, Augustus. *Catalogue of Manuscript Music in the British Museum*. London: Printed by Order of the Trustees, 1906–1909.

Jackson, Stanley W. *Melancholia and Depression: From Hippocratic Times to Modern Times*. New Haven, Conn.: Yale University Press, 1986.

Jensen, H. James. *The Muses' Concord: Literature, Music, and the Visual Arts in the Baroque Age*. Bloomington: Indiana University Press, 1976.

Jobe, Thomas Harmon. "The Devil in Restoration Science: The Glanvill-Webster Witchcraft Debate." *ISIS* 72 (September 1981): 343–56.

———. "Medical Theories of Melancholia in the Seventeenth and Early Eighteenth Centuries." *Clio Medica: Acta Academia Internationalis Historiae Medicinae* 11 (1976): 217–31.

Jones, Ann Rosalind, and Peter Stallybrass. "Fetishizing Gender: Constructing the Hermaphrodite in Renaissance Europe." In *Body Guards: The Cultural Politics of Gender Ambiguity*, ed. Julia Epstein and Kristina Straub. New York: Routledge, 1991.

Jorgens, Elise Bickford. "The Singer's Voice in Elizabethan Drama." In *Renaissance Rereadings: Intertext and Context*, ed. Anne J. Cruz, Maryanne Cline Horowitz, and Wendy A. Furman, 33–47. Urbana: University of Illinois Press, 1988.

Kantorowicz, Ernst H. *The King's Two Bodies: A Study in Mediaeval Political Theology*. Princeton: Princeton University Press, 1957.

Kerman, Joseph. "A Glimmer from the Dark Ages." In *Dido and Aeneas: An Opera*, ed. Curtis Price, 224–28. New York: W. W. Norton, 1986.

Kiefer, Christian. "Music and Marston's *The Malcontent*." *Studies in Philology* 51 (1954): 163–71.

Kiefer, Frederick. "The Dance of the Madmen in *the Duchess of Malfi*." *Journal of Medieval and Renaissance Studies* 17 (1987): 211–33.

Klibansky, Raymond, Erwin Panofsky, and Fritz Saxl. *Saturn and Melancholy: Studies in the History of Natural Philosophy, Religion, and Art*. New York: Basic Books, 1964.

Lancashire, Anne. "*The Witch*: Stage Flop or Political Mistake?" In *"Accompanying the Players": Essays Celebrating Thomas Middleton, 1580–1980*, ed. Kenneth Friedenreich, 161–81. AMS Studies in the Renaissance. New York: AMS Press, 1983.

Laqueur, Thomas. *Making Sex: Body and Gender from the Greeks to Freud*. Cambridge, Mass.: Harvard University Press, 1990.

Levine, Laura. *Men in Women's Clothing: Anti-Theatricality and Effeminization, 1579–1642*. Cambridge: Cambridge University Press, 1994.

Limon, Jerzy. *The Masque of Stuart Culture*. Cranbury, N.J.: Associated University Presses, 1990.

Lindley, David. "The Politics of Music in the Masque." In *The Politics of the Stuart Court Masque*, ed. David Bevington and Peter Holbrook, 273–95. Cambridge: Cambridge University Press, 1998.

Long, John H. *Shakespeare's Use of Music: The Final Comedies*. New York: Da Capo Press, 1977.

Lowenthal, Cynthia. "Sticks and Rags, Bodies and Brocade: Essentializing Discourses and the Late Restoration Playhouse." In *Broken Boundaries: Women and Feminism in Restoration Drama*, ed. Katherine M. Quinsey, 219–33. Lexington: University Press of Kentucky, 1996.

Lowerre, Kathryn. "Gothic Elements in English Theater Music." Paper presented at the annual meeting of the American Musicological Society, Columbus, Ohio, 2003.

———. "Music in the Productions at London's Lincoln's Inn Fields Theater, 1695–1705." Ph.D. diss., Duke University, 1997.

MacDonald, Michael. *Mystical Bedlam: Madness, Anxiety, and Healing in Seventeenth-Century England*. Cambridge: Cambridge University Press, 1981.

Major, John M. "Desdemona and Dido." *Shakespeare Quarterly* 10, no. 1 (Winter 1959): 123–25.

Maravall, José Antonio. *Culture of The Baroque: Analysis of a Historical Structure.* Trans. Terry Cochran. Vol. 25 of *Theory and History of Literature.* Minneapolis: University of Minnesota Press, 1986.

Marcus, Leah S. "Politics and Pastoral: Writing the Court on the Countryside." In *Culture and Politics in Early Stuart England,* ed. Kevin Sharpe and Peter Lake, 139–59. Houndsmills, UK: Macmillan, 1994.

Martensen, Robert. "The Transformation of Eve: Women's Bodies, Medicine and Culture in Early Modern England." In *Sexual Knowledge, Sexual Science: The History of Attitudes to Sexuality,* ed. Roy Porter and Mikulas Teich, 107–133. Cambridge: Cambridge University Press, 1994.

Maus, Katharine Eisaman. " 'Playhouse Flesh and Blood': Sexual Ideology and the Restoration Actress." *ELH* 46, no. 4 (Winter 1979): 595–617.

McClary, Susan. "Excess and Frame: The Musical Representation of Madwomen." In *Feminine Endings: Music, Gender, and Sexuality,* 80–111. Minneapolis: University of Minnesota Press, 1991.

McGeary, Thomas Nelson. " 'Warbling Eunuchs': Opera, Gender, and Sexuality on the London Stage, 1705–1742." *Restoration and 18th-Century Theatre Research* 7 (1992): 1–22.

Mellers, Wilfrid. "The Tragic Heroine and the Un-Hero." In *Dido and Aeneas: An Opera,* ed. Curtis Price, 204–213. New York: W. W. Norton, 1986.

Moore, Robert E. "The Music to *Macbeth.*" *Musical Quarterly* 47 (January 1961): 22–40.

Murray, Peter B. *A Study of John Webster.* The Hague: Mouton, 1969.

Music in the Western World: A History in Documents. Selected and annotated by Piero Weiss and Richard Taruskin. New York: Schirmer Books, 1984.

Neely, Carol Thomas. *Distracted Subjects: Madness and Gender in Shakespeare and Early Modern Culture.* Ithaca, N.Y.: Cornell University Press, 2004.

———. " 'Documents in Madness': Reading Madness and Gender in Shakespeare's Tragedies and Early Modern Culture." *Shakespeare Quarterly* 42 (Fall 1991): 315–38.

Norton, Rictor. *Mother Clap's Molly House: The Gay Subculture in England 1700–1830* London: GMP Publishers, 1992.

Notestein, Wallace. *A History of Witchcraft in England from 1558 to 1718.* New York: Russell and Russell, 1965.

Orgel, Stephen. *Impersonations: The Performance of Gender in Shakespeare's England.* Cambridge: Cambridge University Press, 1996.

Page, Christopher. *Discarding Images: Reflections on Music and Culture in Medieval France.* Oxford: Clarendon Press, 1993.

Parker, Patricia. *Shakespeare from the Margins: Language, Culture, Context.* Chicago: University of Chicago Press, 1996.

Paster, Gail Kern. *The Body Embarrassed: Drama and the Disciplines of Shame in Early Modern England.* Ithaca, N.Y.: Cornell University Press, 1993.

Pearson, Jacqueline. *The Prostituted Muse: Images of Women and Women Dramatists, 1642–1737.* New York: Harvester-Wheatsheaf, 1988.

Pinnock, Andrew. "Book IV in Plain Brown Wrappers: Translations and Travesties of Dido." In *A Woman Scorn'd: Responses to the Dido Myth,* ed. Michael Burden, 249–71. London: Faber and Faber, 1998.

Plank, Steven E. " 'And Now about the Cauldron Sing': Music and the Supernatural on the Restoration Stage." *Early Music* 18 (1990): 392–407.

Porter, Roy. *Mind-Forg'd Manacles.* London: Athlone Press, 1987.

Price, Curtis. "*Dido and Aeneas* in Context." In *Dido and Aeneas: An Opera,* ed. Curtis Price, 3–41. New York: W. W. Norton, 1986.

———. "*Dido and Aeneas:* Questions of Style and Evidence." *Early Music* 22 (1994): 115–25.

———. *Henry Purcell and the London Stage.* Cambridge: Cambridge University Press, 1984.

———. *Music in the Restoration Theatre: With a Catalogue of Instrumental Music in the Plays 1665–1713.* Ann Arbor, Mich.: UMI Research Press, 1979.

Price, Curtis, and Irena Cholij. "Dido's Bass Sorceress." *Musical Times* 127 (1986): 615–18.

Purkiss, Diane. "The All-Singing, All-Dancing Plays of the Jacobean Witch-Vogue: *The Masque of Queens, Macbeth, The Witch.*" In *The Witch in History: Early Modern and Twentieth-Century Representations,* ed. Diane Purkiss, 200–222. London: Routledge, 1996.

Ravelhofer, Barbara. "Unstable Movement Codes in the Stuart Masque." In *The Politics of the Stuart Court Masque,* ed. David Bevington and Peter Holbrook, 244–72. Cambridge: Cambridge University Press, 1998.

Rogers, John. *The Matter of Revolution: Science, Poetry, and Politics in the Age of Milton.* Ithaca, N.Y.: Cornell University Press, 1996.

Rooley, Anthony. "New Light on John Dowland's Songs of Darkness." *Early Music* 11 (1983): 153–65.

Rosand, Ellen. "The Descending Tetrachord: An Emblem of Lament." *Musical Quarterly* 65 (July 1979): 346–59.

———. "Operatic Madness: A Challenge to Convention." In *Music and Text: Critical Inquiries,* 241–87. New York: Cambridge University Press, 1992.

Rosenberg, Marvin. *The Masks of Macbeth.* Berkeley: University of California Press, 1978.

Salkeld, Duncan. *Madness and Drama in the Age of Shakespeare.* Manchester: Manchester University Press, 1993.

Savage, Roger. "Producing Dido and Aeneas." In *Dido and Aeneas: An Opera.* Ed. Curtis Price, 255–77. New York: W. W. Norton, 1986.

Schiesari, Juliana. *The Gendering of Melancholia: Feminism, Psychoanalysis, and the Symbolics of Loss in Renaissance Literature.* Ithaca, N.Y.: Cornell University Press, 1992.

Schmalfeldt, Janet. "In Search of Dido." *The Journal of Musicology* 18, no. 4 (Fall 2001): 584–615.

Seaward, Paul. *The Restoration, 1660–1688.* New York: St. Martin's Press, 1991.

Seng, Peter J. "The Earliest Known Music for Desdemona's 'Willow Song.'" *Shakespeare Quarterly* 9, no. 1 (Winter 1958): 419–20.

———. *The Vocal Songs in the Plays of Shakespeare: A Critical History.* Cambridge: Harvard University Press, 1967.

Sharpe, James. *Instruments of Darkness: Witchcraft in England, 1550–1750.* London: Hamish Hamilton, 1996.

Sharpe, Kevin. *Criticism and Compliment: The Politics of Literature in the England of Charles I.* Cambridge: Cambridge University Press, 1987.

———. *The Personal Rule of Charles I.* New Haven, Conn.: Yale University Press, 1992.

Showalter, Elaine. "Representing Ophelia: Women, Madness, and the Responsibilities of Feminist Criticism." In *Shakespeare and the Question of Theory,* ed. Patricia Parker and Geoffrey Hartman, 77–94. New York: Methuen, 1985.

Shullenberger, William. "'This for the Most Wrong'd of Women': A Reappraisal of *The Maid's Tragedy.*" *Renaissance Drama* 13 (1982): 131–56.

Smith, Bruce R. *The Acoustic World of Early Modern England: Attending to the O-Factor.* Chicago: University of Chicago Press, 1999.

Smith, Rochelle. "Admirable Musicians: Women's Songs in *Othello* and *the Maid's Tragedy.*" *Comparative Drama* 28, no. 3 (Fall 1994): 311–23.

Spink, Ian. *English Song: Dowland to Purcell.* New York: Taplinger, 1986.

Stallybrass, Peter, and Allon White. *The Politics and Poetics of Transgression.* Ithaca, N.Y.: Cornell University Press, 1986.

Sternfeld, F. W. *Music in Shakespearean Tragedy.* London: Routledge and Kegan Paul, 1963.

———. "Ophelia's Version of the Walsingham Song." *Music and Letters* 45 (1964): 108–113.

Stevens, John. *Words and Music in the Middle Ages: Song, Narrative, Dance, and Drama, 1050–1350.* Cambridge: Cambridge University Press, 1986.

Straub, Kristina. *Sexual Suspects: Eighteenth-Century Players and Sexual Ideology.* Princeton: Princeton University Press, 1992.

Thomas, Keith. *Religion and the Decline of Magic.* London: Weidenfeld and Nicolson, 1971.

Tomlinson, Gary. *Music in Renaissance Magic: Toward a Historiography of Others.* Chicago: University of Chicago Press, 1993.

Traub, Valerie. *The Renaissance of Lesbianism in Early Modern England.* Cambridge: Cambridge University Press, 2002.

Trumbach, Randolph. "London's Sapphists: From Three Sexes to Four Genders in the Making of Modern Culture." In *Body Guards: The Cultural Politics of Gender Ambiguity*, ed. Julia Epstein and Kristina Straub, 112–41. New York: Routledge, 1991.

———. "Sodomitical Assaults, Gender Role, and Sexual Development in Eighteenth-Century London." *Journal of Homosexuality* 16, no. 1 (1989): 407–429.

———. "Sodomy Transformed: Aristocratic Libertinage, Public Reputation and the Gender Revolution of the Eighteenth Century." In *Love Letters between a Certain late Nobleman and the Famous Mr. Wilson*, ed. M. S. Kimmel, 105–124. New York: Harrington Park Press, 1990.

Underdown, David. *Revel, Riot, and Rebellion: Popular Politics and Culture in England, 1603–1660.* Oxford: Clarendon Press, 1985.

Van Lennep, William. *The London Stage 1660–1800, Part 1: 1660–1700.* Carbondale: Southern Illinois University Press, 1960.

Veevers, Erica. *Images of Love and Religion: Queen Henrietta Maria and Court Entertainments.* Cambridge: Cambridge University Press, 1989.

Walker, D. P. *Spiritual and Demonic Magic from Ficino to Campanella.* University Park: Pennsylvania State University Press, 2000.

Walkling, Andrew R. "Political Allegory in Purcell's *Dido and Aeneas.*" *Music and Letters* 76 (November 1995): 540–71.

———. "Politics and the Restoration Masque: The Case of *Dido and Aeneas.*" In *Culture and Society in the Stuart Restoration: Literature, Drama, History*, ed. Gerald MacLean, 52–69. Cambridge: Cambridge University Press, 1995.

Walls, Peter. *Music in the English Courtly Masque, 1604–1640.* Oxford: Clarendon Press, 1996.

Ward, John M. "Joan Qd John and Other Fragments at Western Reserve University." In *Aspects of Medieval and Renaissance Music: A Birthday Offering to Gustave Reese*, ed. Jan LaRue, 832–55. New York: W. W. Norton, 1966.

Weil, Rachel. "Sometimes a Scepter Is Only a Scepter: Pornography and Politics in Restoration England." In *The Invention of Pornography: Obscenity and the Origins of Modernity, 1500–1800*, ed. Lynn Hunt, 125–56. New York: Zone Books, 1996.

Wells, Robin Headlam. *Elizabethan Mythologies: Studies in Poetry, Drama, and Music.* Cambridge: Cambridge University Press, 1994.

Westrup, Jack. "A Flawed Masterpiece." In *Dido and Aeneas: An Opera*, ed. Curtis Price, 195–203. New York: W. W. Norton, 1986.

Wilkin, Rebecca May. "Feminizing Imagination in France, 1563–1678." Ph.D. diss., University of Michigan, 2000.

Willis, Deborah. *Malevolent Nurture: Witch-Hunting and Maternal Power in Early Modern England*. Ithaca, N.Y.: Cornell University Press, 1995.

Wills, Garry. *Witches and Jesuits: Shakespeare's Macbeth*. New York: Oxford University Press, 1995.

Wood, Bruce, and Andrew Pinnock. " 'Unscarr'd by Turning Times'? The Dating of Purcell's *Dido and Aeneas*." *Early Music* 20 (1992): 373–90.

Index

Page numbers in italics indicate figures and musical examples.

AMANDA EUBANKS WINKLER is Assistant Professor in the Department of Fine Arts at Syracuse University, specializing in early music. Her articles and reviews have appeared in *Cambridge Opera Journal*, *The Journal of Musicology*, *Notes*, and *Journal of Seventeenth-Century Music*. She is author of *Music for Macbeth*.

www.ingramcontent.com/pod-product-compliance
Lightning Source LLC
Chambersburg PA
CBHW070447100426
42812CB00004B/1226